PRAISE FOR 9 LEA
AND LEADER-F

9 Leader Touchstones is full of valuable, practical, and important insights and tips. I can't think of a single leader who wouldn't draw immediate value from this book, just as I did. It's potent, powerful, and personal!

BILL TREASURER
Chief Encouragement Officer, Giant Leap Consulting
Author of International Best Seller *Courage Goes to Work*

In *9 Leader Touchstones*, Jes offers actionable, honest advice for leaders navigating the current generational shift and growing leadership crisis. Now more than ever, we need Jes's guidance, backed by her many years of consulting experience, to build enduring organizations. That starts by looking and leading beyond the bottom line. Inevitably, today's labor challenges will pass, but Leader-First Leadership will timelessly guide us well into the future.

MELANIE SCHILD
Chief Executive Officer, Association of Junior Leagues Intl.

Jes is a phenomenal leader and team coach who advocates for enhancing team performance and healthy organizational cultures. Her work transformed my leadership approach and drove foundational changes in my organization. Her thoughtful and authentic style resulted in sustainable impacts that continued to produce positive outcomes even after I moved on from the organization. *9 Leader Touchstones* is a must-read for any leader who cares about embracing culture change and building healthy organizations focused on sustainable results and enduring growth.

LIEUTENANT COLONEL KADY GRIFFIN
United States Air Force

With stories that are inspiring and compelling, Jes gives us a refreshing view on leadership, marrying the human insights of Brené Brown with the pragmatic guidance of Jim Collins. *9 Leader Touchstones* is a new look at modern leadership for organizations of today and the future.

PAULA BOOKIDIS
Chief Executive Officer, Girl Scouts of Central Texas

I lead a global team of lawyers and other legal professionals and am passionate about their development. *9 Leader Touchstones* offers new perspectives and insights on personal leadership and professional development. The ripple effects of micro adjustments can have a significant compounding effect. Jes's book inspires each of us to make a ripple to create big change.

DALE J. DAVIS
Deputy General Counsel & Chief IP Counsel, Cummins, Inc.

Leader-First Leadership opened my eyes to the importance of focusing on my own resilience, then building a Culture of Vitality to encourage my team members to do the same. It also provided me the insight to lead with courage when faced with challenging team and organizational dynamics.

ELIZABETH GILBERT
Owner & Managing Principal, Clark Condon

Beyond academic theory, Jes has spent thousands of hours working with leaders and teams. She uses her gift of storytelling to break down the complexity of systems dynamics so that, as leaders, we can see and understand the interconnection of business, behavior, and life. Reading *9 Leader Touchstones* feels like one moment, sitting on the back porch sharing stories, and then the next, in the classroom, changing our entrenched thinking on business and leadership.

JAMES LOVAAS, MBA, FCA
Founder, Freefall Consulting
Director of DTC Operations, Korbel Champagne Cellars

When I first met Jes, I was impressed by her willingness to serve others and her honesty and integrity in everything she does. Whether from the sidelines or together on the field of play, she's cheered me on through the formation and growth of my career. The Leader-First Leadership approach comes from how Jes lives and breathes and is imbued with her hard-pushing, joyful spirit. It's a resource any leader should have at their side!

ANNE MANNER-MCLARTY

President & Lead Consultant, Heurista

This is a must-read book for anyone who is a leader or aspires to be one. Brilliantly written, captivating, inspiring, and backed up by fascinating neuroscience and personal stories, *9 Leader Touchstones* will make you rethink leadership.

ABRAHAM THOMAS

Management Consultant and Advisor, Global Projects Americas, EMEA & APAC Regions

In *9 Leader Touchstones*, Jes weaves a water-tight tapestry for bringing about a culture of work that is reaffirming and rewarding for everyone in the organization. Is it doable? Yes. Is it transformational for your organization? Absolutely.

JENN HULTING OSMAN, BA, MNA

Leadership & Organizational Development Consultant

Between Baby Boomer retirements and the Great Resignation of the past few years, many organizations face a critical loss of institutional knowledge and key relationships. Into this gap, flourishing leaders and teams are needed even more than ever. *9 Leader Touchstones* combines proven research with stories from remarkable leaders to provide a compass to help you navigate this change. Trusting the wisdom within your team requires a Leader-First approach.

WINSTON FAIRCLOTH

Founder, For Love of Team

Jes's ability to write with authenticity and vulnerability makes 9 Leader Touchstones an approachable and joyful read while giving readers a strong foundation in proven methods to ensure sustained success. This is not a theoretical book – it's a practical guide that provides valuable insights and strategies for anyone who wants to lead with excellence and build resilient organizations.

MELISSA MARCELISSEN, MBA
Founder, Vision Leadership Consulting Inc.

Jes walks the talk in *9 Leader Touchstones*. Her personal stories ignite passion, and her research revolutionizes the way leaders need to think in the 21st century and beyond. This book will redefine you as an authentic, purpose-driven leader by showing you how to live and breathe the touchstones.

JOHN MIKOS
President & Chief Executive Officer, YMCA of Middle Tennessee

My expectations of leaders have changed due to understanding the Leader Touchstones. Learning how culture is created in organizations has caused me to change my actions and approaches to being part of a team and pushing others to behave in ways that reinforce trust and empathy. Thanks, Jes, for bringing this into the world! Even if you've read dozens of leadership books, the approach and wisdom in *9 Leader Touchstones* will make leadership and your team's success tangible in a new way.

JADA TULLOS ANDERSON
Program Manager, Wildlife Conservation Society

In *9 Leader Touchstones*, Jes shows you how to create the blueprint to build a dynamic organization that not only prospers at the moment but endures.

ROBERT KLEPPER
Global Insurance Executive & Strategic Advisor, Betterview

LEADER

TOUCHSTONES

Unleash your team's unique potential and
build a dynamic, enduring organization

Jes DeShields, PhD
The Creator of Leader-First® Leadership

Name: Jes DeShields, Author
Title: 9 Leader Touchstones
Unleash your team's unique potential and build a dynamic, enduring organization
Description: First Edition | Taylors, SC | Leader-First Publications
Cover Design: Cassandra Porter, Director of Design, Taylor Brand Consulting
[2023] includes biographical references

IBSN 979-8-9885141-0-7 (Hardcover)
IBSN 979-8-9885141-1-4 (Paperback)
IBSN 979-8-9885141-2-1 (e-Book)
IBSN 979-8-9885141-3-8 (Audio)

For more information, visit: www.9leadertouchstones.com.

DEDICATION

To Beth and Harry:
You gave me the chance to live an inspired life.

To Mom:
You planted the seeds.

To My Daughters, Madi and Emily:
I'll never stop fighting for a future where, as
women, you won't have to fight so hard to
be heard and be seen as the magnificent,
brilliant creatures you are.

To My Husband, Brian:
My heart, my soul, and my mind find
respite in your unconditional love, kindness,
and unwavering support. I would adventure
to the end of the world and back with you.

To Leaders who play the long game:
Together, we can change the world.

TABLE OF CONTENTS

A NOTE FROM THE AUTHOR

For nearly ten years, I've analyzed existing research, synthesized data, collected stories, and incorporated findings into my daily work. Last year, I finally got serious about bringing this research to you. Since starting to write *9 Leader Touchstones*, friends, colleagues, and family members have asked me a simple question. "What is your book about?" I started writing this book to help you understand which leader behaviors reliably create the conditions for enduring organizational growth. That has not changed. What has changed is my perspective.

Building healthy organizational culture is the most essential tool in a leader's tool belt. But to build enduring organizations in a *Volatile*, *Uncertain*, *Complex*, and *Ambiguous* world, we must look at learnings from the past through a new lens and look to the future with fresh eyes. The Leader-First® Leadership model and the research in *9 Leader Touchstones* encourage you to think differently about organizational growth. Creating the right conditions inside the organization starts with you. It also challenges you to think differently about how you lead people and how your leadership approach affects you personally. You lead during a time like no other. How we've led people during the last 30 to 40 years no longer works in our current reality.

Taking this trek means challenging the status quo, which is sometimes a difficult and lonely road. I often think of Robert Frost's poem, *A Road Not Taken*, when I need to summon my *Courage* to take the more challenging path. Leader-First® Leadership equips you with the foundation to build dynamic, enduring organizations, but to do it, you must courageously take the road less traveled. This work will challenge you. And it will change you if you'll let it. When you do, indeed, it will make all the difference.

Yours in Leadership,

Founder and Principal Consultant
Crescent Leadership

THE ROAD NOT TAKEN

By Robert Frost

Two roads diverged in a yellow wood,
And sorry I could not travel both
And be one traveler, long I stood
And looked down one as far as I could
To where it bent in the undergrowth;

Then took the other, as just as fair,
And having perhaps the better claim,
Because it was grassy and wanted wear;
Though as for that the passing there
Had worn them really about the same,

And both that morning equally lay
In leaves no step had trodden black.
Oh, I kept the first for another day!
Yet knowing how way leads on to way,
I doubted if I should ever come back.

I shall be telling this with a sigh
Somewhere ages and ages hence:
Two roads diverged in a wood, and I—
I took the one less traveled by,
And that has made all the difference.

PROLOGUE
Look *First* to Self—An Ode to My Mother

There is always light if only we're brave enough to see it.
If only we're brave enough to be it.
~Amanda Gorman

We are a reflection of our life experiences—the good ones and the hard ones. How those stories shape and guide us has less to do with whether the stories are good or bad and more about how we interpret them. Growing up in the backcountry of Arkansas and the Panhandle of Texas wasn't easy. I grew up in poverty, surrounded by drug and alcohol addiction. My

Phyllis Alexander 1959-2012
Mom is pictured here at age 16
with my father and sister.

young mother, who experienced a far more difficult life than me, divorced my father shortly after I was born. She never finished high school, and from her late teens, she wrestled with raising two girls and two boys before she was 25 years old. Reflecting on Mom's experience, I think about how hard it is for me to raise one stubborn, brilliant little girl. I am educated and have a steady flow of income. I have a loving, supportive partner in my husband, Brian. And without reservation, I will admit to you that I struggle daily. But my mom, Phyllis, without a high school education and always searching for work, had to figure out how to manage four of us. She was a force.

My mom would work long hours in factories and convenience stores, sometimes working two or three jobs simultaneously. We lived in a never-ending string of rundown trailers. I have visceral memories of these trailers. The thing that always comes back so vividly is the empty refrigerator. For some reason, I can only ever remember eating macaroni and cheese and Vienna sausages. Even though we were eligible to receive food stamps and commodities, my mom had too much pride to stand in line at the church parking lot to get our rations of milk, cheese, and bread. We were hungry—all the time. I was skin and bones. It's funny how food insecurity follows you your entire life, even when food is at your fingertips. Once you've been hungry, *really hungry*, you never stop feeling hungry. I don't blame my mom. She did everything she knew how to do. I know she gave us everything she had. She wanted so desperately to be a great mother to her babies. But she was just a baby.

Unfortunately, in her early thirties, she experienced several setbacks. Her beloved mother, my grandma Ruby, died from complications related to diabetes. Her husband, my stepdad, left Mom only a few days after Grandma Ruby's funeral. Even though it left us in a lurch, I welcomed the separation. My mom and stepdad had a complicated, emotionally, and sometimes physically abusive relationship. Despite that, she loved him deeply, and I know it rocked her. At the time, my sister, Cyndi, lived with my dad, stepmother, and brother, Anthony, a few towns away. It was just my mom, me, and my two youngest brothers. Mom tried to pull it together for us, but she was devastated by these two losses. I had a front-row seat to her spiral into depression and addiction.

Within a few weeks, the power company had turned off our electricity, and our cupboards were bare. During the frigid winter of my 8th-grade year, we pulled all the mattresses from the beds into the living room. We tacked blankets to the door frames to keep in as much heat as possible. We'd burrow ourselves into the living room nest at night and then rush to school the next morning for warmth and free breakfast. Luckily, this part of my story didn't last long. A few weeks later, my aunt said that she was moving back to Texas. She told my mom about an available job there if she wanted it. Looking back at how our lives unfolded from that decision, I know Mom buried every hope she had left into that job offer. It promised a new start away from the pain she didn't know how to manage.

We packed a few belongings and moved to the tiniest town I've ever known, Booker, Texas. The day after we arrived, Mom left the trailer to walk to her new job. It was the first time I'd seen her smile in months. She arrived only to discover that the person who offered her the job based the offer on his purchase of the business. That sale fell through while we were driving to Texas.

At the time, I was 14 years old, the same age as my mom when she dropped out of school. Soon after, she got pregnant with my sister, Cyndi. By 17, she was pregnant with me. As an inexperienced, uneducated, and unsupported young woman with a desire to be a great mother and provider, it shattered her when she fell short. This last setback was too much—the straw that broke the camel's back. In tiny Booker, where the 1,214 people knew everyone and everything that happened, Mom felt her failures magnified for the world to see.

She started using hard drugs and abusing alcohol. As her depression deepened, she faded further and further into a dark place I couldn't travel with her. The mother I deeply loved became unrecognizable to me. In her early thirties, my mom's addictions took hold of her. This time was the most challenging period of my young life. My mom would leave for days, sometimes weeks at a time. My sister and I did what we'd watched our mom do for years. We got jobs to feed ourselves and care for our two baby brothers. And then, one day, ten weeks before the end of my sophomore year of high school, she packed up my brothers and left for good. Then my forever family, Beth, Harry, and Cody, took me in and gave me a chance for a different kind of life.

Sometimes when I share this story, I think about how many young people go through the very thing we did. I think about how they succumb to the pressure and fall victim to their environments. They get sucked into the vicious cycle of poverty, addiction, and crime. Unfortunately, this was the case for my brothers. But for some reason, my sister and I found ways to pull ourselves out of it. For me, the lessons Mom engrained in me from the early days of my young life took root.

Before things devolved, Mom would use every spare moment between working hours to support us. She would always tell me how smart I was. She gushed about it to everyone she met. Mom took such pride in my success at school. Looking back now, I know that my success started with her putting words in front of me. She would save her coins and buy me tattered books from yard sales. By the time I was in second grade, I was reading 400- to 500-page novels. She'd never question me when I asked to walk to the library. I'd stay for hours, sitting in the rows surrounded by knowledge. I still love the smell of books and am overcome with nostalgia when I walk into a library. Mom came to every spelling bee and would stay up late at night learning new words with me. Once, she tried to secure funds from a benefactor to send me to a fancy private school because she knew my school didn't challenge me. I never got to go to that school, but I also never forgot that she fought to give me the opportunity.

While I didn't know it then, I was developing my strong work ethic and *Resilience* from her. Even after she was gone, making Mom proud became a subconscious driver of my success. Years later, while completing my Master's Degree and working for Eaton Corporation in Houston, Mom found her way back into our lives. When she left Booker, she had taken my brothers back to the place that was the source of much of her pain. Within a couple of years, she hit rock bottom and was arrested with a group found manufacturing drugs. She spent two years in prison, paying for her decision of being in the wrong place at the wrong time with the wrong people. It gave her all the time she needed to find herself again. She got clean, and the mom I remember from our early childhood came back to us.

Even though it took some time for us to mend what was broken between us, we did. Mom resumed her role as my biggest cheerleader and encouraged me to apply to a doctoral program. I was four months pregnant with Madi and two chapters away from completing my dissertation when Mom became suddenly ill. She called me out of the blue on a Friday. I remember the call like it was yesterday. It was the day after Thanksgiving—November 23, 2012. We had ventured into the mountains with some friends and were standing in the middle of a self-cut Christmas Tree farm. The reception was terrible. All I can remember from the call were these words, "The doctor has given me three to six months." And my head couldn't help but do the math. Madi was still five months away.

Thirty-six days later, she lost her fight. On her deathbed, Mom never stopped apologizing for the pain she'd caused us and for the experiences of our childhoods. In one of our last conversations, I had the chance to change the narrative of our history. I finally found the words to tell her what she'd meant to me. I had the opportunity to tell her I got my grit from her and learned how to work hard because of her example. I told her that she's the one who taught me to always look to myself first before blaming others for my situation or asking someone else to fix it.

There were some other important lessons weaved in there as well. While we must *first* look to ourselves, I also learned that we can't always do hard things alone. Mom learned this too late and wanted me to avoid making the same mistakes.

She taught me that we need to connect and engage with people. We need to extend trust, even when it is scary and requires us to tap into our vulnerability or when it pushes us to take risks that nudge us out of our comfort zones. Sometimes the most uncomfortable space is where our most significant growth happens.

Those experiences from my adolescence—the good and the bad—planted the seeds of my leadership philosophy. My experiences working for and with nonprofit and for-profit organizations have cultivated that philosophy. But my mom's simple yet poignant message—look *first* to yourself—has become the maxim of my life and led me to where I am today.

Thanks, Mom.

PART ONE

LEADER-FIRST® LEADERSHIP
Leaders *first* look to themselves.

INTRODUCTION
Restore the Distinctive Nature of Leadership

In periods where there is no leadership, society stands still. Progress occurs when courageous, skillful leaders seize the opportunity to change things for the better.
~President Harry Truman

"Are you here to fire us?" I turned my head and came eye-to-eye with the employee who'd asked the question every other person in the room was too afraid to ask. I scanned the room and studied the faces of the beleaguered employees. Emotions of apprehension, anxiety, and fear filled their eyes.

Before that day, I'd never worked with this company. The employees knew me only by name and that the Board of Directors had hired me as an external consultant to work with them over the next few months. They wanted me to "take a look under the hood" following the abrupt resignation of their longtime CEO. For anonymity, let's call him Leo from Company XYZ. Leo had moved on to another CEO position in a different state, and the Board worried he had left some risk exposure to the company in his wake. In the two weeks since Leo's departure, whispers of the toxic culture he had created started seeping out to the public. Until then, the Board had let Leo's seven-year tenure as CEO pass by unchallenged and unchecked.

While I've experienced my share of toxic cultures in my lifetime, it still shakes me when I witness the effects firsthand. It confounds me that those responsible for an organization and the people who work for them allow things to devolve so significantly before they take meaningful action to make the right changes. That day, as I looked around the room, this was like nothing I'd personally experienced. You get used to reading the signs—physical and emotional manifestations of fear. In this room, the fear was palpable. I tried to reassure the team quickly. "I'm not here to fire anyone. That's not the job the Board brought me here to do. I am here to listen, learn, and hopefully help your company get back on track."

Specifically, the Board hired me to achieve two objectives. First, they wanted me to look deep into the company's inner workings. They wanted to know what they didn't yet know. The Board gave me complete access to everything and every person I felt I needed. Then, based on the discovery process, I would provide a report of findings and recommend a CEO candidate profile to guide the executive search. Judging by the first day at Company XYZ, this job would challenge me like no other had. Over the next several weeks, I conducted exploratory interviews with each employee individually and in groups. I evaluated the financial statements, historical sales results, policies, procedures, and customer service metrics. I visited stores and offices, talked to external stakeholders, and interviewed former team members.

On paper, the company looked strong. The staff team met increasing sales quotas year after year. Flush with money through tight expense control and revenue generation, the company appeared *healthy*. Throughout Leo's tenure, he focused on feeding shareholder interests and improving his financial position. He delivered results—the numbers consistently increased on quarterly reports. The Board asked very few, if any, questions about *how* Leo's team achieved such consistent and impressive results. In an interview with a Board member, I asked, "Why didn't you ask more questions about *how* Leo and the team achieved the results?" He responded, "Why would we? Leo was persuasive and charismatic. He convinced us that things were on track and the numbers were great. However, I'm not placing the blame fully on him. The results shuttered us to the company crumbling right under our noses."

SLEIGHT OF HAND

Good magicians create illusions that thrill an audience for the length of an evening performance. Magicians take painstaking efforts to present the reality they want us to believe. However, to create this incredible reality, they have to conceal the tangible reality — the one that reveals all the variables that make their magic tricks work. If we have paid for the ticket to the magic show and leave wowed by the experience, we rarely demand to know how the magician achieved the result. We got exactly what we wanted.

A collection of underlying variables, not just a singular result, reveals the tangible reality. In the case of Company XYZ, Leo had created an incredible, magical reality of consistent growth. His performance thrilled the audience. My report to the Board revealed a very different state of the company — the tangible reality. Pressured by the CEO and other members of the executive team to produce highly unrealistic sales targets, team members falsified customer accounts and, with creative accounting, manipulated earnings by as much as 50% in a given year. They were so busy fabricating results that they had little time for customer retention. This created the *Pac-man®* *Anomaly* — increasing sales plotted over decreasing customer retention.

Suppose the organization is doing the bare minimum in customer care, due to the general nature of sales and the cost of acquiring new customers, retention should grow or remain steady because there are significantly more customers. Steeply declining customer retention against increasing sales would likely reveal internal staff burnout and exhaustion years before the board realized there was a problem. If the team members at Company XYZ had done everything by the book, they would need to *seriously* hustle to create enough new business growth. In the case of Company XYZ, the *Pac-man® Anomaly* (see Figure 0.1) revealed a more significant problem. It creates a nearly impossible scenario. A company would have to double

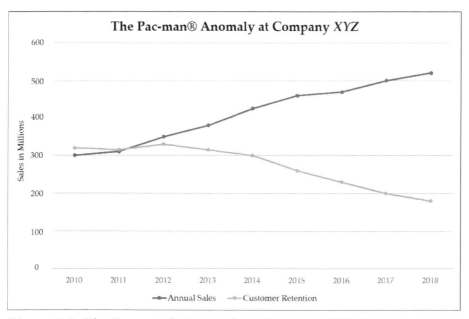

~KEY DEFINITION~

The *Pac-man® Anomaly* occurs when independent yet correlated metrics should have the same behavior—to increase or decrease—but one increases while the other decreases. This should signal an underlying problem with delivery, service, or measurement.

or even triple the size of its sales team to overcome this much customer attrition with new business and achieve the kind of sales growth that Company XYZ achieved.

Figure 0.1: The Pac-man® Anomaly at Company XYZ

My exploratory interviews revealed a darker situation that had metastasized inside Company XYZ. Leo used company resources, including staff labor, to support his outside interests. Most team members followed the CEO-mandated protocol impetuously out of fear of retribution. Team members worried about losing their jobs in a volatile employment market. They felt shackled to the company even as Leo increasingly intensified his fear tactics to protect his scam. As I developed the human narrative for this organization, it turned out that each team member who stayed had a unique situation binding them to the company. Some dealt with ailing elderly parents who needed their care and financial support. There were single parents with children who relied on their sole income. Some team members had graduated from college under a mountain of burdensome debt. Leo terminated any team member that questioned his tactics and decisions. One former team member reported sending an anonymous letter to the Board before resigning. Because the Board had adopted the practice of only investigating complaints from known sources, they did not pursue the lead. The company had no system for employees to safely report potential ethical violations.

Leo had surrounded himself with "yes" people — unqualified individuals given fancy titles and matching salaries who would carry out his plans without questions. These executives adopted Leo's toxic, fear-based management tactics. Leo and his team hid actual losses behind creative expense suffocation. Company XYZ had underinvested in innovation, capital, and workforce development for years. Stores and offices were in disrepair and, in some cases, dangerous. Technology was outdated and dysfunctional. Team members resorted to using their personal technology when they could not get functional replacements from the company. Aside from Leo and his executive team, staff members had no performance evaluations or merit increases for at least the previous seven years. When executives did hold performance evaluations, they were prejudicial and inconsistent.

Internally, the organization was in chaos. And that internal chaos had finally started to seep externally. Pressure mounted, and when Leo knew he could no longer keep up the subterfuge, he used his yet unblemished record of "success" to pursue his next opportunity. When Leo left, he removed the layer he had built between his executive team and the Board. The executive team members were less convincing and charismatic. It took mere weeks before the Board finally started asking the right questions, leading them to hire our team.

BASTARDIZATION OF LEADERSHIP

I probably could have picked a nicer word. In fact, I tried to use a nicer word. However, experiences like the one with Company XYZ kept pushing me to bring the word back. I can't think of any other word that fully articulates how far leadership has fallen. I have to acknowledge that not all bad leaders are toxic Leos. Some people take on the responsibility of leading others before learning *how* to lead people well. They are not toxic. They are inexperienced and ineffective. Others report to Leos and must make impossible choices between their livelihoods or engaging in bottom-line focused management. The behaviors of bottom-line executives can range from anything along this continuum:

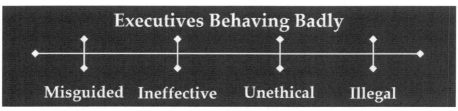

Figure 0.2: Bottom-Line Executive Behavior

On the other hand, when I think of the best leaders who have guided me on my journey, they remind me of skilled orchestra conductors. They perpetually develop their team members' competencies and skills through intentional practice, risk-taking, failure, and growth. They selflessly share everything they have learned with those they lead. Always looking *first* to themselves, they beautifully guide those under their care to achieve a shared purpose. Leadership, at its essence, is distinctive. So, the current state of leadership leaves me frustrated.

You can't scroll a news feed or flip a page in a business book without hearing about the importance of "people" in making an organization successful, and that success *starts with leadership*. I 100% agree. But it's not that simple. By focusing so heavily on the concept of people-centered organizations, even if unintentionally, we have taken the spotlight off the responsibility of organizational executives to self-reflect, personally grow, and lead people well. This has led to the misguided use of "human resources" to improve the bottom line. The shifted focus chips away at a growing chasm between achieving results and ensuring those results endure. The word "leader" has become so commoditized—so bastardized—that its distinctive nature is lost in the noise. Our limited attention spans and needs for immediate gratification push us to simplify, simplify, simplify. But leadership is not simple.

Leadership is not a destination. The word, leader, is not a title. It is not a job you get or even earn through hard work and achieving results for your company. Yes, you have to work hard, but hard work alone is not all that's required of a leader. I tell my students, "The moment you think you've arrived in leadership is the moment when you start to fail your organization." At that very moment, you have lost sight of what it means to be a leader.

~BOTTOM-LINE EXECUTIVE BEHAVIOR~

*The moment you think you've arrived in
leadership is the moment when you start
to fail your organization.*

Leadership *is* an ever-evolving, endless journey. Leadership is unique for each person because it's defined by a collection of personal life experiences. Warren Bennis, a leadership pioneer, said, "The most dangerous leadership myth is that leaders are born—that there is a genetic factor to leadership… that's nonsense; in fact, the opposite is true. Leaders are made rather than born." What makes leadership so unique? It is a choice. Day in and day out, you have to choose to show up for your people and earn the designation of *leader*. This takes commitment to self-reflection, growth, vulnerability, intentional practice, failure, and persistence. Leadership is hard.

While the actions of excellent leaders reinforce healthy culture dimensions for enduring growth, leadership itself is not about numbers or metrics. Leadership is about human connection and improving the human condition. True leaders set the standard for others to follow. The most important responsibility of a leader is to build more leaders. *Building more leaders* is the reward for exceptional leadership, not a gold-plated plaque, a raise, or stock options.

For enduring growth to happen, we have to put the focus back on the *leader*. That requires restoring the distinctive nature of leadership and the very word "leader." Throughout the remainder of this book, I intentionally differentiated people managing others into two categories—leaders or bottom-line (BL) executives. By stating the difference, I intend to illuminate the distinction between people who lead well and those who have been given the power to supervise another person but have not earned the title of "leader."

~LEADER-FIRST SPOTLIGHT~

For enduring growth to happen, we have to put the focus back on the leader.

In an organizational system, there is one thing you can control—your behaviors. The research presented in *9 Leader Touchstones* shows that the behaviors of those managing people have either a fertile or chilling effect on an organization's success. While you need to follow an intricate map to get there, your behaviors ultimately positively *or* negatively impact the bottom line. Leader-First® (LF) Leadership is your map. The Leader Touchstones™ serve as the compass to guide you on the journey to achieve sustainable results and build dynamic, enduring organizations. In its purest form, leadership represents the heart of organizational growth presented in this book. So, we need to start here. The current

~KEY DEFINITION~

A *bottom-line (BL) executive* is a person who has been given the power to supervise others but is doing it poorly because other BL executives are misguiding them, they have not received the proper training to teach them how to lead people well, or they are engaging in unethical or illegal activity. BL executives focus on bottom-line results at the expense of everything else and fail to define the behaviors necessary to achieve the desired results.

state of leadership reveals why LF Leadership is not only important, but essential.

THE GROWING LEADERSHIP CRISIS

There has never been a more critical time in history to work together to restore the distinctive nature of leadership. Only when we do that can we put people back at the center of organizational success. I know. It is pretty easy for me to write this in the pages of a book. The effort to do so is extraordinarily more challenging. However, we need to start, no matter how difficult the work is. In the past few decades, especially the last few years, the workplace landscape has changed more rapidly than at any other time in history. Unfortunately, with the Fourth Industrial Revolution upon us and technology shaping every aspect of our lives, the internal workings of organizations, including how we lead people, have not broadly changed in response.

~LEADER-FIRST SPOTLIGHT~
There has never been a more critical time in history to work together to restore the distinctive nature of leadership.

The Great Awakening

In 2021, when 47 million people left their jobs, Dr. Anthony Klotz of the University College of London coined the phrase "the great resignation." While *the great resignation* did not start with the coronavirus pandemic, it did increase the speed to get to where we find ourselves today.[1] This, coupled with public outrage over racial injustice, is forcing organizations to change their business models and approach to leading people. Those choosing not to are experiencing the decisive action of people who have been voiceless or mistreated in the workplace for far too long.

I was one of the 47 million. But to me, leaving my job felt less like a resignation and more like an awakening. The pandemic changed me, as I know it changed many people. I watched people I love get sick and die. I spent long days at home, trying to figure out how to teach common core math to my then 7-year-old daughter, Madi, while juggling the constant pull of a position where I was overworked and undervalued.

I balanced those difficult moments with as many good ones as possible, including when I married my husband at a sunrise wedding on top of a mountain in June 2020. This culmination of good and bad experiences was the metaphorical shot in the arm I needed to awaken me. It made me realize how much meaningful time I had lost throughout my career doing work that didn't help me ultimately fulfill my purpose. Unfortunately, I sometimes worked at the expense of my relationships, health, and happiness. I decided to stop waiting and start living. My story is one of millions like it.

While people left their jobs for different reasons, one thing is irrefutable. The pandemic opened minds enough for people to assess their relationship with their jobs, their companies, and the people managing them. McLean and Company reported that in 2023 companies need to recruit the right talent in a highly competitive employment market *and* give meaningful focus to retaining that talent.[2] The modern workplace demands well-being, improved employee experience, and Diversity, Equity, and Inclusion (DEI) strategies that go beyond mere compliance. This means fixing what's broken on the inside. To do this, it will require that leaders of people acknowledge how their behaviors ultimately impact the path to get there.

The Leadership Gap

While the pandemic provided heightened awareness of the state of work, we have been barreling toward a paradigm shift for a while now. In 2015, The World Economic Forum published the results of its Survey on the Global Agenda. 86% of respondents proclaimed that we are in the midst of a leadership crisis.[3] Since the 2015 results were published, Baby Boomers have held tightly to leadership roles across all sectors, probably longer than anyone expected they would. "Boomers still hold most of the CEO jobs at top public companies, most of the seats in Congress, and most of the votes in the academy that hands out Oscars."[4] That's a good thing if we look at it from the perspective that we have failed to adequately prepare enough next-revolution leaders to take the helms of organizations. But now, the workplace generational shift is upon us, and we are not ready.

As many as five generations work together in several organizations—Gen Z, Millennials, Gen X, Baby Boomers, and Traditionalists.[5] Millennials are the largest living adult generation. By 2025, they will represent 75% of the workforce and occupy many available leadership roles. While we see this happening already, Millennials will increasingly challenge traditional leadership and organizational culture standards. Millennials eagerly desire to make a difference. 63% of Millennial team members believe that the purpose of a company is to improve society more than to generate profit.[6] If their organizations do not give them the chance to improve society and strive for a greater purpose, they will go to a place that will.

When our team works with organizations undergoing a leadership transition, smooth succession is rarely realistic. With the considerable challenges leaders have faced over the past several decades, well-planned succession has yet to reach the top of most strategic plan priorities. Time and again, we discover that the next layer of leadership is woefully unprepared to step into leadership roles. Unfortunately, poor leadership evolves as supervisors continue to take on more and more "people" responsibilities without truly understanding what it takes to lead people. Supervising people and leading people are exceptionally different. High-performing individual contributors get thrust into supervisory roles, unequipped with the knowledge and skills to lead people well. As a result, leadership devolves, and organizational distress becomes more complex and convoluted.

~BOTTOM-LINE EXECUTIVE BEHAVIOR~

Poor leadership evolves as supervisors continue to take on more and more "people" responsibilities without truly understanding what it takes to lead people. Supervising people and leading people are exceptionally different.

Last year, while facilitating a leadership team coaching session, a junior leader appropriately described her company's succession challenge as, quite literally, a gap in leadership. With 50% of the company's senior partners retiring within one to two years, the junior partners had not been adequately prepared to step into the spaces left by the departing senior partners. I looked around the room at the faces of these junior partners and saw fear in their eyes. They knew they weren't ready, and it made them worry about the long-term future of the company they stood to inherit.

Leadership Ethics and Bottom-Line Mentality

Over the past several decades, the leadership crisis has deepened and expanded, but not simply because of poor succession planning. What was once only concern about the leadership gap left in the wake of one of the largest generations aging out of the workforce has morphed into something more regrettable. We have witnessed the crisis of leadership play out time and again. Corporate empires collapse due to ethics violations, corruption, and mismanagement. Nonprofit organizations and entire movements crumble surrounded by scandal or negligence. Political institutions have become more polarized and less focused on advancing the greater good.

Company XYZ did not implode or plummet off a cliff. When the board acted quickly and meaningfully, it saved this organization from becoming a headline. However, the company still has not fully recovered. It will take years for the new leaders to untangle the damage caused by this internal scandal. Sadly, these days, this type of situation feels more like the norm than the exception. The scandals that make the headlines should guide all leaders on how to do better. However, history shows that either we miss the point altogether, or we pick and choose what we learn and what gets implemented. Piecemeal efforts only deepen the problems in an internally struggling organization. The statistics do not lie. In 1958, the average company lifespan on the S&P 500 Index was 61 years.[7] By 1980, the average lifespan had dropped to 36.4 years.[8] By 2020, the average lifespan had plummeted to 21.4 years. Success built on a shaky foundation will fail, sometimes slowly and sometimes disastrously.

Repeated scandals rocked the global economy in the first decade of the 21st century. Following the exposure of the Enron fiasco in 2001 came a slew of others—WorldCom and Tyco in 2002, HealthSouth and Freddie Mac in 2003, and AIG in 2005. In 2008, when Lehman Brothers declared bankruptcy, it set off the most significant economic downturn since the stock market crash of 1929. The 2010 BP and the Deepwater Horizon oil rig explosion killed 11 people, injured another 17, destroyed the local ecosystem, and had a devastating, long-term impact on wildlife.

The past decade hasn't improved much with scandals at Volkswagen in 2015, Wells Fargo in 2016, Kobe Steel, Apple, Uber, Equifax in 2017, and Silicon Valley Bank in 2023—just to name a few. For-profit organizations aren't the only ones engaging in shady practices. Nonprofit organizations have also engaged in their fair share of scandals—the Red Cross in 2010, the Sierra Club in 2012, and Boy Scouts in 2015. Sadly, these lists are not comprehensive. I could fill a book with summaries of scandals that made headlines over the past several decades. Case study after case study confirms that BL executives have become less interested in doing the right things to build enduring organizations and more focused on improving the bottom line at any cost. Can you count the number of times you have heard this question:

Did we hit our numbers?

As a manager of people, can you count the number of times you have asked it? The truth behind these five simple

~KEY DEFINITION~
Bottom-line mentality is one-dimensional thinking that revolves around securing bottom-line outcomes while neglecting all other competing priorities and failing to define the behaviors that achieve desired bottom-line outcomes.

words is an evolving history that has eroded the relationship between organizations and their team members. *Bottom-line mentality* is one-dimensional thinking that revolves around securing bottom-line outcomes while neglecting all other competing priorities and failing to define the behaviors that achieve desired bottom-line outcomes.[9] Even though profit maximization is reserved for the corporation, bottom-line mentality has seeped into nonprofit, education, and public sectors as well.[10]

Every type of institution has a bottom line. For corporations, it's shareholder value. For nonprofits, it's charitable donations. For educational institutions, it's standardized test scores. For membership organizations, it's the number of members. For governments, it depends on the administration, but rest assured, some quantifiable bottom line influences priorities and decision-making. During the LF Leadership program, getting to the bottom of their organization's bottom line and how it gets achieved is one of the most eye-opening experiences for our participants.

Throughout my career, I have watched countless organizations focus on the wrong things—measuring KPIs, hitting the numbers, and driving for results. Don't get me wrong. Measuring performance and achieving results are crucial outcomes to ensure that organizations grow. The problem is this. "Our culture, obsessed with numbers, has given us the idea that what we can measure is more important than what we can't measure. Think about that for a minute. It means that we make quantity more important than quality."[11] Leaders must overcome decades of reinforcement that *focusing on achieving results* is a strategy in and of itself.

When results become the *output* (the behaviors that achieve a result) instead of the *outcome* (the desired result), the

~KEY DEFINITIONS~
Outputs are the behaviors that produce *Outcomes*—desirable and measurable results.

organization will achieve superficial gains and unsustainable growth, at best. Bottom-line mentality and increasing shareholder value, at any cost, have conditioned executives to make decisions that only affect the near term. The breakdown happens when people in positions of power fail to meaningfully define the behaviors necessary to achieve those results. Their focus on short-term wins ultimately derails enduring growth. The need to *make the numbers* becomes the driving force behind all decision-making, planning, and prioritization.

~BOTTOM-LINE EXECUTIVE BEHAVIOR~

"Our culture, obsessed with numbers, has given us the idea that what we can measure is more important than what we can't measure. Think about that for a minute. It means that we make quantity more important than quality." ~Dana Meadows

We must look back into our history to fully understand how we have moved so far away from building enduring organizations that achieve ethical and sustainable growth. In 1776, Adam Smith first introduced the concept of capitalism in his book *The Wealth of Nations*.[12] He believed that humans are, by nature, self-serving—a central tenet of capitalism. However, he also knew that if we could harness the ethical fulfillment of our self-interests, collectively, we could meet the needs of society.

Nearly two centuries later, in 1970, the New York Times published *The Friedman Doctrine*.[13] With his philosophy on shareholder primacy, Milton Friedman, who would win the Nobel Memorial Prize for Economic Sciences in 1976, established a precedent that has permeated board rooms and business schools for decades, especially in the United States. Friedman's message was clear—business entities have zero social responsibility to better society. Instead, a business's sole responsibility is "to use its resources and engage in activities designed to increase its profits."

Friedman's nod to a single source of measurement made it easier for BL executives to perform. Unfortunately, their morphed view of capitalism gave them a twisted rationale to exploit ethical gaps so they could fulfill their duty to increase shareholder value. As short-termism evolved over the past 40 years, the metaphorical or actual bottom line has become the most crucial thing—*the only thing*—no matter the cost. When the sole focus of an organization's strategy is to improve the bottom line with no meaningful roadmap to achieve it, the internal challenges of an organization grow in complexity. An organization's strategy should guide team members on the actions necessary to achieve the results, not vice versa. This is the thing—organizational behavior is collective human behavior. Ignoring the human side of organizational health is a recipe for disaster.

I have woven stories and case studies throughout *9 Leader Touchstones* to demonstrate what happens when BL executive behaviors flood the organizational system. These stories illustrate the damning impact of bottom-line mentality on the organization and all its stakeholders.

~BOTTOM-LINE EXECUTIVE BEHAVIOR~

Organizational behavior is collective human behavior. Ignoring the human side of organizational health is a recipe for disaster.

BE THE ANCHOR. TAKE THE RISK.

Leaders who desire to build enduring organizations that transcend market disruptions, competition, and existential crises treat their organizations like dynamic systems. They consider the unique parts but have the vision to see the whole. They understand that *people forces* have the most significant impact on the long-term success of an organization. So, they nurture relationships with *all* the organization's stakeholders — employees, customers, partners, communities, the environment, and greater society. These leaders courageously challenge the status quo by relinquishing short-term, unsustainable results and, instead, put in the hard work to build organizations that not only endure but thrive. If this is you, you are a leader that desires to play the long game.

I wrote this book for you.

Everything I have learned about leadership came from observing and learning with others and then reflecting on those experiences. Of course, the rows of books on my bookshelves have shaped the leadership philosophy in *9 Leader Touchstones*, but nothing rivals when an experience converts to learning. The leadership model presented in these pages originates from an experience that sparked a curiosity that led to hours, days, or years of research. I've taken the time to supplement experiences with the fun stuff—research, case studies, brain and body science, and tools to help you turn your learnings into action— to bring it to you in a single source. But the experiences, both personal and witnessed, bring this book to life. Leadership is personal. So, in some ways, this book, while packed with science and guidance for leaders at all stages of their journeys, is also a memoir.

I spent the first 20 or so pages explaining why bold action is necessary. Now, I am shifting my message directly to you for the rest of the book. Throughout the rest of these pages, I will take some time to introduce myself to you by sharing some important stories that have shaped my life and leadership philosophy—not because I think my stories will influence yours. It's quite the opposite. All leaders must own their stories by embracing experiences— good and bad. These stories have made you who you are. I will tell you my stories to make it easier for you to say yours out loud. I'm going to tell you my stories to build trust with you. I will get vulnerable enough with you so that you know it is OK to be a leader and be vulnerable. In fact, to be the kind of leader I'm going to ask you to strive to be, you have to get vulnerable.

~KEY DEFINITION~

An *enduring organization* is a dynamic system that learns, evolves, innovates, and optimizes, fueled by the behavior of people through carefully and ethically cultivated relationships. It stands the test of time by sustainably growing over its lifespan and transcending destructive external interferences.

You must peel back the layers of who you are to put yourself on the path you were meant to travel.

If you decide to join me on this journey to become an LF Leader, I need to tell you now that it will not be easy. It will be some of the most challenging work you have done during your trek in leadership. But I will commit to you three things. First, this journey will be rewarding—both professionally and personally. Second, along the way, you will learn what it means to truly *lead people well*. And third, as a result of your commitment to the process, you will unleash your team's unique potential to build a dynamic, enduring organization.

CHAPTER ONE
Look to the Past Through a New Lens

*To be responsible inventors and discoverers, we need
the courage to let go of the old world, to relinquish
most of what we have cherished, to abandon our
interpretation about what does and doesn't work.*
~Margaret Wheatley

Developing a model that could quell the unique challenges of the current state of work meant first examining everything we already know about leadership. I developed Leader-First (LF) Leadership through inductive modeling based on field research, analysis of prevailing cases, and synthesis of existing literature. It embodies tenets of three established leadership disciplines—systems leadership, behavioral leadership, and shared leadership. However, it builds from this fundamental premise—leaders *first* look to themselves.

I want to dispel any misguided interpretations of that phrase. LF Leadership is not about putting the leader first. It's about putting people first, which can only happen when leaders introspectively examine their behavior's profound influence on shaping bottom-line outcomes. Even though leaders must first look to themselves, LF Leadership is not about leadership in isolation—isolation in action, achievement, or celebration. It is the exact opposite. If leadership *feels lonely at the top*, you're probably doing it wrong.

At Crescent Leadership, we live and breathe LF Leadership. The *Leader-First Leadership Manifesto* guides our team members and represents the theoretical underpinning and definition of LF Leadership. I have included it in this chapter to help you understand the model's essence.[1]

LEADER-FIRST LEADERSHIP MANIFESTO

- The word "**Leader**" is overused and misunderstood.

- "**Leader**" is not an entitlement that someone bestows upon you. It is an earned honor, and it must be earned again day after day.

- **Leaders** are naturally curious and know that their leadership journey never ends.

- **Leaders** know wellness matters and that their holistic health is inherently linked to how well they lead others.

- **Leaders** do what is right, not what is expedient.

- **Leaders** see *difference* as the essential thread that weaves together the fabric of their extraordinary teams.

- **Leaders** are steady in the face of crisis and fearless in the face of stagnation.

- **Leaders** are unafraid to get vulnerable, embrace who they are, and connect authentically.

- The personal mission of **Leaders** is to build more **Leaders**.

More than any other line in the manifesto, the final line embodies the materialization of leadership success. To endure, leaders who embrace LF Leadership must perpetuate its ideology throughout their organizations. *The personal mission of leaders is to build more leaders.*

LEADER-FIRST LEADERSHIP—THE MODEL

In the remaining chapters of Part One, I will take you through each element of the LF Leadership model so you understand how to put it to work. I included a brief overview here as a preview:

Figure 1.1: The Leader-First® Leadership Model

The first model integration is *systems leadership*. When you employ systems thinking, you see the whole, not just the parts of the organization. You understand that your behavior fuels how the system gets shaped and, ultimately, how it behaves. You constantly seek to interpret the dynamic environmental context in which your organization operates and catalyze shared leadership to identify relevant systematic transformations that solve the most complex organizational problems. You adapt approaches using evolving external and internal information to inform real-time decisions.

~KEY DEFINITION~

A *Systems Leader* sees the whole, not just the parts of the organization. They understand that their behavior fuels how the organizational system gets shaped and, ultimately, how it behaves. They constantly seek to interpret the dynamic environmental context in which their organizations operate and catalyze shared leadership to identify relevant systematic transformations that solve the most complex organizational problems. They adapt approaches using evolving internal and external information to inform real-time decisions.

The second integration is *behavioral leadership.* In the Introduction, I told you that "organizational behavior is collective human behavior." I've studied systems and human behavior for over two decades. Organizational system models rarely explore human behavior as a primary system inflow, thus missing its most pervasive modifier. Human behavior is complicated but comprehensible

~KEY DEFINITION~

Behavioral Leadership is leader success based on a set of learned behaviors.

through the lens of brain-body science. You can use what you learn in *9 Leader Touchstones* and already know about human behavior to intentionally shape an organization that endures and thrives.

Behavioral leadership, modeled after John Watson's behaviorism movement, suggests that leadership success results from a set of learned behaviors.[2] Most leadership models describe leadership behaviors, styles, or skills. The LF Leadership model goes a step further. My original primary research question asked:

Which leader behaviors reliably create the conditions for enduring organizational growth.

Based on the findings, I identified nine behaviors—the Leader Touchstones. Once I defined those, I probed deeper:

How do the behaviors accomplish the work?

In Part Two, we will explore how each Leader Touchstone individually and collectively reinforces healthy culture dimensions capable of unleashing each team member's unique potential. In this state, sustainable results flourish, and the organization can more capably resist and overcome external destructive forces. At the same time, bottom-line (BL) executive behaviors fuel stagnant, declining, and toxic organizations. Both realities demonstrate the pervasive behavioral influence of *people in charge*.

Organizations become unyielding, dysfunctional systems by giving BL executives formal authority through hierarchy but minimizing their behavioral accountability. I'm not shaming organizational structures. Structures are helpful when used appropriately—to define ultimate *behavioral* accountability. However, we've drifted too far away from the fundamental principle that leaders serve as the ultimate point of accountability, either for a team, a team of teams, or the entire organization. As the leader, behavioral responsibility flows from you. And that responsibility starts well before the bottom line improves.

~BOTTOM-LINE EXECUTIVE BEHAVIOR~

*Organizations become unyielding,
dysfunctional systems by giving BL executives
formal authority through hierarchy but
minimizing their behavioral accountability.*

Finally, LF Leaders *share leadership*. Expanding on behavioral accountability, shared leadership shifts responsibility for organizational success away from the single-power hierarchical model. When you share leadership, an ultimate point of accountability still exists, however, the leader collaboratively shares responsibility and accountability throughout the organization's leadership structure. Sharing leadership demonstrates your dedication to the long game. As you go, you also prepare those who will lead after you.

~KEY DEFINITION~
In a *Shared Leadership* model, a single point of ultimate accountability still exists, however, the top-level leader collaboratively shares responsibility and accountability throughout the leadership structure in an organization.

Playing *the long game* means building dynamic organizations that not only endure but sustainably thrive by ethically creating value for *all* of the organizations' stakeholders. You acknowledge that consideration for the human element will maximize results to the highest degree possible over time. Always looking *first* to yourself, you reflect and act on your behavioral influence in shaping your organization's future. You seek long-term success that you may never have the opportunity to see, carried out by those leaders you have cultivated along the way.

LF Leadership development focuses on supporting you, as a leader of people, to *first* look to yourself. Once you embrace the Leader Touchstones and feel equipped to continue your personal growth journey, I will show you how to nurture growth in your team members. By cultivating the touchstones in your team members, you create a natural succession environment. LF Leaders recognize that organizational

~KEY DEFINITION~

Playing *the long game* means building dynamic organizations that not only endure but sustainably thrive by ethically creating value for all of the organizations' stakeholders. You acknowledge that consideration for the human element will maximize results to the highest degree possible over time.

sustainability and enduring growth are more important than the success of a single leader or group of leaders at a specified point in time.

CHAPTER TWO
The Stubborn Brilliant System

*Pull a thread here, and you will find it's
attached to the rest of the world.*
~Nadeem Aslam

Last year, I anxiously sat reclined in the tan leather dental chair, waiting for the doctor to make her appearance. My dentist referred me to an Endodontist when I felt severe pain in my molar following a small filling. After a second look, my dentist suspected I needed a root canal. I get that root canals are standard procedures performed on more than 15 million people each year. Today alone, 41,000 brave souls have reclined in their Endodontists' leather chairs and let their docs go in for a dig. But at 45 years old, I did not even have my first cavity until last year. I am somewhat of a newbie to dental procedures and dental pain, for that matter. So yes, I nervously waited for Dr. Rebecca Steffens to arrive and tell me the bad news.

Once Dr. Steffens reviewed my x-rays, did tooth taps and cold tests, and made me bite down on some tasty cardboard, she swiveled my chair so that I could see the enlarged image of my second molar. She said, "I think we have several issues at play here, but I don't think we have a problem with the root." Dr. Steffens then taught me much more about my teeth than I had ever hoped to know. As she talked, my brain connected the dots. I had a systems problem at play.

Before I explain what was happening with my tooth, I need to acknowledge the elephant in the metaphorical room. Usually, phrases like "systems thinking" or "systems problem" conjure images of complicated computer-generated diagrams and models. I will not deny the complexity of systems thinking, but I can't eliminate it from the model either. Systems leadership is the integration that makes Leader-First (LF) Leadership work so exquisitely. It's impossible to build dynamic, enduring organizations that withstand constantly changing, uncontrollable forces without taking a systems approach. I get excited to think about you geeking out on systems leadership as much as I do. So, my desire is to make it consumable and intriguing for you while maintaining the integrity of its beautiful complexity.

Dana Meadows was my hero when I wrote my dissertation on how systems interactions impact a community's ability to eradicate social problems. I may be biased, but Dr. Meadows was possibly one of the most brilliant systems scientists of my lifetime. She explained it with a simple definition that helps us to apply systems concepts to everyday situations. In her book, *Thinking in Systems*, she described a system as "an interconnected set of elements coherently organized in a way that achieves something."[1] Her definition tells us that a system is functional and has a purpose. It also tells us that the *relationships among the parts* of a system are more important than *the parts* themselves. Before I explain why this matters for an organizational system, let's get back to my tooth.

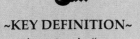

~KEY DEFINITION~
A *system* is "an interconnected set of elements coherently organized in a way that achieves something."
~ *Dana Meadows*

In the case of my second molar, the interconnection of several compounding issues had made my dental situation more complicated and was causing intense pain. The problem wasn't my root. The problem was the relationship between several issues at play. So, Dr. Steffens asked me, "How long and how much pain can you endure?" She was hedging a bet on my toughness. This would give her the time she needed to take a step-by-step approach to fix the core problem. I told her, "If it means I get to keep my root, I am all in."

You may already be a systems leader and intuitively understand how systems work. If you do, you also know that haphazard innovation, short-term fixes, and bottom-line mentality weaken the organizational system and produce unsustainable results vulnerable to the next crisis. If you are not a systems leader, you don't need to get a degree in Systems Dynamics, but you do need to understand your behavior's power to untangle vulnerabilities and strengthen the system. I'm going to show you how.

In this chapter, I will decomplexify systems principles and focus on the elements most relevant to helping you understand how a system operates. I will steer you to the organizational system element where you yield the most control—your behaviors. Finally, I will demonstrate how the inflow of Leader Touchstones (healthy, constructive leader behaviors) fuel the dynamic, enduring organizational system to produce sustainable, bottom-line growth. But I need you to trust the science enough to keep going, even when you don't see immediate results.

Dr. Steffens offered to *untangle the flawed system* so that she could provide a step-by-step solution to address the core problem. She wasn't looking for a payout. In fact, for the work she did on my molar, I paid her 10% of the original estimate for the root canal. Dr. Steffens also wasn't looking for a quick fix to my pain. She wanted to get to the root cause—no pun intended—and fix the problem for the long term. Dr. Steffens may not know it, but she is a systems leader. If she *does*, she also understands that her approach negatively impacted her bottom line on the day of my appointment. However, she recognizes that her actions will have a greater return for her business over the long term. Dr. Steffens has made me a loyal customer for life. Not only will I be back, but I like to share the good news of excellent service with everyone I know. New customers are likely to follow.

Dr. Steffens made one thing crystal clear—solving my problem for the long term would take time, patience, methodical action on my part, and more pain than I might typically be willing to endure. But once I understood *the why* behind her recommendations, I knew I had to do it. Now I'm going to make *you* the central figure of that statement. When you play the long game, it takes time, patience, methodical action on your part, and more pain than you might typically be willing to endure. Untangling any broken or suffering system is complicated and doesn't happen overnight. In the same way, building an enduring organization isn't a quick-win growth strategy. Ultimately it comes down to your decision and the type of legacy you want to leave.

SYSTEMS 101—THE RELIABLE BEHAVIOR OF SYSTEMS

Meteorologist Edward Lorenz, the father of Chaos Theory, first discovered the butterfly effect in 1972. He showed us how the flap of a butterfly's wings could ultimately impact something as significant as a tornado's speed and trajectory or prevent it from happening altogether thousands of miles away.[2] In the same way, when you drop a stone in water, ripples flow outward and expand incrementally. A *ripple effect* creates a chain reaction, starting with a single action. The effect organically grows unless something interrupts it. Small causes have big effects. To realize the ultimate transformation, you must suppress your hard-wired human need to see the effect materialize quickly after the cause. The effect *does* materialize, but it does so gradually, then pervasively, then exponentially.

Organizations are interconnected, dynamic, functional, and self-maintaining systems. Like the ripple effect, a system produces reliable outflows (outcomes or results) unless something interrupts it. Infusing constructive leader behaviors into the system shapes healthy culture dimensions, but systems do not discriminate in how they function. Toxic *or* thriving organizational systems evolve in the same way. The phrase, *what you put in is what you get out,* aptly describes the reliable nature of systems behavior. The elements inside a *system* have the capability to reciprocally influence each other. When this happens, it creates a context that intensifies with each reinforcement. The reciprocal influence and reinforcing context breed conditions for sustainable growth, stagnation, gradual decline, or failure. To understand how each gets shaped, you must first understand the system's primary elements.

~KEY DEFINITION~

A *ripple effect* creates a chain reaction, starting with a single action. It flows outward and expands incrementally. The effect organically grows unless something interrupts it.

SYSTEMS 102—ELEMENTS OF THE SYSTEM

Understanding how system elements operate can help systems leaders identify intervention points that optimize organizational performance. This section will explore *inflows, stocks, interconnections* and *feedback, outflows,* and the system's *purpose.* I've provided standard system element definitions adopted from the research of Meadows.[1] Later in this chapter, I'll show you how these elements form a blueprint for how to build a dynamic, enduring organization system.

Inflows (or inputs) come into the system through various sources—raw materials, labor, financial capital, and technology, as well as intangibles like information, behavior, and knowledge. Inflows initiate and sustain the system-shaping process. The functioning and performance of the system depends on the nature and quality of the inflow.

Think of a system *stock* like a reservoir. Reservoirs store information like memories of historical events and experiences. Inflows into the stock shape its characteristics. Because of the self-sustaining nature of a system, its memory resists efforts to change it quickly, even when inflows change suddenly. Stocks regulate the flow of internal resources and determine the system's capacity to achieve its purpose.

Interconnections represent the dependent, influential relationships between inflows, stocks, and outflows. Understanding the interconnections gives you the potential leverage to optimize the system. Changes or disturbances in one part of the system can negatively affect or augment other elements. *Feedback loops* are pathways where information about system performance feeds back to influence future inflows, processes, or decisions. Positive or reinforcing feedback loops amplify or reinforce changes within a system, potentially leading to exponential growth or instability. Negative feedback loops can act as stabilizing forces or can counteract changes.

System processes generate *outflows* (or outputs) from the stocks. Depending on the system, stocks can create products, waste, emissions, results, or feedback to other systems. Outflows are indicators of whether or not the system is achieving its *purpose*. The system realizes its purpose when it accomplishes its intended function. The purpose represents the reason *why* the system exists and provides a sense of direction.

SYSTEMS 103—CHANGE THE SYSTEM, NOT THE PARTS

It's human nature to expect a relatively close or timely cause-and-effect relationship. A situation I've witnessed repeatedly is bottom-line (BL) executives having a knee-jerk reaction to decreasing revenue. Nine times out of ten, they immediately cut training and development (T&D) funding. However, the underlying reason for decreasing revenue may directly relate to the need for the T&D line item. Sales team members may lack key competencies to sell effectively. Therefore, cutting T&D would create a bigger problem. Left without the funding to pay for needed training, sales team members continue to perform at a deficit, and sales continue to decrease. Perhaps customer experience team members have not received the proper training or knowledge transfer to support customer needs. Over time, loyal customers become passively committed, eventually detracting from the organization's success. Instead of referring new customers to the organization, detractors now ward off potential new customers from ever buying the company's product. The budget is balanced just long enough to make it through the end of the fiscal year—a close cause-and-effect relationship—but the true source of the problem goes unidentified. A BL executive ignores or fails to consider the detrimental long-term impact of quick, unvetted decisions that address the immediate problem of decreasing revenue. As a result, the issue of ill-prepared team members grows and causes even more problems.

I shared this same example in an article I wrote last year. Ed Devore, a CFO with whom I'd worked for several years before moving into consulting, was the first to reach out. He asked me a great question, but knowing Ed, I recognized it was rhetorical. *"Often, the reaction to a downturn is that it's an expense problem, so what can we cut?"* He was not challenging the example. He knows it's a question that teams face every day—one, in fact, that we'd faced together many times. But when we worked together, Ed was always open to helping me get to the bottom of the *real* problem so that we could develop and invest in *real* solutions, even when the budget was tight.

Ed's rhetorical question represents what I want leaders to consider differently. I want you to stop making this your first question: *What can we cut?* Instead, I want you to ask: *Why do we need to cut in the first place?* A problem evolves when a threat elicits knee-jerk reactions. BL executives start to slice and dice without taking meaningful time to investigate the core problem. Using this scenario, when you take the time to evaluate the issue effectively, you discover that the core problem is actually *unprepared team members*, not the budget. The budget issues are symptoms of the core problem. You start solutioning at *"unprepared team members"* instead of immediately slashing the budget.

Ultimately, you might cut the T&D budget anyway because there are other ways to build competencies without investing vast sums of money in training. But so often, that conversation never happens. I recognize that this may not occur because of poor leadership or even poor management. I can say this because I've been there. I've sat in the conference room with a team of senior leaders, trying to figure out how to close the gap. Often leadership teams get so tangled up in the freneticism of the job that they go for the solution with the quickest return. By *quick-fixing* the problem, they can shift focus back to the work that must be done immediately to keep the doors open.

As a leader, I know you have to contend with competition, changing technology, external crises, and any number of other external forces. I am not minimizing those trials with what I am about to say next. The problems that challenge you rarely result from *outside* forces. It is easier—and quicker—to blame organizational problems on uncontrollable external influences. However, most problems originate *inside* the organization. Internal issues evolve because of human behavior. This makes problems far more complex to untangle, so core problems often get partially addressed, misdiagnosed, or avoided altogether.

BL executives focus their energy and the energy of their team members on camouflage solutions. *Camouflage solutions* are quick, easily-controllable fixes to organizational problems that typically have nothing to do with the actual problem. Some camouflage solutions I regularly see include needlessly rebranding or upgrading technology, heavily monitoring competition, reorganizing or restructuring the organization, constantly micromanaging metrics, launching unnecessary new products, and conducting random training (but then not engineering the relevant system changes to sustain learning from training).

Camouflage solutions can be cost-prohibitive, time-consuming, and futile in an internally-damaged or broken organization. They may create a short-term boost. However, these temporary fixes only perpetuate the actual problem, complexify other problems, or create new problems to untangle down the road. Because of feedback delays inside organizational systems, BL executives won't immediately know which problems are evolving and what new ones are developing. This creates an organization in chaos—a tangled mess exceptionally challenging to fix.

~KEY DEFINITIONS~

Camouflage solutions are quick, easily-controllable fixes to organizational problems that typically have nothing to do with the actual problem.

Restorative solutions heal the organization by addressing the core problem and simultaneously addressing the interconnected system problems.

As with any self-sustaining system, a toxic organization maintains in a state of internal disorder. The self-preservation mode and evolutionary nature of systems can keep any organization—toxic or thriving—afloat even through significant internal strife. However, the outside experience eventually reflects what is happening inside the organization. Where there is chaos internally, clients will feel that chaos. Team members will disengage if BL executives micromanage, stoke fears, and suppress growth. Disengagement manifests in various forms—poor client management, withholding critical insight, absenteeism, and turnover. The organization declines, even if slowly over time, eventually drifting into irrelevancy.

On the other hand, leaders work with team members to develop restorative solutions. *Restorative solutions* heal the organization by addressing core problems and simultaneously addressing interconnected problems within the system. Table

2.1 shows an example that demonstrates the difference between camouflage and restorative solutioning.

PROBLEM: DECLINING CUSTOMER RETENTION
STATED CAUSE
Outside Force: *Increased competition*
CAMOUFLAGE SOLUTION
Develop and release a new product.
ACTUAL CAUSE
Inside, Human Force: *Employee fatigue and disengagement causing to poor customer service, heavy turnover, and absenteeism*
RESTORATIVE SOLUTION
Step One—Identify the core problem: *Obscured to top-level leaders, poorly trained mid-level team managers create cultures of fear and fatigue.*
Step Two—Investigate why the problem is happening *(eliminate the fear of retribution): Team managers micromanage result production because they don't know how to coach well or empower team members.*
Step Three—Develop a restorative solution *(solution addresses core problem plus connected issues): Leaders establish behavioral expectations of all team managers and members. Leaders model the behavior they want to see and hold all team members accountable to the expectation. Team leaders attend leadership training that includes essential competencies such as coaching, emotional intelligence, Trust-building, and energy management. Team managers create personal action plans and meet with their leaders, who regularly review progress and coach them as they progress. Leaders provide safe spaces for team leaders and members to express concerns.*
Step Four—Implement a restorative solution *ensuring quality and persistence. As the conditions inside the organization change, customer service and, subsequently, customer retention organically improve.*

Table 2.1: Camouflage Versus Restorative Solutioning

Jada Tullos Anderson, Program Manager for the Wildlife Conservation Society and Crescent Leadership Collaborator, shared a powerful story about how camouflage solutioning in systems has the potential to impact not only livelihoods but lives.

·ı||ıı·ı·

A LEADER-FIRST STORY
A Systems Approach—Regenerative Livelihoods, Food, and Ecosystems
~Contributed by Jada Tullos Anderson~
Program Manager, Wildlife Conservation Society
Crescent Leadership Collaborator

Our work at the Wildlife Conservation Society is simple. We "save wildlife and wild places." But we work with remarkably complex systems. Sometimes "fixing" one problem can create another if we don't understand how everything works together. I work with small-scale fisheries that serve as vital food sources and livelihoods for millions of people.

In 2016, over 60 million people (50% are women) were employed part or full-time along the small-scale fisheries value chain. Fisheries provide employment opportunities, income generation, and food security for communities, contributing to poverty alleviation, especially in rural areas. While engaging in fishing activities, coastal communities pass down cultural traditions and knowledge from generation to generation.

While small-scale fisheries generally employ more sustainable fishing practices, there are instances where their activities can inadvertently damage coral reefs and coastal ecosystems. These habitats serve as essential breeding grounds and feeding areas for numerous marine species. Using inappropriate fishing gear, homemade bombs, and poisons that stun fish to increase the catch can disturb and destroy these habitats. Long-term, this leads to the loss of biodiversity and the degradation of coastal ecosystems. Ultimately, communities lose their source of income, food, and an essential part of their culture.

The solution seems straightforward—prevent people from using destructive and dangerous means to catch fish. However, the issue is more complex. Fishing is often the only way people can make money or provide food. If they stop, they can't afford to pay for their kids' school uniforms, and their kids won't be allowed to attend school. At worst, the family won't have food. Mothers and children primarily suffer from a lack of vital nutrients that fish provide.

Working with them to better understand the full scope of the system gives us more insight into why they use destructive techniques. Our community members often tell us they can't afford better gear. Sometimes, we learn that because there are no local banks or none that will lend money to poor fishers, they are constantly in debt with the buyers who fund their fishing. So, our interventions may stop them from using destructive fishing for a while, but during tough times the system reverts to business as usual— destructive fishing.

To fix the system, we have to change the system, not just provide a camouflage solution that tweaks it. This means helping them find alternative ways to make money or teaming up with the buyers to change how they do business. In some places, this means working with the buyers to provide better gear to their fishers, creating agreements between buyers and fishers to forbid bomb-fishing, and supporting communities to work with local governments to write laws that prohibit destructive fishing. Sometimes we bring community members to visit areas that have stopped destructive fishing. They can talk directly to their peers about how they changed the system. Sometimes it's easier to play the long game when you can see the proof of future actions right in front of you—vibrant reefs and abundant fish.

To protect the resilience of coastal ecosystems and the nutrition and livelihoods of millions of people worldwide, we must understand how the behavior of all people in the system interacts. When we learn why someone is doing something that may not initially make sense, we learn where in the system the problem exists and with whom we need to work to realize long-term, meaningful change. Undertaking a change process like this takes much longer and is significantly more tedious. But the process is inclusive, equitable, and yields the most enduring and meaningful results for all the stakeholders in the system, including wildlife and the wild places we all need, for the generations we have yet to meet.

THE DYNAMIC, ENDURING ORGANIZATION SYSTEM

As promised, I have focused systems exploration on the elements relevant to understanding how an organizational system operates, specifically, the dynamic, enduring organization system. These elements explain what happens when leaders *first* look to themselves by cultivating and then demonstrating the Leader Touchstones.

- ❖ *Inflows* (the nine Leader Touchstones)
- ❖ *Stocks* (the four healthy culture dimensions)
- ❖ *Interconnections* and *Feedback Loops*
- ❖ *Outflows* (results or outcomes)
- ❖ *System's Purpose* (build a dynamic, enduring organization)

Flooding the organization with Leader Touchstones creates ripple effects that positively shape every part of the system. Figure 2.1 shows a high-level linear diagram. This figure simplifies the system to a single inflow and outflow. However, each of the nine touchstones shapes the system in unique and powerful ways, ultimately creating abundant, positive results.

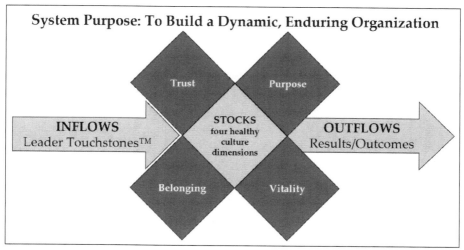

Figure 2.1: The Dynamic, Enduring Organization System

System Purpose—Enduring Growth

When I published my dissertation in 2014, we were just starting to scratch the surface of systems leadership.[3] I had spent the previous six years of my doctoral program studying the interplay of systems dynamics and leadership to understand its impact on organizational or system-wide change. My early research focused on using a systems approach to eradicate community problems. When I started my research in 2010, I had difficulty finding case studies of successful community change efforts that solved problems to the point of eradication. While many efforts had delivered excellent progress, over and over again, I discovered that communities, organizations, and leaders would change focus before achieving eradication of a core problem. Transforming large, complex systems to realize problem eradication takes the sustained coordination of many stakeholders.

To provide you some context, my case study examined the effort undertaken by Dane County in Wisconsin over nine years to eradicate the racial achievement gap. 3rd-grade reading levels represent the most critical indicator of a child's future success. In 4th grade, students shift from "learning to read" to "reading to learn." Scores serve as indicators for academic trajectories, specifically graduation rates. Vulnerable populations are especially at risk, and which populations qualify as vulnerable will vary from community to community. In a longitudinal study, researchers found that across the general population, male students, African American students, and students who ever spent time in the foster care system represented the most significant gap to their peers.[4] These children typically read at lower levels and improve at a slower rate.

The community I studied did eradicate the problem. At the time of the Dane County effort, African American children experienced the most significant achievement gap compared to their peers. And between 1996 and approximately 2004, the community reduced the achievement gap from 21% to the point of statistical insignificance measured by 3rd-grade reading scores. At the point of eradication, this nationally recognized work was heralded as one of the most important efforts in the community's history, but students, families, and the greater community would not realize the long-term implications for years.

I spent time in Madison in February 2012, conducting hundreds of in-person interviews and reviewing thousands of historical documents. Nearly eight years after the community had met its goal, the timing of my study exhumed a critical dynamic that shaped my findings and recommendations. On the 14th day of interviewing, a participant, whom I'd already interviewed two times in the weeks leading up to this final meeting, arrived noticeably frustrated. This leader shared with me the front-page headline from the morning paper. From his vantage point, the article implied that the achievement gap had never been addressed. He said, "It's like the community forgot about what we did." He had since retired from his leadership role and had become less involved in community work. When the people that had collaboratively led the effort shifted focus to other problems, the achievement gap started to reopen. It had not reached the levels of 1996, but the eradication had not sustained either.

This revelation has since guided my work with leaders and organization. A system's purpose is vital in shaping *sustainable* system behavior. When the purpose changes, it can drastically change how the system functions. In the case of the Dane County effort, new leaders chose to focus community resources on different efforts, thereby changing the purpose.

How does this relate to building a dynamic, enduring organization? Without carefully cultivated succession, leadership changes can impede progress in realizing the system's purpose. When I introduced the LF Leadership model at the beginning of Chapter One, I told you that for an organization to endure, you must perpetuate its ideology throughout your organization. *The personal mission of leaders is to build more leaders*—leaders that share the purpose of building a dynamic, enduring organization. That's why a vital component of the model is to share leadership and ensure the next leaders are ready to carry forth the work, even in your absence.

Inflows—Leader Behaviors

A complex, self-sustaining system resists isolated attempts to change it, and leaders can't control or plan for every contingency. As systems, organizations have countless internal influencers on team member behavior—executive behaviors, goals, budgets, procedures, measurements, technology, and policies, to name a few. LF Leadership heavily focuses on the element where you yield the most control over the system— your behavior. Human behavior has the power to shape all other system elements. When healthy, constructive behaviors— the Leader Touchstones—flow into the system, they indirectly but inevitably create the desired outflows of the system— sustainable results. However, you don't see an immediate cause-and-effect between your actions and the outcome. That is why untangling a toxic or broken organizational system is painstakingly hard and relies on faithful implementation.

The nine Leader Touchstones presented in these pages are the leader behaviors that make enduring growth possible in the current state of work. I include the definition of each on the following page, but Part Two of the book is devoted to exploring them in greater detail—*Curiosity, Emotional Intelligence, Courage, Integrity, Authenticity, Empathy, Gratitude, Inclusivity,* and *Resilience.* The Leader Touchstone chapters explain the progressive and reinforcing nature of each

~KEY DEFINITIONS—THE TOUCHSTONES~

Curiosity is the insatiable desire to know and understand unfamiliar things and then to put wonder into action.

Emotional Intelligence (EI) is the motivation to understand and the ability to apply emotional knowledge in a way that brings about positive outcomes for yourself and others.

Courage is acting on what is right, despite being afraid or uncomfortable, when facing situations involving pain, risk, opportunity, uncertainty, or intimidation.
(Definition adopted from Bill Treasurer)

Integrity is adhering consistently to morals, ethical principles, and values to do what is right, not expedient.

Authenticity is the daily practice of letting go of who you think you're supposed to be and embracing who you are through the interpretation and ownership of your life experiences.
(Part of the definition adopted from Brené Brown)

Rooted in sincere care for others' well-being, *Empathy* is the ability to understand and share someone else's emotions and perspectives.

Inclusivity is fostering an environment that values authentic contributions and empowers the full participation and acceptance of all people.

Gratitude is reflecting an appreciation for what brings meaning to your life and recognizing and expressing that the source of value falls outside of yourself.
(Part of the definition adopted from Robert Emmons)

Resilience is your capacity to overcome adversity by systematically renewing the four energy wellsprings—physical, emotional, mental, and spiritual.

touchstone and explore how each individually and collectively shapes the organizational system. I've also included the brain and body science that illuminates their unique relationships and reinforcing powers, case studies, and guidance on how to cultivate the them in yourself and then nurture them in your team members.

Stocks—Culture Dimensions

I've had the opportunity to work with some excellent leaders throughout my consulting career. One, in particular, took the helm of an organization following a toxic BL executive. The new CEO has worked methodically to untangle the unhealthy culture left behind by the former executive. After several years, the fruits of her labor are starting to materialize. It has been a slow process, but this leader plays the long game and knows it takes time to fix a broken system. She also knows she must build the right internal culture to produce sustainable results.

The dynamic, enduring organization system includes four stocks (healthy culture dimensions). The linear view of the model from Figure 2.1 shows how Leader Touchstones flow into the culture dimensions. In this view, I've not included all the resulting interconnections and reinforcing feedback loops. When I explore the Leader Touchstones in greater detail, we will look at the interconnections of each inflow, resulting outflows, and how different touchstones initiate reinforcing feedback loops that strengthen the culture dimensions. Keep in mind that the type of behavior (constructive or toxic behaviors) flowing into the system will determine which culture dimensions grow.

Creating a model that would reliably produce the right outcomes meant first understanding how the brutal realities of the past few years have reshaped the workplace. To thrive, organizations and their leaders must shift to meet people where they are now, not where they were decades ago. Before defining the Leader Touchstones, I asked this question:

What do team members need right now *to be successful?*

Once I knew that, I identified the dimensions capable of creating the ideal state—a thriving internal culture. These culture dimensions include *Trust, Belonging, Purpose,* and *Vitality*. But keep in mind that organizations are somewhere along the Unhealthy→Healthy culture continuum at any given time. Healthy culture-building leader behavior accomplishes two things. First, it untangles unhealthy culture dimensions. Second, it reinforces healthy culture dimensions. Fittingly, the antithesis occurs when BL executive behavior reinforces *fear, isolation, apathy,* and *fatigue,* untangling healthy culture in the process (See Figure 2.2).

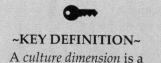

~KEY DEFINITION~

A *culture dimension* is a measurable continuum that describes the properties and characteristics of an organizational system stock.

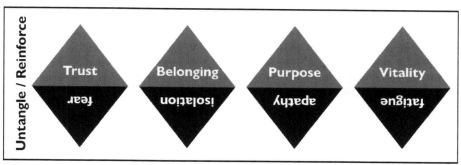

Figure 2.2: Healthy Versus Unhealthy Culture Dimensions

At Crescent Leadership, we developed the *Dynamic, Enduring Organization Culture Assessment (DEOCA)* to provide organizations with a baseline and ongoing measurement of where they are on the continuum for each culture dimension (see Figure 2.3). DEOCA gives teams insight into growth and decline indicators based on their culture's overall health and health in each dimension. The baseline report helps provide leaders with a starting point for prioritizing their culture-building efforts.

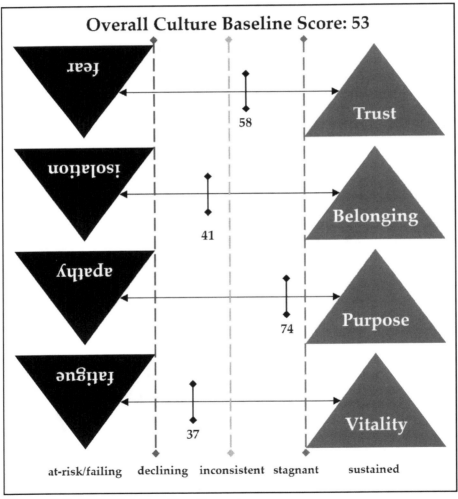

Figure 2.3: DEOCA Baseline Report

Healthy culture dimensions produce sustainable growth. However, unhealthy cultures can still produce results, and sometimes quickly. That's why some BL executives opt for the easy approach. Unfortunately, unhealthy culture limits growth, yields unsustainable results, and comes at a high price to team members and the organization. Even though a toxic organization may stay afloat in uneventful external conditions, it cannot respond effectively when destructive external forces threaten—economic downturns, societal shifts, competition, and environmental crises. Instead, the organization responds in a way characteristic of its internal self—chaotically, disjointedly, and insipidly.

Figure 2.4 shows how antithetic behavior (LF Leaders versus BL executives) shapes organizational systems. If a leader demonstrates *Inclusivity*, it reinforces the *Culture of Belonging*

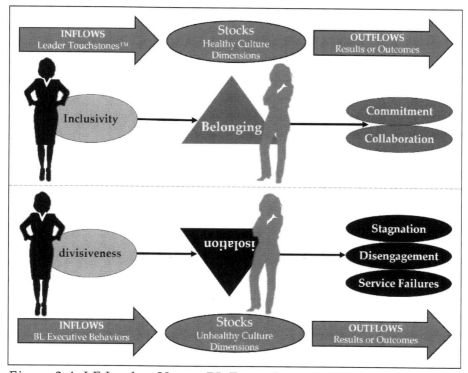

Figure 2.4: LF Leaders Versus BL Executives

and results in commitment and collaboration. However, if a BL executive encourages divisiveness, it reinforces the *culture of isolation*, resulting in stagnation, disengagement, and avoidable service failures. Either effect intensifies when the behavior creates a reinforcing feedback loop. Reinforcing feedback loops, explored later in this chapter, can amplify system behavior, creating a vicious or virtuous cycle. Eventually, this causes the system to stabilize and grow sustainably *or* decline and self-destruct.

The Four Culture Dimensions—A Deeper Look

I defined the four healthy culture dimensions of dynamic, enduring organizations to leave no ambiguity about what it looks like to have a thriving culture. The definition of each provides a clear destination for you as you start the work to reshape your organizational culture. When you review each healthy dimension, consider the other end of the continuum— its antithesis description. Unhealthy culture dimensions offer insight into what you untangle as you go and what is possible when you elevate the wrong person to manage a team of people without properly cultivating and developing them.

REINFORCE *TRUST*, UNTANGLE *FEAR*

The surest way to extinguish the passion of a motivated and highly-competent employee is to signal to them that their expertise and knowledge have no value to you as a leader. To build an enduring organization, *Trust* is essential. A *Culture of Trust* is an environment where multi-directional feedback flourishes, risk-taking and safe-fail zones encourage learning, and team members feel empowered to express ideas and concerns.

~KEY DEFINITIONS—THE CULTURE DIMENSIONS~

A *Culture of Trust* is an environment where multi-directional feedback flourishes, risk-taking and safe-fail zones encourage learning, and team members feel empowered to express ideas and concerns.

A *culture of fear* is a low transparency, psychologically-unsafe environment where micromanagement, compulsion, silos, and politics prevent the organization from making forward progress.

A *Culture of Belonging* is an environment where human connection thrives, diversity is valued, and team members are encouraged to lean into their *Authenticity* by showcasing their unique advantages.

A *culture of isolation* is a disconnected, self-focused environment of information hoarding, favoritism, ego, and suppression of individuality.

A *Culture of Purpose* is an environment where team members feel that they make meaningful contributions, and each takes ownership of helping the organization realize its reason for existence.

A *culture of apathy* is a disconnected environment where mediocrity and avoidance rules and team members are detached and reclusive.

A *Culture of Vitality* is an environment of *Resilience* where physical, mental, emotional, and spiritual energy renewal is prioritized above "time" and exhaustion. Team members feel appreciated for their efforts, and *Gratitude* is openly expressed and received.

A *culture of fatigue* is an environment where exhaustion is worn as a badge of honor, team members are disengaged, and executives micromanage time through rigid and inflexible expectations that reward effort over impact.

Paul Zak, professor at Claremont Graduate University and founding director of the Center for Neuroeconomics Studies, discovered that giving "people discretion in how they do their work" increases outcomes of motivation and innovation.[5] In his book, *The Trust Factor*, he cited a Citigroup and LinkedIn survey that revealed at least 50% of employees would forego a 20% pay increase if it meant they could enjoy greater control over how they do their work.[6] Allowing people to utilize the expertise you paid for when you hired them is a no-brainer way to reinforce the *Culture of Trust.*

~BOTTOM-LINE EXECUTIVE BEHAVIOR~

The surest way to extinguish the passion of a motivated and highly-competent employee is to signal to them that their expertise and knowledge have no value to you as a leader.

General George S. Patton said, "Never tell people how to do things. Tell them what to do, and they will surprise you with their ingenuity." This World War II legend believed leaders should focus on the strategy—*what* needs to be accomplished. However, the people doing the work should define *how* to achieve the goal.

REINFORCE *BELONGING*, UNTANGLE *ISOLATION*

Belongingness is a basic human need. Social scientists have studied its importance and implications for decades. In the 1940s, when Abraham Maslow introduced us to the hierarchy of needs, he ranked only physiological and safety needs higher than social belonging (see Figure 2.5).[7]

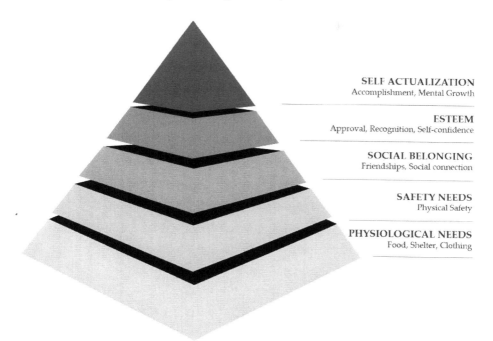

SELF ACTUALIZATION
Accomplishment, Mental Growth

ESTEEM
Approval, Recognition, Self-confidence

SOCIAL BELONGING
Friendships, Social connection

SAFETY NEEDS
Physical Safety

PHYSIOLOGICAL NEEDS
Food, Shelter, Clothing

Figure 2.5: Maslow's Hierarchy of Needs

Researchers have discovered relationships between belonging and decreased depression, suicidal thoughts, and morbidity. BetterUp surveyed 1789 employees across industries and found that team members who felt a strong sense of belonging at their workplaces performed 56% higher than those who did not.[8] Belongingness increases self-esteem and motivation. A high sense of belonging decreased turnover risk by 50% and the number of sick days by 75%. Employees who felt they belonged were also 167% more likely to recommend their company to others. On the other hand, researchers found that a single incidence of exclusion resulted in as much as a 25% decline in team member performance. Exclusion and isolation increase aggression and decrease *Empathy*.[9] While humans desperately need belonging, these findings confirm that it is also good for business, but a lack of it can impair performance.

At its most elemental level, belongingness is a basic human need for meaningful social connection. However, achieving belongingness goes beyond connectedness. In *Braving the Wilderness*, Brené Brown distilled the concept further by emphasizing the distinction of true belonging.[10] Belonging is not just *fitting in*. In fact, fitting in can be a barrier to true belonging. To belong requires us to be our authentic selves. This distinction is critical when building enduring organizations.

A *Culture of Belonging* includes three essential components—connection, contribution, and *Authenticity*. It is an environment where human connection thrives, diversity is valued, and team members are encouraged to lean into their *Authenticity* by showcasing their unique advantages. Real connection is only possible when we acknowledge and value difference. That starts with a desire to understand it. For the conditions of true *Belonging* to thrive, team members must feel valued *and* believe that they bring value to the team. When one of these conditions goes unmet, belongingness is impossible to achieve.[11] In the same way, a team member can feel connected to others on the team and not feel valued.

To feel like you truly belong, you must feel comfortable being authentic. In a *Culture of Belonging*, team members can lean into their natural advantages and realize the distinct value they bring to the organization. In this age of constant change, shifting operational environments, and disruption, teamwork remains the one sustainable competitive advantage that goes largely untapped. However, teamwork that creates a competitive edge is not just about having solid team dynamics. It also means harnessing the best of each team member to contribute to the power of the collective group. As a leader, equipped with this knowledge, you can tap the right talent at the right time to create a recipe for success.

REINFORCE *PURPOSE*, UNTANGLE *APATHY*

Patagonia is the embodiment of a purpose-driven company.[12] In 2018, the organization changed its purpose to ensure it sent a clear message. "Patagonia is in business to save our home planet." You may be saying, "But they're an outdoor clothing company." Yes, they are, and making and selling outdoor clothing is what they do very well. But the company's reason for existence is different. Patagonia has been working to save the planet since 1985. Each year they donate a *self-imposed Earth tax* of 1% of sales to preserve and restore the natural environment. They also encourage other companies and individuals to join them in the work. Their website has a page dedicated to environmental activism touting this message:

Start Small, Go Big, Give Back

If you're doom-scrolling the climate crisis, know that it doesn't have to be this way. You can get involved with grassroots groups working in regenerative agriculture, renewable resources, or conservation to meet the climate crisis head-on. Don't give in, give back and find a group today.

An organizational purpose statement and a *Culture of Purpose* are very different things. It's like the difference between self-awareness and *Emotional Intelligence (EI)*. Becoming self-aware is the first step to growing your *EI*, but just because you are self-aware does not mean you are emotionally intelligent. *EI* requires putting what you know about yourself and your emotions to work. The same distinction is true when it comes to purpose.

Every organization should define its purpose by creating a statement that says, *this is why we exist.* Indeed, having a compelling purpose is the best first step for any organization. But, when an organization has a *Culture of Purpose*, it puts that statement to work. An exceptionally written purpose statement is powerless if the organizational culture can't breathe life into it. A *Culture of Purpose* is an environment where team members feel that they make meaningful contributions, and each takes ownership of helping the organization realize its reason for existence.

In a *Culture of Purpose*, team members accomplish something more meaningful than creating a product or improving the bottom line. When team members align around a common purpose, it energizes them, guides actions and decision-making, and motivates them to reach their highest potential.

The *North Stars*—Purpose, Vision, Mission, and Values—functionally drive high performance in a *Culture of Purpose*. If well-developed and used to guide action and decision-making, the North Stars can significantly and positively influence outcomes. When we work with organizations that want to define their path forward and align their team, we start by refreshing or establishing their North Stars. Sometimes the four North Stars get interchanged, or one gets omitted

~KEY DEFINITIONS~
Organizational Purpose is *why* you exist.

Organizational Vision is *where* you ultimately want to go. It represents a future state.

Organizational Mission is *what* you do each day. It represents the current state.

Organizational Values are the filters for *how* you do your work.

altogether, but each North Star has a specific job. I've included the most precise definitions to clear up misperceptions and put them at your fingertips. I've also included Crescent Leadership's North Stars to show you the difference.

The *Purpose* defines *why* you exist. At Crescent Leadership, our *Purpose* is:

> *"To develop Leader-First® Leaders committed to building enduring organizations that improve the human experience."*

The *Vision* paints the picture of *where* you want to go. It defines a future state that you still need to reach. Your *Vision* is intentionally aspirational and ambitious. It sets a standard of excellence. Our *Vision* is:

> *"To restore the distinctive nature of leadership."*

The most commonly misused North Star is *Mission*. The *Mission* defines the current state and represents *what* you do every day that helps your team reach the *Vision* and achieve the *Purpose*. At Crescent Leadership, the *Mission* defines our daily work through consulting and coaching practices. Our *Mission* is:

> *"To transform the systems that inhibit organizations from learning, evolving, innovating, optimizing, and enduring."*

Finally, *Values* set behavioral standards. They guide *how* your team delivers the work. When I first started Crescent Leadership, I was a solo entrepreneur. The company values were built from my core values, and as we grew our team, we adopted these. Our five Living Value Statements are:

"Be annoyingly curious. Own our nerd."
"Protect health like our life depends on it."
"Laugh-cry more."
"Live just beyond our comfort zones."
"Love first. Period."

We use *Living Values* to guide our actions. And all of the North Stars provide a filter for decision-making and prioritization.

To put the *Culture of Purpose* to work, leaders must learn the unique potential each team member can contribute to realizing the organization's purpose. Empowering team members to use their gifts not only benefits the organization. Ultimately, when team members feel connected to and inspired by the work, it aids in their energy renewal and *Resilience*—it feeds their souls. And this helps to build the *Culture of Vitality*.

Reinforce *Vitality*, Untangle *Fatigue*

My husband, Brian, is a chiropractor and holistic wellness expert. He also coaches healthcare professionals through Crescent Leadership to support them in learning how to better connect with their patients so they can deliver better care. His patients love him. They will drive from other states once or twice a month to receive his care because he is literally a miracle worker. I speak from experience. I have seen his work up close and personal. Following a terrifying car accident in 2013, I lived with chronic lower back pain for over three years. When I met Brian, my back pain had become so debilitating that I could barely sit in my car for my 50-minute commute to North

Carolina each day. As my daughter grew, I struggled to lift her. My health had suffered for several reasons, and it negatively affected me in countless ways that, at the time, I didn't fully understand.

I have since learned so much from my husband about how the body has the capacity to renew and heal itself in indescribable ways, how the health of the body affects our mind's ability to process information, and how the health of the body affects our ability to regulate our emotions and use them in ways to facilitate our performance, rather than destroying it. As my research for *9 Leader Touchstones* evolved, it became abundantly clear that a *Culture of Vitality* is essential to building dynamic, enduring organizations. When leaders focus here, they create an environment of *Resilience* where mental, physical, spiritual, and emotional energy renewal is prioritized above "time" and exhaustion. *Gratitude* is openly expressed and received, and team members feel appreciated for their efforts.

Health and wellness are very much personal accountabilities. However, as a leader, you have the responsibility to cultivate organizational cultures that value the wellness and vitality of the people you lead if you genuinely desire to build organizations that endure. To build a *Culture of Vitality*, leaders must model behaviors that signal to the team— *my health and energy matter, and yours matter to me too.* Teams cannot perform without energy. Instead of figuring out how to squeeze more time out of your people, shift your focus to energy. Time is finite, but *energy is exponentially renewable.*

~LEADER-FIRST SPOTLIGHT~
Time is finite. Energy is exponentially renewable.

Interconnections and Feedback Loops

A system's stubborn and self-sustaining nature illuminates why it can take years to change the culture inside an organization following a BL executive. Feedback loops can initially resist efforts by leaders who attempt to change the system. Yet, with consistency, those same feedback loops reinforce the leader's intended change. Eventually, feedback loops and a consistent inflow of the Leader Touchstones stabilize the system by establishing behavioral norms that ultimately enable sustainable outflows or results.

Daniel Coyle introduced Dr. Jeff Polzer's "vulnerability loop" in *The Culture Code*.[13] Coyle says, "Normally, we think about *Trust* and vulnerability the way we think about standing on solid ground and leaping into the unknown. First, we build *Trust*, then we leap. But science is showing us that we've got it backward. Vulnerability doesn't come after *Trust*—it precedes it." He shares this concept as an essential step for building *Trust* in teams and organizations. Polzer says, "At some level, we intuitively know that vulnerability tends to spark cooperation and *Trust*."

Dr. Polzer's Vulnerability Loop (see Figure 2.6) shows how with consistency and patience, a leader's constructive behavior creates a healthy reinforcing environment inside the organization. This is how it works:

1. Person A sends a signal of vulnerability.
2. Person B detects the signal.
3. Person B responds by signaling their own vulnerability.
4. Person A detects the signal.
5. Repeat as necessary to deepen *Trust*. This repeated action establishes a norm, and *Trust* increases.

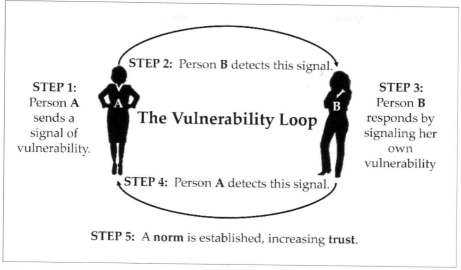

Figure 2.6: The Vulnerability Loop

The caveat is that a single act doesn't change the *Trust* dimension immediately. The receiver must take the step to return vulnerability. The vulnerability loop serves as a guiding concept for LF Leadership and affirms what we know about the general nature of systems. For the system to stabilize and establish a norm, the reinforcing feedback loop may need to occur several times. You and your team of leaders must consistently flood the right behaviors into the system to untangle, the damaging memories from the previous system. As the stock changes to reflect the inflow of healthy culture-building leader behavior, the outflows—sustainable results—will eventually reflect the nature of the stock.

Outflows—Sustainable Results

For organizations to sustain and grow, achieving results is vital. But we've been thinking about results the wrong way for far too long. When results *become* the strategy, with no meaningful roadmap to achieve them, the internal problems within the organization increase in complexity. Strategies should guide team members on what it takes to achieve the results, not vice versa.

High-level strategies and actionable tactics are outputs. In Chapter One, I defined *outputs* as the behaviors that produce *outcomes*—desirable and measurable results. When outcomes or *results* get erroneously and dangerously labeled as outputs or *strategies*, the organization will achieve superficial gains and unsustainable growth, at best. At worst, employees crippled by *cultures of fear* and *fatigue* will sometimes go to any length to "achieve the result." That's why the dynamic, enduring organization system puts results in their rightful place—as the outflow (see the expanded view of the system in Figure 2.7). This still simplified view shows all the Leader Touchstones as inflows and results as outflows.

Do something for me. Take a break from reading this book, and if it's available to you, look at your organization's current strategic plan. Read the top-line strategies. Do any of the strategies include expressions of quantity, such as increase/add or decrease/reduce percentages, numbers, or dollars? If so, your team members will be hard-pressed to achieve them. When executives focus solely on quantitative performance values—measuring KPIs, hitting the numbers, and driving for results—they issue the death sentence for endurance and sustainability. Organizations and the people that manage them have become paralyzed and, in some cases, hypnotized by the results they want or need to achieve—increased sales revenue, higher profitability, new customer acquisition, less customer attrition, and net profit growth.

Accomplishing sustainable results is the final evolution of system behavior before realizing enduring growth. To achieve results, you must first fuel the system stocks with the Leader Touchstones to reinforce healthy culture dimensions.

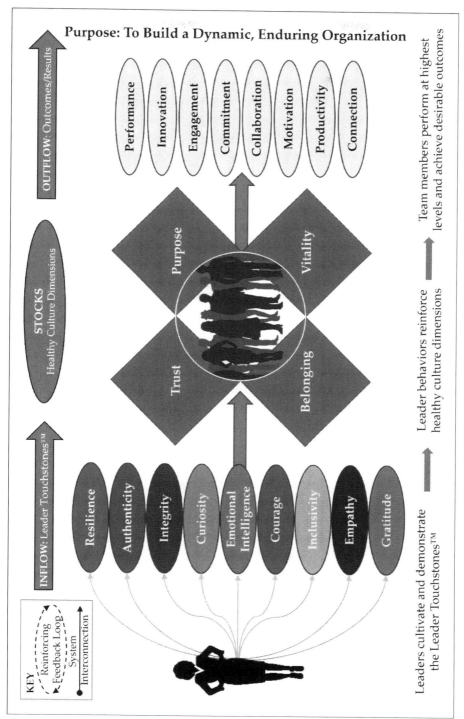

Figure 2.7: Dynamic, Enduring Organization System—Expanded

This unlocks your team's unique potential and creates a breeding ground for prolific results and sustainable growth. The gray box below defines organic results you can expect by first creating the right conditions inside your organization.

~KEY DEFINITIONS—THE RESULTS~

Performance is a team member's ability to consistently deliver exceptional quality, timely, and relevant work products.

Innovation is a team member's identification and implementation of fresh ideas, processes, products, or services that identify cost savings or create a competitive advantage for the organization.

Engagement describes team members' emotional and intellectual investment in delivering high-quality work and achieving the organization's goals.

Commitment reflects team members' dedication and loyalty toward their work to go the extra mile, take ownership, and stay focused on realizing the organization's purpose.

Collaboration refers to team members working harmoniously towards shared goals by leveraging diverse skills, knowledge, and perspectives.

Motivation is a team members' internal drive and desire to excel in their jobs.

Productivity refers to team members' astute prioritization and effective energy management to maximize high-quality work output.

Connection is a team member's ability to foster trust-based, internal relationships through respect and effective, transparent communication.

CHAPTER TWO | 67

PLAYING THE LONG GAME

I opened the section on stocks with a story about an exceptional CEO who has worked methodically to untangle the toxic culture left by the former CEO. After several years of consistent focus, she is finally seeing her efforts materialize into tangible results. The day I was editing this part of the book she called me unexpectedly. She was excited and wanted to share some news. She shared some stories about how the environment inside her organization was starting to resemble the very definitions of healthy culture dimensions. She said that "during a planning meeting, team members respectfully told me that my idea would not work based on the situation."

I told her that she had made it safe for team members to give multi-directional feedback, including to her, two layers up from their positions! The outcome? Together they developed a plan where all possible ramifications were considered, and the team walked away committed to shared accountability in executing the plan. She laughed as she told me this, and I knew it was out of sheer joy. Her hard-won effort was showing signs of working. Some leaders who play the long game do not get to enjoy seeing the fruits of their labors. This particular CEO is getting the chance to experience it right now.

By playing the long game, your team's performance will be higher, more sustainable long-term, and at a lower cost to everyone's health and wellness. When the organization reaches a healthy culture state, and the conditions for *Trust, Belonging, Purpose,* and *Vitality* are met, you no longer need to tell your team members to *be accountable* and *take responsibility*. In this state, team members feel a sense of ownership to help achieve the organization's purpose. And they are motivated to carry on the work, even when you are gone.

CHAPTER THREE
Culture is a Verb

Culture eats everything.
~Marc Benioff, CEO and Co-Founder, Salesforce

I have long shared Peter Drucker's famous quote when talking to teams about the impact of culture on organizational performance—*Culture eats strategy for breakfast.* Then I read the words—*Culture eats everything*—in Marc Benioff's book, *Trailblazer.*[1] Yes! That about sums it up. Researchers and management gurus have studied the link between performance and culture since the early 1950s. Known as the originator of the term *corporate culture*, Elliott Jaques published *The Changing Culture of a Factory* in 1957.[2] His revolutionary research revealed how the company's focus on positive social forces drove effective production and employee collaboration.

John Kotter, who has studied organizational change and culture for decades, gave us one of the most significant research-backed demonstrations of the bottom-line impact of culture. He and James Heskett studied 200 companies and found that strong culture increased net income by 756% over 11 years.[3] A Columbia University study further affirmed this. Of 1,300 executives from major organizations surveyed, 92% answered that improved culture would increase the value of their companies.[4]

Through our work with all types of organizations, I've come to realize that executives are less and less skeptical about the impact culture can have on bottom-line performance *because of* the significant research proving otherwise. The hesitation to see through culture-building efforts comes from two sources—

confusion about *how* to do it and concern about *how long* it will take. Culture-building can feel complex and overwhelming, especially for executives running entire organizations. Since the burden of leading culture starts with them, sometimes intentional culture-building gets pushed to the side.

The other source of skepticism is the amount of time it takes for culture-building to produce sustainable performance impact. Kotter found that significant culture change efforts can take as long as four to ten years.[3] In the dizzying, face-paced digital age, anything that can't be quickly and easily implemented, measured, and proven gets tossed out with the morning garbage. If you think bottom-line (BL) executives are skeptical about culture today, imagine how Jaques's revelations went over 70 years ago!

Most culture-building efforts get pawned off to Human Resources (HR). Before I say anything else on this, I have to stop. That may sound like a snub, and that's far from how it's intended. I want to give a huge shout-out to all my good friends in the HR profession because your positions could not be more critical, complex, and underappreciated. A few years back, one of my students perfectly summed up the profession. She said, "Being in HR, it is assumed that we are bubbly people who love giving out birthday cakes and raises. That's about .02% of the job while the rest is ensuring the company doesn't end up on 60 Minutes."

Some of the most vital internal work—culture, wellness and *Vitality*, and DEI—gets framed as "initiatives" and pushed to HR instead of framed as growth strategies methodically worked by every leader in the organization. There could not be a more important relationship than the one between HR and leadership when it comes to building a healthy culture. However, successful culture-building starts with the leader.

Culture-building *is not* an initiative. Culture-building *is* the most important growth strategy leaders should adopt if they desire to play the long game. The verb form of culture, *culturing*, comes from biology, which means creating and maintaining conditions suitable for growth.[5] This accurately describes the work leaders must do to build a dynamic, enduring organization. So, I've adopted this definition for the Leader-First (LF) model.

~KEY DEFINITION~
Culturing creates and maintains conditions suitable for growth through methodical and intentional planning, execution, cultivation, and measurement.

CULTURING *IS NOT* AN INITIATIVE

I love to bake cakes. Even when I'm only going to indulge in a single bite, the process of baking the cake is my reward. It feeds both sides of my brain. I get to use my right brain to develop innovative designs. Creating something unique that wows the recipient feels like such an achievement. But I also get to use my left brain.

Baking a scratch-made cake correctly is well-planned, complex, painstaking work. It takes patience and insight to give each step in the process the time it needs for the cake to develop properly. If you overmix ingredients, your cake will get too dense. If you undermix, your cake may rise but fall as it cools. Opening the oven during baking can also cause your cake to sink. You can't eyeball measurements when baking the cake like you can when making lasagna. When you don't measure cake ingredients correctly, you can ruin your cake's flavor, stability, and consistency. If your ingredients are too cold, your cake bakes faster on the outside, and you end up with raw centers and burnt edges. It *does* matter if your baking powder expired in 1992. Expired leaveners can cause your cake to flatten in the oven. I could write a book on cake tips based on the lessons I learned in the kitchen while baking.

One chilly morning in November 2020, my *culture-cake* metaphor was born. I was eyeballs deep in flour. The smells of vanilla, and buttercream, and coconut were wafting from my kitchen. I was baking my husband's favorite cake for his birthday—Italian Cream. As I meticulously added one egg at a time, each warmed perfectly to room temperature, this was the moment it hit me. Culturing is a lot like baking a delicious scratch-made cake. But most of the time, companies either focus on covering a poorly made cake with some delicious frosting or opt for the quick-and-easy, boxed cake altogether.

~LEADER-FIRST SPOTLIGHT~
Culturing is a lot like baking a delicious scratch-made cake.

When organizations frame and treat culturing as an initiative versus a growth strategy, the internal culture becomes haphazard efforts fashioned with cool perks like dress-down Fridays, pot-luck Wednesdays, foosball in the breakroom, and Bring-Your-Furry-Friend-to-Work Day. These things *are* cool and lighten the sometimes-challenging environments where we have to spend a fair portion of our lives. Joy in the workplace *is* essential. But when joy and fun become the entirety of the company's culturing effort, these things are just *frosting*. Don't get me wrong, delicious frosting is my favorite part of the cake. But culture is far more than just the frosting.

CULTURING *IS* A GROWTH STRATEGY

I've worked with some BL executives that force feed "fun" to their team members—required happy hours, company retreats, and other perks. At the same time, they overworked their people to the point of exhaustion and burnout. They limited growth opportunities and failed to provide team members with the tools, meaningful feedback, and coaching they needed to be successful. They micromanaged work, sucking up energy and productivity like vacuums. BL executive behavior creates environments where required "fun" gets met with resentment and even anger.

On the other hand, I get to work with some pretty incredible teams who understand that fun is just part of the equation. A few years ago, a company hired me to help their leadership team break through some dynamics preventing them from being a great team. These leaders got in the trenches with me and did some of the most challenging work I have teams do together. We spent time doing what I call *metaphorical Trust falls*. No one is actually falling, and no one is actually catching. However, by the end of the first day, everyone is talking about the hard things that, in the past, have made them uncomfortable, and everyone is there to *catch* what their peers are sharing. By the end of the second day, they've built enough *Trust* to learn how to engage in healthy ideological conflict, as well as share and give multi-directional feedback. The work is not for the faint of heart. When leadership teams willingly take it on and commit to doing it well *after* I leave, they embrace their most untapped competitive advantage—teamwork.

A few months later, these team leaders brought me back to help them scale this work throughout the entire organization. Because our work requires some vulnerability by participants, I kicked off our full-team session with a *Trust*-building exercise.

This particular exercise is not a full "fall," but it is a low-level vulnerability exercise designed to warm team members up to engage openly with one another.

Within minutes of the assignment, several team members had pulled out crates of props from the storage closet. I wish I could show you the pictures of the outcome. Company owners threw on wigs and boas. Entire teams formed moving trains with rolling office chairs. I looked around the office and felt their contagious energy. This team enjoyed working together. Some leaders surprised the team during the afternoon break by commissioning an ice cream truck. We could hear the chimes from a block away. The truck pulled up to the backdoor, and everyone had the chance to pick their childhood favorite. I had a Strawberry Shortcake Crunch… and maybe a Push-Pop.

THE SIX FUNDAMENTALS OF CULTURING

A few years ago, I was facilitating a workshop for a room of CEOs, and I asked a simple question:

Who here has made culture-building a strategic priority?

Nearly every hand in the room pridefully shot up in the air. And then I asked, *"How are you doing it?"* and *"Would you be willing to share a copy of your culture-building strategy or plan with me?"* A blanket of bewilderment fell across the room. Hands slowly returned to laps. A bit perplexed, one of the CEOs said, "It's not written out, but it is so important." Another said, "Our senior leaders have made it a priority." Again, I asked, *"How?"*

I want you to take a moment and think about the last time you led a major change implementation. Perhaps you were launching a new product, integrating a new curriculum, or expanding into new markets. Maybe you were reorganizing your governance structure or planning a major capital campaign. Without a step-by-step plan, you wouldn't take a new product to market or even cultivate a high-impact, prospective client without a laser-focused strategy. You would also equip your team members with the right tools, competencies, and knowledge. Without a tangible approach and the right behaviors, your organization has far too much exposure to variables that could derail your effort. So why would you leave something as important as culture to chance? My recommendation? *Don't.*

If you heed my advice, culturing may initially feel daunting, especially if you have existing internal culture challenges. But don't wait. Just start where you are. Keep in mind that the longer you take to start, the more tangled and convoluted your unhealthy culture becomes. When you take the leap and decide you're ready to make culturing your priority growth strategy, there are some non-negotiable fundamentals that every leader must follow. Doing so improves adoption and sustainability. Each fundamental followed strengthens your culturing effort. The act of culturing itself helps to untangle toxic culture dimensions and reinforce thriving ones.

~BOTTOM-LINE EXECUTIVE BEHAVIOR~
The longer you take to start culturing, the more tangled and convoluted your unhealthy culture becomes.

Even though we cover the Leader Touchstones in depth in Part Two of this book, I want to draw some connections for you now. You will internalize each culturing fundamental more meaningfully when you see it through the lens of the LF

Leadership model. As I go through each fundamental, I will also show you how some of the Leader Touchstones shape desirable, healthy culture dimensions.

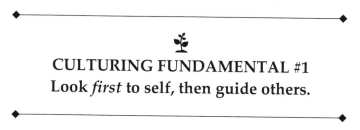

CULTURING FUNDAMENTAL #1
Look *first* to self, then guide others.

This means that you must start with and continue developing the touchstones in yourself before successfully reinforcing those behaviors in others. The act of introspection, personal development, and continual improvement is *Curiosity*. *Curiosity* alone can reinforce healthy culture dimensions. When you demonstrate *Curiosity*, you signal to the team that you care about how you lead them. That subtle signal strengthens the *Culture of Trust*.

Remember that your behaviors reinforce some element of culture when witnessed by team members. Each time you demonstrate a Leader Touchstone, you're also signaling to the team how they should act and what they should prioritize. In Chapter Four, I'll show you how to use culture signals to support your efforts to create a thriving organizational culture.

CULTURING FUNDAMENTAL #2
Never culture alone—share leadership.

Fundamental #2 is vital for a couple of reasons. Earlier in the book, I told you that if it feels lonely at the top, you're probably doing it wrong. Culturing is not a single-player game.

To safeguard the longevity of the thriving culture you will work to create, you must share accountability with every team leader and then make it the responsibility of every person in the organization.

Secondly, if you communicate behavioral expectations, but someone who leads people in the organization doesn't follow those expectations, it signals to the team that you are not serious about the culture changes you want to make. Acts by rogue executives can untangle the *Culture of Trust* you are working so hard to reinforce.

CULTURING FUNDAMENTAL #3
Invite team members to co-create culture.

When you involve your most essential stakeholders—your team members—in developing the most important strategies, you demonstrate the Leader Touchstone, *Inclusivity*. *Inclusivity* is a powerful touchstone. It reinforces every culture dimension—*Trust*, *Belonging*, *Vitality*, and *Purpose*. Including team members in the co-creation process accomplishes three things. First, relying on insight from a diverse team member group ensures that all stakeholders' perspectives are represented. Embracing diversity is not just the right thing to do, it is the smart thing to do. In Chapter Twelve, I will show the bottom-line impact of creating diverse, inclusive organizations. Without perspectives from people with diverse backgrounds and life experiences, you build strategies with holes. Strategies with holes may work for a while, but ultimately, they won't survive the diverse needs of your wider group of stakeholders.

Second, relying on insight from those closest to the experience ensures that you're building an internal culture that supports what your team members need to be successful. Third, when you involve your team members in the co-creation process, you endear them to the resulting strategy and deepen their commitment to ensuring its success.

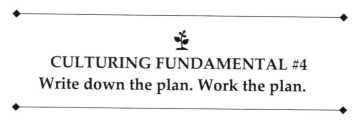

CULTURING FUNDAMENTAL #4
Write down the plan. Work the plan.

To untangle a toxic culture and build a thriving one, you and your team leaders must work your plan like any other major change strategy. Create milestones, set up regular check-ins, allow for plan adjustments if new information becomes available, and celebrate the big and small wins along the way.

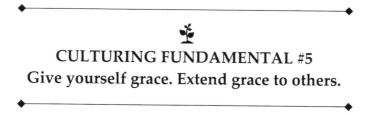

CULTURING FUNDAMENTAL #5
Give yourself grace. Extend grace to others.

Know that you're never going to get it right every time. You're human. Change is hard. Leadership is harder. In these moments, when things go wrong, the very best thing you can do is own up to it. Learn from it. Laugh about it. Make the right shifts to keep it from happening again. Demonstrating the Leader Touchstone—*Integrity*—builds your credibility as a leader. This reinforces the *Culture of Trust*. Remember, just as you are human, so are your team members. Extend them the same grace you give yourself. Extending grace to others is a demonstration of the Leader Touchstone—*Empathy. Empathy* directly reinforces *Cultures of Belonging* and *Trust,* and indirectly reinforces *Cultures of Vitality* and *Purpose.*

CULTURING FUNDAMENTAL #6
Be patient.

Remember that culturing is not a quick-win growth strategy, but it is the only sustainable one. Kotter told us it could take ten years to see the performance impact of culture-building efforts. However, a single infusion of healthy culturing leader behavior starts to change the system immediately—untangling toxic culture dimensions and tangling up the good ones. Just as toxic culture is difficult to untangle, healthy culture resists destructive forces that attempt to damage it.

Let's go back to the team whose story I shared earlier in this chapter. Even though this team does have fun and keeps things light, they also know they had to do some work to resolve some of the more tangible issues facing the company when we first started our work together. They were and still are actively working on building a dynamic, enduring organization today. I titled this chapter *Culture is a Verb* to get you to think about culture differently. I want you to stop thinking of culture as a stagnant noun. Culturing is action—painstaking and intentional work that must be methodically planned, executed, cultivated, and, yes, measured.

~Leader-First Leader Insight~

Paula Bookidis, CEO, Girl Scouts of Central Texas

"I appreciate the human side of business and spent the earliest parts of my career learning what drives and deters people in their work. My leadership philosophy centers on delivering success by focusing on teams and people. I believe that a leader inspires others to dream more, learn more, do more, and become more. As a consultant improving performance for Fortune 100 and 500 companies, I focused on instilling this human-focused mentality into our consulting work, inspiring my teams to help make clients' lives better. This approach to business creates a ripple effect, where deep customer relationships and human-focused policies lead to success time and time again.

As I moved from manager to executive leader to chief decision-maker, I continue to value the benefits of developing human capital. When I became the CEO of Girl Scouts of Central Texas, this was the first organizational challenge I tackled. I evolved human resources policy, improved internal communication and collaboration, and focused on building a healthy culture before anything else. At my organization, we have cultivated respect, empathy, and team member development—critical steps in improving employee relations and, subsequently, our ability to continuously provide high-quality programs and services to girls in our community. Our external success starts and ends with internal culture."

CHAPTER FOUR
The System Fuel—Leader Behaviors

Behavior is the end result of a prevailing story in one's mind—change the story, and the behavior will change.
~Dr. Jacinta Mpalyenkana

The lowest point of my leadership journey happened months before I made a significant professional transition. In fact, this experience was a precipitating event in a series of experiences that culminated in my decision to make the change. To understand the full weight of my action, I'll describe the context surrounding my spectacular failure. At that particular moment in my career, I had a Doctorate specializing in Leadership and Organizational Change. I was teaching executive leadership to global leaders at one of the best Ivy League schools in the country. In my role, I *led* a team of other leadership experts. I preached daily about leadership, to my students, to my clients, and even to my husband when he would listen. I'd tell them things like "leaders never arrive," "leaders are always learning," and "a leader can fail but still rebuild." While this may seem like a high point in my career, this is when I failed my team members as their leader. My failure also served as the most important lesson on my leadership trek. It was humbling, and it was the wake-up call I needed to put me back on my path.

Several years earlier, as a Chief Operating Officer, I was leading a large team within an organization. I was honored to interview *the* rockstar candidate for an open Vice President position on my team. She was the kind of person you would hire on the spot, and you would take with you anywhere you go. She was a candidate who would give you hope that the pile of seemingly unachievable goals could be accomplished if only she would join your team. I did make her an offer. But just before she could accept, her husband received an offer they couldn't refuse in another state. I was devastated, but we had a great connection and decided to stay in touch.

Over the years, we would cheer each other on and check in occasionally through social media. When I posted about an open position on my team, she reached out and expressed interest in applying. She said she'd always wanted to work with me and that my leadership style resonated with her. Of course, I hired her. Unfortunately, what she and my other team members didn't know, and what I had not yet realized, was that the layers of bottom-line (BL) executives above me were influencing and shaping my personal leadership style.

The new executives had a command-and-control style of management, which of course, is 100% their prerogative. However, before these management changes took place, team leaders were trusted to drive their bodies of work and lead teams based on their expertise. After the shift, team leaders no longer had that freedom. Instead, those at the highest levels micromanaged what team leaders and team members did. They also managed *how* we executed the work product, including how we managed personnel issues.

The new management style made it impossible for us to utilize our amassed expertise and knowledge, or to lead authentically. Essentially those at higher levels would manage *through* team leaders. This changed approach starkly contrasted with the expectations set for me when I was hired. It also undermined the experience I brought to the position. In a short period of time, it seemed as though my expertise had little value to the new group of executives and the direction of the organization.

The consultant I hired is a person I respect and with whom I share a high-*Trust* relationship even to this day. During a regularly scheduled one-on-one call, she put a mirror up to me. She said, "Jes, I came to work for this organization because of your leadership. But you are not showing up as the leader I thought you were." In an instant, my heart sank. I was mortified. After digging in with her more and asking her to give me specific, tangible feedback, I realized I had lost my way. I had mindfully cultivated my leadership approach over two decades of leading teams of all sizes and levels of experience. I was no longer leading according to my leadership philosophy or my personal values. I was exhibiting BL executive behavior and managing my team the way I was being managed.

THE DARK SIDE OF AUTHORITY INFLUENCE

No integration has a more significant impact on the effectiveness of the Leader-First (LF) Leadership model than leader behavior and its capacity to influence the behaviors of others. We have known the power of behavioral influence for some time, going back to John Watson's introduction of behaviorism as the prevailing driver for learning.[1] Regrettably, many executives have used their influence as a control mechanism to achieve the desired result.

In the 1960's Stanley Milgram, a Yale University Psychologist, conducted his controversial and well-known study, the *Milgram Experiment*.[2] Milgram initiated his study to answer the question, "*How could the German people allow the Nazis to massacre the Jews?*" More broadly, he intended to understand the conditions that would influence people to obey authority when those in authority commanded actions that went against their conscience.

Milgram recruited 40 men between the ages of 20 and 50 through newspaper advertisements. Each recruit received $4.50 for their participation in the experiment. Participants would enter a room with other individuals who they believed were also participants. These individuals were actors with advanced knowledge of the experiment's intent.

Researchers assigned participants the role of *teacher*, with the actors taking on the role of *learner*. Experimenters instructed teachers to deliver shocks to the learners in an adjacent room when they gave incorrect answers. Before the start of a session, one actor went so far as to tell the teacher that he had a heart condition. The teachers didn't know that learners were actors in the experiment, only pretending to be shocked. They also didn't realize that they were actually the subjects of the experiment. The intent was to see how much influence the experimenter, positioned in the room as an authority figure, could have on the participants' behavior and action.

Milgram's daunting shock generator appeared to give shock levels from 15 to 450 volts, increasing in 15-volt increments. To increase the intimidating nature of the machine, experimenters labeled terms like *slight shock, moderate shock, strong shock, very strong shock, extreme intensity shock,* and finally, the ominous, *XXX–danger: severe shock.* In reality, the experiment was rigged. Teachers were not delivering shocks at all. Learners would provide primarily incorrect answers, with predetermined reactions to increasing shock levels. In the video of the experiment, you can hear the learners pleading with teachers to be released. One learner becomes silent, refusing to answer additional questions. The experimenter instructs the teacher to treat the silence as an incorrect response and continue to deliver the shock.

As the experiment progresses, the experimenter prods the teachers to continue through a series of commands:

"It's absolutely essential that you continue."
"Please continue."
"You have no other choice."
"Go on."
"The experiment requires that you continue."

I've studied the video several times. The teachers become noticeably distressed, conflicted, and uncomfortable, asking the experimenter if they should continue. Some react with resistance, some yell and refuse to continue, and some respond with nervous or inappropriate laughter. But 65%, or 26 of the 40 participants, delivered the highest level of shock. Only 14 participants stopped before reaching the highest levels of voltage.

Milgram's study has been a recurring source of criticism. The controversy comes from the unethical, damaging treatment of his participants due to the level of anxiety they experienced during and after the study. The study would not adhere to ethical treatment standards for human subjects in today's research landscape. However, more ethical replications of the study, even as recent as 2009, have yielded similar results. Whether you agree with Milgram's methods, the outcome still gives us insight into the behavioral influence of people in authority. He demonstrated the dark side of behavioral obedience. Milgram's study and subsequent research provide awareness of how those in authority can have a damaging effect on the behavior of those under their care. When BL executives are driven by results at any cost, they can directly and negatively influence the behaviors of their team members.

The good news is that obedience and behavioral change are not inevitable or absolute. The experiences of the person and the circumstances of the situation *do* have a bearing on what stirs someone to question authority, act against it, or walk away from it. For me, the feedback my team member provided shook me awake and pushed me into introspection. From there, it quickly became apparent that I had fallen off my leadership path. Fortunately for me, I had cultivated enough healthy leader behaviors in my career to *hear* my team member when she trusted me enough to give me tough feedback. In Part Two, when we explore the Leader Touchstones in-depth, we'll examine how *Integrity, Emotional Intelligence, Courage,* and *Authenticity* help leaders and team members gauge appropriate behavioral influence. When cultivated, these Touchstones provide the foundation leaders and team members need to battle the disturbing realities of behavioral influence and *ethical fading*.

~LEADER-FIRST SPOTLIGHT~
Integrity, Emotional Intelligence, Courage, *and* Authenticity *help leaders and team members gauge appropriate behavioral influence.*

Tenbrunsel and Messick introduced the concept of ethical fading to explain pervasive unethical behavior in organizations at the turn of the century.[3] Sometimes unwittingly, humans will engage in self-deception, making trade-offs between self-interest or self-preservation and moral principles. We focus heavily on one aspect of a decision other

~KEY DEFINITION~
Ethical fading is a cognitive phenomenon in which people fail to recognize or consider all the ethical ramifications of their decisions. They become so focused on other aspects, such as financial gains, personal interests, or behavioral pressures, that they unintentionally overlook or downplay the moral implications of their actions.

than the ethical ramifications of the decision. Our brains signal us to see what we want to see by interpreting information that supports our pre-existing beliefs, self-interests, and expectations. As this happens, the other aspects of the decision fade into the background. We may choose unethically, even if we intensely desire to do otherwise.

USE CULTURE SIGNALS FOR GOOD, NOT EVIL

Early trait theory suggested that behaviors are innate or inherited. Trait philosophy gave rise to the Great Man Theory of Leadership—*great leaders are born with traits unique to leaders, not found in all people*. Thank goodness for the behaviorism movement of the 1900s! Behavioral leadership explains how behaviors are learned and reinforced through experiences in our environments. This means that, for better or worse, culture gets reinforced through the actions and inactions of people in positions of power.

BL executives approach behavioral influence differently than leaders. BL executives attempt to change the people inside a system. They see team members as pawns in a game and reinforce toxic *cultures of fear, fatigue, isolation,* and *apathy,* even if sometimes unintentionally. This type of environment suffocates *Authenticity* and squanders the unique gifts of team members. On the other hand, leaders look *first* to themselves, knowing that their behaviors have the power to shape every element in the system. Instead of trying to change the people in the system, leaders change the system. By changing the system, leaders create environments that positively enhance and complement team members' advantages rather than trying to change the team members themselves. This is how you unleash your team members' unique potential.

Reinforcing behaviors, good and bad, are called culture signals. *Culture signals* are intentional or subconscious behaviors—channeled through communication, actions, or decisions—by top-level executives that signal to team members how they should act and what they should prioritize. Before exploring culture signals in more depth, let's look at the odious Wells Fargo fake account scandal. No recent case study more succinctly illustrates the destructive consequence of culture signals negatively shaping team member behavior.

Wells Fargo—Losing its Way

In a 2020 press release, the US Department of Justice detailed the egregious actions of the company over fourteen years. In order to meet unrealistic sales goals, Wells Fargo team members illegally used customers' private information—addresses, social security numbers, birthdates—without consent to open more than 3.5 million banking product accounts such as credit cards, additional bank accounts, direct deposits, and even loan accounts.[4] Wells Fargo's fall from grace starkly contrasts the heritage and folksy brand the banking institution

~KEY DEFINITION~

A *culture signal* is an intentional or subconscious behavior—channeled through communication, actions, or decisions—by a top-level executive that signals to team members how they should act and what they should prioritize.

built on a 170-year history of customer confidence and public trust. The Wells Fargo website proudly touts its legacy:

On March 18, 1852, our founders—Henry Wells and William G. Fargo—built an innovative start-up to help customers build businesses and manage money in a rapidly changing world. Their dedication to finding creative solutions and advocating for more inclusive communities continues to inspire generations of change-makers to build the history of what's next.[5]

In 2008, during the financial crisis, Wells Fargo was one of the only major financial institutions that did not take significant government bailouts. During a difficult economic time, the company was known as a vital, well-run, safe financial institution. This reinforced confidence in Wells Fargo so much that federal regulators helped engineer its acquisition of Wachovia. So how did America's most reputable, trusted, longstanding banking institution lose its way?

THE "GREAT 8" CROSS-SELLING CRUCIBLE

Cross-selling became a badge of honor at Wells Fargo. The company appeared to perfect the art of cross-selling, and Wall Street touted it as the go-to bank. CEO John Stumpf and high-level executives at Wells Fargo framed cross-selling as a way to deepen long-term client relationships. In reality, it bound customers so tightly to the bank that they had difficulty getting out of the banking relationship even when dissatisfied with service. The compensation structure for team members and multiple levels of management depended on cross-selling success. Personal bankers were compensated with a base salary plus bonus and commission pay. Once personal bankers achieved their cross-sell goals, branch managers would receive theirs, regional managers would receive theirs, and so on. The company also framed cross-selling as an organizational health indicator and used its success to entice investors. Stumpf personally pocketed more than $200 million tied to increasing shareholder value due to cross-selling during the fake account scandal.

While Wells Fargo bankers were expected to cross-sell four banking products to every household, management pushed bankers to open at least eight accounts. CEO John Stumpf revealed the catchy "Great 8" benchmark in Wells Fargo's 2010 Annual Report. The eight accounts benchmark was not based on data or specific research indicating that households needed eight accounts, but rather, he liked that eight rhymed with great. Stumpf's nod is a powerful example of a culture signal that communicates to the rest of the organization, "This is what we're going to do."

PERFORMANCE MYOPIA

When managers set narrowly-defined goals focused on quantitative outcomes to drive team member performance, it can create *performance myopia*. Performance myopia is a type of cognitive bias that occurs when team members excessively focus on short-term performance metrics or goals, often at the expense of long-term sustainability and overall success. It involves a narrow focus on quick results, such as financial gains or meeting specific targets, while neglecting broader considerations, such as ethical concerns, employee well-being, customer satisfaction, or the organization's long-term viability. Similar to bottom-line mentality, performance myopia causes decision-makers to make choices that optimize short-term performance but undermine long-term growth, strategic thinking, adaptability, innovation, and reputation.

Performance myopia increases when the goals are devoid of reason or the "why" behind the goals. At the onset, BL executives fail to consider the dynamic drivers of the goal, and team members focus on achieving the goal in the short term. When BL executives fail to coach team members on how to achieve obscure goals, team members focus on the goal itself instead of the long-term ramifications for the organization. Harvard researchers uprooted the long-held management belief that

~KEY DEFINITION~
Performance myopia is a type of cognitive bias that occurs when team members excessively focus on short-term performance metrics or goals, often at the expense of long-term sustainability and overall success.

goal-setting drives high performance.[6] Their study revealed the harmful, systematic side effects of over-prescribed goal-setting. "Goal setting has been promoted as a powerful motivational tool, but substantial evidence demonstrates that in addition to motivating constructive effort, goal setting can induce unethical behavior."

In Netflix's Dirty Money documentary, *The Wagon Wheel*, a former personal banker from St. Helena, CA, Yesenia Guitron, gave a firsthand account of her experience working for Wells Fargo.[7] She broke it down to a problematic 4th-grade math problem. St. Helena is a five-square-mile Napa Valley community with just over 5,000 residents. Yesenia worked at a Wells Fargo branch that employed five bankers. Bank managers expected bankers to open at least eight accounts a day. That is 40 accounts every day. Meeting sales quotas based on the number of community residents would require everyone in the town to open an account within 125 days. This math does not even consider pre-existing account holders at Wells Fargo or other competitor banks in the community.

The drive to achieve these sales quotas created a pressure cooker culture throughout the company.[8] Managers would coach employees on how to inflate sales, endlessly badger them when they could not produce unrealistic sales quotas, force them to work unpaid overtime when they fell short, then fire them if they reported the fraudulent activity to the Wells Fargo ethics hotline.

As the scandal unfolded, BL executives acknowledged their awareness of the illegal actions dating back to 2002. For fourteen years, bankers targeted the elderly, naïve college students, immigrants with language barriers, and desperate entrepreneurs as low-hanging fruit for fraudulent accounts. As early as 2010, there were more than 700 whistleblower complaints on file that regulators blatantly ignored. Some whistleblowers were fired within weeks of filing complaints or were blocked, making finding employment in the financial industry nearly impossible.

A COMPLETE FAILURE OF LEADERSHIP

During Senate and Congressional hearings, Stumpf was repeatedly reproached because while he claimed to "take responsibility" for the fraudulent activity, he continued to isolate the blame on the fired 5,300 bankers and tellers who committed the acts. However, he fell short of calling out the systematic leadership failures that cultivated a culture capable of such actions. Elizabeth Warren's famous rebuke of Stumpf describes how something as simple as Stumpf's culture signals and poorly-developed goals unraveled the internal environment at Wells Fargo (full transcript at end of this section). Inside the organization, BL executives created a *culture of fear* capable of inducing performance myopia and ethical fading in its team members while lining pockets all the way up to the shareholder. Stumpf ultimately resigned under pressure in October 2016 with a $130 million payout. Customers whose identities were stolen and who had accounts created in their names received, on average, $100 per claim.

In 2018, the Federal Reserve sent a resounding message to Wells Fargo when it issued unprecedented sanctions for its criminal action and widespread consumer abuse. "This case illustrates a complete failure of leadership at multiple levels within the bank," said Nick Hanna, U.S. Attorney for the Central District of California.[4] "Wells Fargo traded its hard-earned reputation for short-term profits and harmed untold numbers of customers along the way." The company has since been forced to pay $3 billion to resolve its criminal action. The Federal Reserve also penalized the company by preventing it from growing its balance sheet beyond $2 trillion until it could prove internal changes had been made to circumvent such criminal activity from taking place in the future.

~BOTTOM-LINE EXECUTIVE BEHAVIOR~
"This case illustrates a complete failure of leadership at multiple levels within the bank."
~Nick Hanna, U.S. Attorney

Stumpf and other top-level executives were fined approximately $90 million, and Stumpf agreed to a lifetime ban from working in the financial industry. However, the broken internal culture, the bank's tarnished reputation, countless lives ruined, and shattered customer trust has been far more costly.

Senate Banking Committee Hearing—October 20, 2016
Full Transcript of Senator Elizabeth Warren's Questioning of Wells Fargo CEO John Stumpf

Warren: Thank you, Mr. Chairman. Mr. Stumpf, Wells Fargo's vision and values statement, which you frequently cite says: "We believe in values lived, not phrases memorized. If you want to find out how strong a company's ethics are, don't listen to what its people say; watch what they do." So, let's do that.

Since this massive years-long scam came to light, you have said repeatedly: "I am accountable." But what have you actually done to hold yourself accountable? Have you resigned as CEO or chairman of Wells Fargo?

Stumpf: The board, I serve...

Warren: Have you resigned?

Stumpf: No, I have not.

Warren: Alright. Have you returned one nickel of the millions of dollars that you were paid while this scam was going on?

Stumpf: Well, first of all, this was by 1 percent of our people.

Warren: That's not my question. This is about responsibility. Have you returned one nickel of the millions of dollars that you were paid while this scam was going on?

Stumpf: The board will take care of that.

Warren: Have you returned one nickel of the money you earned while this scam was going on?

Stumpf: And the board will do...

Warren: I will take that as a no, then. Have you fired a single senior executive? And by that, I don't mean regional manager or branch manager. I'm asking about the people who actually led your community banking division or your compliance division.

Stumpf: We've made a change in our regional, to lead our regional banks...

Warren: I just said I'm not asking regional managers. I'm not asking about branch managers. I'm asking if you have fired senior management, the people who actually led the community banking division, who oversaw this fraud, or the compliance division that was in charge of making sure that the bank complied with the law.

Stumpf: Carrie Tolsted...

Warren: Did you fire any of those people?

Stumpf: No.

Warren: No. OK, so you haven't resigned, you haven't returned a single nickel of your personal earnings, you haven't fired a single senior executive. Instead, evidently your definition of "accountable" is to push the blame to your low-level employees who don't have the money for a fancy PR firm to defend themselves. It's gutless leadership.

In your time as chairman and CEO, Wells has been famous for cross-selling, which is pushing existing customers to open more accounts. Cross-selling is one of the main reasons that Wells has become the most valuable bank in the world. Wells measures cross-selling by the number of different accounts a customer has with Wells. Other big banks average fewer than three accounts per customer. But you set the target at eight. Every customer of Wells should have eight accounts with the bank. And that's not because you ran the numbers and found that the average customer needed eight banking accounts. It is because "Eight rhymes with great." This was your rationale right there in your 2010 annual report. Cross-selling isn't about helping customers get what they need. If it was, you wouldn't have to squeeze your employees so hard to make it happen. No. Cross-selling is all about pumping up Wells' stock price. Isn't it?

Stumpf: No. Cross-selling is shorthand for deepening relationships. We only do well...

Warren: Let me stop you right there. You say no? Here are the transcripts of 12 quarterly earnings calls that you participated in from 2012 to 2014, the three full years in which we know this scam was going on. I would like to submit them for the record, if I may, Mr. Chair. Thank you.

These are calls where you personally made your pitch to investors and analysts about why Wells Fargo is a great investment. And in all 12 of these calls, you personally cited Wells Fargo's success at cross-selling retail accounts as one of *the main reasons to buy more stock in the company. Let me read you a few quotes that you had.*

- *April 2012 — "We grew our retail banking cross-sell ratio to a record 5.98 products per household." A year later…*
- *April 2013 — "We achieved record retail banking cross-sell of 6.1 products per household."*
- *April 2014 — "We achieved record retail banking cross-sell of 6.17 products per household."*

The ratio kept going up and up. It didn't matter whether customers used those accounts or not. And guess what? Wall Street loved it. Here is just a sample of the reports from top analysts in those years. All recommending that people buy Wells Fargo stock, in part, because of the strong cross-sell numbers. I would like to submit them for the record.

Chair: *No objections.*

Warren: *Thank you, Mr. Chair. When investors saw good cross-sell numbers, they did, while this scam was going on. That was very good for you, personally, wasn't it, Mr. Stumpf? Do you know how much money, how much value your stock holdings in Wells Fargo gained while this scam was underway?*

Stumpf: *First of all, it was not a scam. And cross-sell is a way of deepening relationships. When customers…*

Warren: *We've been through this, Mr. Stumpf. I asked you a very simple question. Do you know how much the value of your stock went up while this scam was going on?*

Stumpf: *It's … all of my compensation is in our public filing…*

Warren: *Do you know how much it was?*

Stumpf: *It's all in the public filing.*

Warren: *You're right. It is all in the public records because I looked it up. While this scam was going on, you personally held an average of 6.75 million shares of Wells stock. The share price during this time period went up by about $30, which comes out to more than $200 million in gains, all for you personally. And thanks, in part, to those cross-sell numbers that you talked about on every one of those calls.*

You know, here is what really gets me about this, Mr. Stumpf. If one of your tellers took a handful of $20 bills out of the cash drawer, they probably would be looking at criminal charges for theft. They could end up in prison. But you squeezed your employees to the breaking point so they would cheat customers, and you could drive up the value of your stock and put hundreds of millions of dollars in your own pocket. And when it all blew up, you kept your job, you kept your multi-million-dollar bonuses, and you went on television to blame thousands of $12-an-hour employees who were just trying to meet cross-sell quotas that made you rich.

This is about accountability. You should resign.

You should give back the money that you took while this scam was going on, and you should be criminally investigated by both the Department of Justice and the Securities and Exchange Commission. This just isn't right. A cashier who steals a handful of twenties is held accountable. But Wall Street executives who almost never hold themselves accountable. Not now, and not in 2008 when they crushed the worldwide economy.

The only way that Wall Street will change is if executives face jail time when they preside over massive frauds. We need tough new laws to hold corporate executives personally accountable and we need tough prosecutors who have the courage to go after people at the top. Until then, it will be business as usual. And at giant banks like Wells Fargo that seems to mean cheating as many customers, investors and employees as they possibly can.

Thank you, Mr. Chair.

Communication — What You Say Matters

Leaders and BL executives channel their behaviors through three types of culture signals—communication, actions, and decisions. This section explores communication tactics in greater depth. Leaders, remember that your team members are always listening—*what you say matters*. These tactics will guide you in structuring communication to effectively signal the behaviors you want to see in your team members.

COMMUNICATION TACTIC #1
Consistent and Clear

Make messages consistent and clear. Important messages should flow from you and then be replicated clearly and consistently throughout the entire structure of leadership. One of the easiest ways for your leadership team to inform or execute important changes is by consistently and clearly cascading messages in a timely way throughout the organization. Weave messages intended to reinforce culture into your daily verbal and written communications. This ensures that key messages shape the ethos inside your organization. These might include messages about the organization's purpose, the brand promise, and standards of behavior.

COMMUNICATION TACTIC #2
Transparent and Accessible

Mind the gaps. When there are gaps in communication and little or no transparency, team members will fill in the blanks with their own stories. When coaching leaders, frequently I find that they misinterpret the transparency needs of their team members. They mistakenly assume team members want to know everything about everything. In leadership positions, I think you'd agree that is impossible. Most team members actually just want to know that you trust them. Transparency is ensuring that your team members know that you will tell them what you can when you can and that you trust them with sensitive information that can move the team forward.

COMMUNICATION TACTIC #3
Purposeful and Pragmatic

If you want your team members to act in a way that advances the organization's mission or helps achieve its purpose, your communications should reflect that intent. When I led teams in a large membership organization, we were held to the standard of growing membership numbers. But our organizational Mission was not about the number of stakeholders we served, it was about their experience and what their membership in our organization would mean for them and greater society long-term. I had to work with my sales leaders to change their language. We shifted focus away from always talking about the numbers. We started sharing the story behind the member. I wanted them to intuitively understand *why they were there* and *why they should care.*

If you struggle to articulate the why yourself, your team members will unlikely connect with the why. When communications focus solely on numeric values—sales figures, budget numbers, numbers of new customers, numbers of returning customers—then your team members will focus on producing a number devoid of purpose. This could also create an environment conducive to performance myopia. Talk about metrics pragmatically. Ask yourself and your team members:

What do the numbers tell us about ourselves?

If the numbers tell you that you could be doing a better job engaging your customers because few are returning to you, then focus your communications on the actions team members should take to solve the problem. But don't muddy your purpose by making success about a metric—unless your organization's purpose is to *increase sales at all costs.*

🌱

COMMUNICATION TACTIC #4
Illustrative and Inclusive

Use vivid, meaningful language and stories to illustrate your message. Storytelling enhances team members' ability to learn by piquing their interests. It allows them to ground something broad, like a theory or an idea, into something specific and tangible. It also aids in opening your team members' minds to integrate new and connected ideas. For instance, I first introduced you to LF Leadership by telling you the story of my childhood and relationship with my Mom. My hope is that you are connected to the more significant meaning of *"look first to self"* and that it reminds you of the context and purpose of its ideology in a meaningful way.

Connecting to the context and purpose of the idea through stories supports the creation of durable memories. Storytelling also taps into the pathos of listeners by appealing to emotions. Engaging by using pathos does aid in persuasion, but your intent should not be to manipulate. Stories go even further to enhance reinforcement when your team members can visualize themselves in the story. When I work with organizations to implement transformational change efforts, I guide change leaders to *make team members the heroes of the change story.* By explaining the role each person plays, you empower them to exercise agency in helping the organization move through change successfully.

Actions—What You Do Matters More

The second culture signal is your *actions* (or inactions). Leaders, actions that align with spoken words reinforce your credibility, but conflicting signals can indicate deception or hidden motives. This can signal to your team members that you're untrustworthy. Although communication *and* actions are both critically important, *what you* do *matters more than what you* say.

Actions create a tangible impact when you actively engage in tasks, make decisions, and implement plans to achieve specific outcomes. They demonstrate your commitment and ability to follow through on your intentions. Your actions create models of action for your team members to follow and telegraph your expectations. Through actions, you not only say your intentions out loud, but you also manifest your values.

To Decide or Not to Decide

The third culture signal is your *decisions*. Leaders, when you make decisions or choose not to decide, both signal to your team members the type of culture you want to build. Decisions are the most under-acknowledged way culture gets reinforced. Many leaders I work with don't initially consider how decisions can reinforce culture. But once the lightbulb is on, I've watched them start to unravel how their decisions, or lack thereof, negatively influenced culturing in their organizations. Three decision areas create the most opportunity for healthy (or unhealthy) culturing—*Policies, People, and Priorities.*

THE POLICY REVIEW

During strategy development work with organizational leaders, as we work through tangible culturing tactics, I always recommend that they review their policy and procedures (P&P) manual. This surprises them because most executives see P&P as a legal requirement and nothing more. They rarely visit it. But P&P manuals and employee handbooks often contain language that can signal something other than the messages they want to send as they work to reinforce healthy culture dimensions. For instance, say your organization allows flexibility to help build *Cultures of Vitality* and *Trust*. It can sow confusion with your team members when your policy on expected time in the office says otherwise. A P&P review is a necessary part of culturing. You can tap into the Society for HR Management and other resources to develop a list of questions to guide you as you complete the review. I've included a few sample questions here to get you started:[9]

⇒ Who is the audience, and what do we want to accomplish with the policy?

⇒ Will the organization benefit from this policy, and if so, how?

⇒ Is a formal rule necessary for this situation?

⇒ How will team members react to this policy, and why?

⇒ Have we taken the time to gather information about this policy and its effect on our team members?

In addition to these types of questions, use the four culture dimensions as a lens for your review.

⇒ If we want to create a *Culture of Vitality*, will this give our team members the support they need to take the necessary time for energy renewal?

⇒ Does this policy make our team members feel like they *belong*, or does it exclude certain groups from full participation?

⇒ How does our organizational *purpose* get realized with this policy in place?

⇒ If we want to create a *Culture of Trust*, does this policy signal that we don't trust our team members?

To wrap up the policy review section, take a look at the Leader-First Story shared by Crescent Leadership Collaborator and Leadership Development Consultant Jenn Osman—*Trust* as a Policy-Making Lens.

··||·||··|·

A LEADER-FIRST STORY
Trust as a Policy-Making Lens
~Contributed by Jenn Osman, BA, MNA~
Crescent Leadership Collaborator
Leadership Development Consultant

I was turning the key to lock my apartment at 6:00 am on a Thursday, and I could hear my phone ringing inside. "Who would be calling me at this hour? I'll let it go to voicemail." I was headed downtown to host a two-day focus group where about twenty high-level subject matter experts were gathered. It was "go time" after several months of planning and preparation. Instantly I remembered the consultant who was in town to help facilitate the event.

Perhaps he needed something! I unlocked the door in a mad scramble to pick up the phone before it stopped ringing. The Caller ID was my grandparents' number.

My grandfather, a WWII veteran and former prisoner of war, spoke in a no-nonsense tone and told me my mother's sister Jean had died at 3:00 am that morning. There was not much information to share at that time. We would learn in the days to come that she had been suddenly stricken with a rare, almost always fatal blood condition and had died just six hours after a neighbor brought her to the emergency room. My grandfather asked me to be the one to let my brother and parents know. Shocked, I said, "Of course," and we hung up. He was not a cold man. He had a job to do and deputized me to get the word out to my family. What he had asked of me was not a simple task. My parents had retired a year prior and were full-time RVers. Being the early days of cell phones, they never turned theirs on unless they would make a call. I wasn't sure how to find them.

I started by calling campgrounds they had mentioned recently. I left tear-filled messages on answering machines describing their vehicles. "They have Illinois license plates…Can you please look for them and have them call their daughter?" It was the hardest and longest morning of my life, knowing that I was about to break my mother's heart and that this news would change her life forever.

That was Thursday. Once I connected with my parents later that day, we had to find a way to get them back to Chicago as soon as possible. I called airlines and even a friend who was a pilot. Ultimately, my parents decided to drive straight through the following day, and I was waiting outside for them when they pulled up to my brother's house. Being together was all that we knew to do. We held each other close and held each other up the best we could that weekend. My Aunt Jean's funeral was scheduled for Monday morning.

Over the course of this unforeseen and traumatic experience for our family, I missed three days of work. I marked those days as bereavement absences when I turned in my timesheet. Later that week, I received a terse and unsympathetic voicemail from our HR staff. "Since it was just your aunt who died, you only get one day off." Our policy did not include aunts as the immediate family (many policies don't), and I was chastised for thinking it did. Hadn't I read the employee handbook? I was hurt, I was grieving, and I was angry at the insensitivity. My Aunt Jean was like my second mom. She was my biggest fan. She lived with us when I was very young. Our families vacationed together every summer. She was immediate family to me.

I had a discussion with my boss, and I asked him, "Of the three days I missed, which two should I have worked? The day I was searching for my parents? The day my mother arrived and crumbled into my arms? Or the day of my aunt's funeral? Which ones?" To his credit, he negotiated with HR to allow me to have three days of paid bereavement, though I suspect he was more afraid of me and my rawness than anything else. Regardless, I will never forget how much that meant to me. He was not a perfect boss and definitely not my favorite boss. Yet, when I needed flexibility, he supported me in a way that he had the power to do.

I spent much time over the following years thinking about that bereavement policy. How many other dedicated employees had experienced something similar, and how had they reacted to it? Did they perceive a message that their grief was not valid, that they were weak, or that someone thought they were trying to get away with something? Had the experience alienated them or impacted their commitment to the organization? Who the heck decides who immediate family is? Why would grief be limited to one-size-fits-all when empirically, it is not? How come these policies aren't flexible? I suspect the answers lie in a mash-up of historically-traditional family structure, outdated Theory X management practices, lack of inclusiveness in the definitions of both family and immediate family, and limited perspectives on grief and expectations for what it means to experience loss. Just a few minor factors, right?

It is impossible to judge what will shatter someone else's heart and make it impossible for them to focus on work. Apart from more "traditional" losses, there are countless personal traumas that policies cannot comprehensively consider. However, they are all valid reasons for being unable to work temporarily.

Consistency and clarity are essential in policies. At the same time, leaders have an opportunity to build in flexibility during policy revision and creation. Doing so codifies and communicates respect for the members of our teams as unique individuals. These policies can serve to reinforce the *Culture of Trust* and normalize vulnerability. There is no better way to empower our team members to use discernment when making professional and personal decisions.

When discussing flexible policies, I get the question, "But what about people who would take advantage of flexibility?" Yes, there may be employees who stretch the policy beyond its intent. That said, when leaders work to build *Cultures of Trust*, staff at all levels demonstrate a greater commitment to the organization, its mission, and the *Integrity* of its relationships. In a healthy organization, abuse of such policies is minimal, and productivity and performance are higher.

My Aunt Jean's premature death changed our family forever. It is one of those experiences that impacts your life not only in the moment but equally in the lasting lessons you carry forward. I could not have learned those lessons without experiencing that loss, and I honor my Aunt Jean's memory when acknowledging the pain of others' experiences. Policies that encourage flexibility and promote *Trust* free us to lead with our hearts through incredibly tough days.

Additional resources on bereavement policies are found in the Notes and References section for Chapter Four.

PEOPLE DECISIONS — GOOD EGGS AND BAD EGGS

Earlier in the book, I told you that organizational behavior is collective human behavior. Because of this, *people decisions* profoundly impact culturing success. When it comes to people, your decisions signal to the rest of the organization the type of organizational behavior you want to perpetuate. Your answers to these questions bear heavily on culture reinforcement:

⇒ Who do you choose to hire, and why?
⇒ Which team members get promoted, and which team members don't?

⇒ Which team members get opportunities for professional development?

⇒ Which team members get held accountable or fired for bad behavior, and which don't?

Most decision-makers start with good intentions. They start by thinking, "We're going to hold out to hire the best candidate for the position no matter how long it takes." "If a team member doesn't embody our values, we will cut ties with them." One of my former leaders called team members either *good eggs* or *bad eggs*. Sometimes in the freneticism of demanding workplaces, the right answers don't come. Bad eggs get to stay because everyone else is overworked and can't take on more responsibility. Unqualified candidates get hired quickly because a *warm body* is more important than *no body*.

Subconsciously, it may feel like you're making the right decision. You think you're protecting your good eggs by not letting a bad egg go when your team members have no capacity to take on more. But keep in mind, typically, the bad eggs are in your organization for the wrong reasons. In the long run, they create more problems and cause you and your team members more work and anxiety. Along the way, you'll lose some good eggs due to your decisions.

NOT EVERYTHING CAN BE A PRIORITY

Leaders, what you prioritize tells your team members what is most important to you and signals to them what they should prioritize. A few years ago, I facilitated a leadership workshop with Crescent Leadership Collaborator Maryann Dwyer. Our message was about prioritizing energy renewal and how energy directly impacts leadership effectiveness. Even then, before I developed the LF Leadership model and identified specific Leader Touchstones, we knew *energy renewal* and *Resilience* were essential to leadership. During the session, we asked, "How do you encourage your team members to prioritize their energy renewal?"

One of the CEOs stood up and said, "It starts with me." She shared that even though she told her team that she cared about them taking the time to renew their energy, she couldn't get them to do it. Prioritizing and then modeling the behavior was the only way she could get her team members to focus on prioritizing healthy decisions. At her workplace, calendar details are shared openly. She added her midday walk as a public entry on her calendar so that her team could see this as an important break in her workday. Once she did this, her team members interpreted this as a priority. Afterward, they felt more comfortable taking needed breaks to renew their energy throughout the day.

By now, you know that your behaviors have a resounding influence on the behavior of those team members under your care. Just as your behaviors can impact the outcome of a product launch or client cultivation, they also reinforce, for better or worse, organizational culture. Like the butterfly effect or dropping a pebble in the water, when you infuse a behavior in the organization today, it creates a ripple in the system that changes it. How the organization's future gets shaped depends on the signals you send today based on the legacy you choose to leave.

CHAPTER FIVE
Shared Leadership—Lend Your Superpowers

*Sometimes leadership is planting tree under
whose shade you'll never sit.*
~ Jennifer Granholm

I can't count the number of times I've heard the phrase, "Jack Welch was one of the world's greatest leaders." I want to offer an amendment to that statement. "Jack Welch was one world's best bottom-line (BL) executives and made lots of money for shareholders." During the 80s and 90s, he was the poster child for increasing shareholder value. Welch was known for his relentless emphasis on short-term financial results. He implemented a strategy called "Neutron Jack," which involved cutting costs and jobs aggressively to improve the bottom line.[1] While this approach boosted profitability in the short term, it undermined long-term investments in research, innovation, and employee development.

Over his twenty golden years at the helm of General Electric (GE), Welch eviscerated the middle class and slashed more than 170,000 jobs with a single goal—push shareholder value higher and higher, and by any means necessary.[2] He implemented a performance evaluation system called *Rank and Yank,* where he annually fired the bottom 10% of employees.[1] This created a cutthroat environment, pitting team members against each other. It might have given him the immediate impact he needed to improve the bottom line, but in the process, he built a *culture of fear*, stifled creativity, and hindered collaboration and teamwork inside the company.

During Welch's tenure, GE experienced several controversies and ethical lapses. GE's fraudulent accounting practices in the late 1990s and early 2000s resulted in a $50 million settlement with the U.S. Securities and Exchange Commission. In 2001, the year of Welch's retirement, the company had achieved record earnings—an 11% increase in earnings and a 12% growth in cash flow from operating activities.[4] GE's market value grew from $15 billion to $594 billion in twenty years. Welch's GE was a Wall Street dream. For nearly a century, GE operated *in the balanced best interests of all*.[5] But Welch changed that. He focused on success in the moment.

Welch's aggressive style and pressure to meet financial targets encouraged the prioritization of short-term gains over ethical conduct, and organizational longevity. The overly complex conglomerate structure he crafted would also become its downfall when he was gone. Welch failed to prepare those that came after him to run the flawed and intricate system he had built. In November 2021, GE announced that it would separate its remaining three business lines—aviation, healthcare, and energy—into distinct entities. Once considered the greatest business conglomerate of all time, GE has now wasted away to a shadow of its former self.[2]

SHARED LEADERSHIP—THE MODEL

Long before GE and Jack Welch, Mary Parker Follett introduced shared leadership in response to the limitations of traditional top-down organizational structures. Follett, the mother of modern management, was an organizational behaviorist ahead of her time. In the 1920s, this social worker and management consultant advocated for collective, inclusive leadership and believed authority should be derived from knowledge and experience rather than hierarchical positions.[6] Follett's approach emphasized cooperation, mutual respect, and collective accountability.

A Pivotal Paradox—Power With, Not Power Over

Shared leadership provides a refreshing alternative to hierarchical leadership structures. By sharing leadership, leaders can unlock the potential of each team member and the organization's collective intelligence. The phrase "share leadership" itself is somewhat of a paradox. A leader's natural inclination to… well… *lead*. To embrace it means to let go of control and opt for collaboration in its purest form.

Unlike traditional models, Follett's shared leadership model emphasized power distribution rather than power concentration. It rejects the idea that leaders exert authority over subordinates and instead promotes a *power-with* approach. In this model, leaders empower team leaders and team members by sharing power and involving them in decision-making.

Beyond the Leader

Raul Yzaguirre is primarily known for his work as a prominent Civil Rights activist for the Latino community. From 1974 to 2004, Yzaguirre led the National Council of La Raza (NCLR), the largest national Hispanic civil rights and advocacy organization in the United States. Yzaguirre expanded the influence and visibility of the NCLR, transforming it into one of the most influential Latino advocacy organizations in the country. Under his leadership, the organization grew from a regional advocacy group to serving 41 states, Puerto Rico, and the District of Columbia.

Leaders across sectors herald Yzaguirre's genius, but they rarely talk about his knack for playing the long game. Perhaps his greatest superpower was his ability to build a high-performing, effective team and his commitment to share leadership. Yzaguirre had the foresight to find people who would complement his strengths and weaknesses. Instead of trying to be everything to everyone or expecting his team members to do the same, he built a dynamic team and then capitalized on their natural advantages.

During an interview, Yzaguirre said, "One of my most important talents is being creative. I have ten ideas, and eight of them are worthless, but the two that are good are what make the organization. And I surround myself with people who are not shy about telling me which are which."[7] He built a competent, collaborative leadership team who put the needs of the organization and the team ahead of personal needs and ego. He also gave them a safe place to learn and experiment. Eventually, through his empowerment, Yzaguirre could let them lead without his direct supervision, freeing him up to execute strategy and grow the organization's external presence.

Yzaguirre's story is a powerful example of how shared leadership can propel an organization forward, even through challenging times. During Yzaguirre's successful 30-year tenure, the organization's growth catapulted. But the true test of a leader's effectiveness happens after they've exited their leadership positions. A review of UnidosUS's financial statements and the organization's cumulative bottom line shows steady growth since 2004. They have not been up each year, but the growth has been stable over time. In 2021, UnidosUS reported net assets of over $95 million, compared to $53 million in 2004. More important than financial health, UnidosUS's annual *Impact Report* details the pervasive influence of the organization.[8]

In 2021 alone, UnidosUS reached 36 million people with important information about COVID-19 vaccines, and 114 thousand people received vaccines through the affiliate network. UnidosUS served more than 60 thousand people with housing counseling and financial coaching. UnidosUS's advocacy for Child Tax Credit expansion and direct support helped to lift 1.4 million children out of poverty. These represent just a few highlights from the report.

Yzaguirre's successor, Janet Murguía, and her team have continued the organization's important work. Not only has the organization endured, but it has also transcended the significant market fluctuations and changing political landscape over the past two decades. Leaders who share leadership make it possible for the organizational system's purpose to continue, even after they are gone.

Tools of the Trade

At Crescent Leadership, when we coach leadership teams to implement shared leadership models, we focus first on building *Trust*. Shared leadership can't thrive in environments without *Trust*, transparent communication, and mutual respect.

From the foundation of *Trust*, we train leaders to use two shared leadership tools—*healthy ideological conflict* and *multi-directional accountability.*

Healthy Ideological Conflict

Instead of avoiding or suppressing it, we work with teams to rethink conflict. *Healthy ideological conflict* is constructive and respectful exchanges of divergent ideas, beliefs, values, or perspectives on a team. It involves a genuine willingness to engage in open and honest discussions, allowing team members to challenge each other and express their viewpoints while maintaining a respectful and tolerant environment. We start by working with them to develop a set of conflict norms that they use during engagements to guardrail their approach. Then we encourage

~KEY DEFINITION~
Healthy ideological conflict is constructive and respectful exchanges of divergent ideas, beliefs, values, or perspectives on a team.

them to *mine* conflict—actively seek it out—as a way to open dialogue and ensure all voices get heard on important issues that impact the entire organization.

When teams engage in healthy ideological conflict, they focus on understanding and critically analyzing diverse perspectives rather than seeking personal attacks or trying to prove their superiority. Buurtzorg, a Dutch healthcare organization, operates with self-managing teams of nurses who collectively make decisions about patient care. The organization's emphasis on autonomy, *Trust*, and group problem-solving has improved patient outcomes and increased job satisfaction among nurses.[9] They approach conflict with the intention to foster intellectual growth, stimulate creativity, and arrive at well-informed decisions or solutions.

Multi-Directional Accountability

Rather than relying solely on top-down accountability, shared leadership emphasizes the value of multi-directional accountability and shared ownership. *Multi-directional accountability* is the practice of holding leaders, colleagues, and yourself responsible for behaviors, performance, and adherence to shared goals and values. Like with healthy ideological conflict, the team must first build a strong *Culture of Trust,* where they feel empowered to provide

~KEY DEFINITION~
Multi-directional accountability is the practice of holding leaders, colleagues, and yourself responsible for actions, behaviors, performance, and adherence to shared goals and values.

feedback, challenge one another, and ensure everyone contributes to the organization's success. Multi-directional accountability operates on the principle that everyone has a vested interest in each other's and the organization's success and growth.

3M encourages team members to take on leadership roles and supports initiatives such as the "15 Percent Culture," where they spend 15% of their time pursuing innovative projects outside their regular responsibilities. 3M's approach has fostered a culture of empowerment, resulting in numerous breakthrough innovations over the years.[10] Semco Partners, a Brazilian conglomerate, implemented shared leadership as a part of its radical workplace transformation.[11] The company quashed traditional hierarchies, encouraged team members to participate in decision-making, and introduced flexible work practices. This shift empowered them to contribute ideas and take ownership of their work, increasing productivity and profitability.

Wash, Rinse, Repeat

Former Ford CEO Alan Mulally, known for leading one of the most brilliant turnarounds in business history, intuitively understood the importance of shared leadership when he took the helm of Ford. Every case study about the Mulally/Ford story is chocked full of compelling findings, and I'll share more of these with you in Chapter Six. Mulally relentlessly pursued transformational change at Ford, in the same way he had at Boeing, and he did this by fixing what was broken on the inside first. In an email to the free press, Ford Executive Chairman Bill Ford said:

I think his greatest achievement was the culture shift he brought to Ford, Alan's genuine interest in people really transcended everything we did and largely was the reason everyone rallied behind him because they could see he was an authentic leader that cared about people and the business.[12]

But Mulally wasn't perfect, and just like any leader, he did make mistakes. Despite a setback here or there derailing his plan, he committed to seeing it through and making adjustments when needed. The most profound conclusion of his epic turnaround is how Mulally left Ford. Mulally transitioned leadership to COO Mark Fields six months earlier than expected. When asked why, he said that Fields and the team were ready.[13]

Mulally planned his succession with the long game in mind. He did two critical things to ensure the work would continue in his absence. First, he prepared his team members to *lead people well* after he was gone. Second, he didn't do the work alone. Mulally included his team in the work of creating the culture he knew they had to perpetuate. Upon taking leadership of the company, Fields talked about knowing the plan and knowing how to work the plan—he called it "wash, rinse, and repeat."

BUILD MORE LEADERS

Even in a shared leadership model, the leader or teams of leaders set the tone and model behavior for the entire organization. The point of a shared leadership model is not that top-level leaders are unnecessary, rather, organizations are more likely to thrive within complex, continuously changing environments when leadership comes from many places within the organization, drawing on the unique advantages of each team member. Leaders aim to identify and build more leaders who embody the Leader Touchstones so they continue to reinforce enduring growth well into the future.

To wrap up this chapter on shared leadership, I have included a powerful Leader-First Story from Crescent Leadership Collaborator Alison Wilcox. Alison is also a successful nonprofit CEO and consultant. Her article brings insight into building both *Cultures of Trust* and *Vitality*. In her experience, when she chose to share leadership so that she could focus on her own energy renewal, she realized the unintentional outcome of building trust with her team.

A LEADER-FIRST STORY
Put Down the Anvil and Put Trust in Those You Lead
-Contributed by Alison Wilcox-
Crescent Leadership Collaborator and Nonprofit CEO

In April 2021, I hit a wall. For over a year, I had been going on pure adrenaline as a nonprofit CEO, board member, and working mom. I was left running on fumes. My mental health counselor asked me to describe the sensations I was feeling. My shoulders clenched. I could feel heavy metal pushing down on my shoulders. An image came to me. I grasped to find the right word. "An anvil," I said. "An anvil is around my neck." "Wow," she said.

We both looked at each other on the video screen and started to laugh. Once I said it out loud, some of the weight of the world I was carrying melted away. After our session, I realized that in the stress of 2020 and early 2021, I had forgotten my own leadership advice. I was going solo, thinking I had to have all the answers, forgetting I was part of a team.

I had already been planning to schedule listening sessions with my leadership team to check in with them, and I decided that this was the most important thing for me to prioritize and to open the sessions up to the whole staff team—anyone who was interested in spending time with me, and sharing what was on their mind. After just one session, I knew this was the wisest use of my time.

I shared a LinkedIn post describing what I was feeling, and the responses told me I wasn't the only one feeling this way. This is what I wrote:

"I've never found leading so hard. I feel privileged to be in a leadership role and grateful to be still employed at this time, and leading, especially now, is hard.

Organizations are about people. People are struggling. And we must support our people to accomplish the missions we set out to do. I can barely keep up with my laundry, let alone feel like I am doing enough to support our team through their different challenges. So instead of sitting alone with the latest "10 things you must do or you're doing it wrong" leadership article, I've been spending time in listening sessions with my staff team. Connecting one-on-one and hearing what they think is the best leadership advice. What keeps them up at night? What are they excited about? What do they wish we could do differently? What could the organization and I do better to support them?

Not only am I learning and hearing great insights and direction, but it's also so nice to spend quality time with awesome people. After an incredibly stressful year, I'm using this time to pause, connect, reset, and realize that I'm not in this alone. If you sometimes feel you're not up to the task, or you are carrying the weight of the world, remember you're not alone."

The responses from my post let me know that others were feeling the same way. That moment marked a turning point for me, professionally and personally. By giving up the mantle of the "smartest person in the room," I unleashed a domino effect.

#1—EMPATHY

I felt more connected to my team, which in turn, made me feel less isolated. That alleviated some of my stress. Being less isolated and less stressed helped me to listen better. By listening better, I became more empathetic and more willing to consider alternate points of view, especially when those ran counter to deeply held beliefs I had about leadership and productivity.

#2—LEARNING

It is a cliché to say that none of us are as smart as all of us, but it is also true. I was overwhelmed because I was worried that I wasn't doing enough or doing the right things to help my team, and I thought I needed to have all the answers. The simplest way to find answers is by asking, listening, and hearing from the people you lead. The collective wisdom of each person who took the time to meet with me shaped the priorities for our organization.

#3—TRUST

As I learned to be more vulnerable, to ask for help, and to give more opportunities for leadership to others instead of clinging to the work myself, my *Trust* in the team grew even more.

#4—BALANCE

As I stopped centering on myself and trusted in the team around me, the weight began to tip back into balance. I had been working far too many hours, and my productivity wasn't better because of it. This balance allowed me to regain a foothold in my personal life.

My son was graduating from high school, and I devoted time to savoring this transition in his life, being present for and with him, and also to what was next for me. I set an intention to write and plan a trip to Scotland in 2022—a three-week vacation that was the sabbatical I needed. Since then, I wrote a chapter about *Courage* which was published in a book, and launched my blog, Birth of Adventure!

By creating space for myself outside of work, I can be more purposeful, present, and empathetic with my team, and in turn, do my best to advocate that they create space for themselves too. Even though I lead a new organization now, that organization's results continue to steadily grow, demonstrating that holding tight and being stressed are not necessary ingredients for productivity.

As a leader or aspiring leader, you have a burning need inside you to make a difference. To lead is to serve people. You can't do it alone. Trusting others, focusing on energy renewal and *Vitality*, collaborating, and finding your purpose, are all essential to leadership.

If you have gotten tired in the past few years, you're not alone, and if you're like me and the last thing you want to do is read a *"10 things you must do, or you're doing it wrong"* leadership article, put down the anvil, and reach out to the people on your team. Find out what they're thinking, worried about, or excited about. Putting the work down and connecting to what excites you in life only improves how you lead people.

PART TWO

THE LEADER TOUCHSTONES™
Leadership is a never-ending journey.

CHAPTER SIX
The Leader-First Leadership Journey

When you are inspired by some great purpose, some extraordinary project, all your thoughts break their bonds; your mind transcends limitations; your consciousness expands in every direction, and you find yourself in a great, new, and wonderful world.
~Patanjali

If the past two years have taught us anything, it's that, as leaders, we cannot control market disruptions, the actions of our competitors, or any other manner of existential crises. What can we control? We can control what happens inside our organizations. Alan Mulally knew this and made it his primary focus at Ford. If the framework for Leader-First (LF) Leadership had existed during his time, Mulally would have represented the embodiment of it. He was a systems leader. He used constructive behavioral influence to methodically shape healthy internal culture. And he shared leadership by building a naturally reinforcing succession environment.

I remember watching Mulally testify at the congressional hearing where he pledged to take an annual salary of $1 until he could turn the business around in the wake of a $14.6 billion company single-year loss. Before he assumed the position of CEO in 2006, the company had lost 25% of its market share.[1] But by 2010, Ford had posted 16 consecutive quarters of growth and ranked as the most profitable automaker in the industry, touting $6.6 billion in profit.[2]

The Mulally/Ford turnaround story inspired the first leadership and culture workshop I developed in the early years of my consulting work. LF Leadership was still evolving in my mind and unfolding in my research. We had not yet experienced the recent pandemic, widespread lockdowns, or the economic recession that followed. I built the components of the workshop based on Mulally's multi-dimensional approach that accentuated systematic culturing. Mulally knew that even amid financial failure, he had to focus on rebuilding the company from the inside first if the organization were to survive *and* thrive long-term. Nothing could fix the external brand experience except repairing what was broken inside the company. Mulally knew that started with his example.

Bottom-line (BL) executives consumed with quick wins and short-termism mistakenly assume that building an enduring organization from the inside out is unrealistic and even impossible during turbulent times. Yet Mulally showed us that transformational change *is* possible during an organization's most merciless moments. He steadily worked to untangle what he described as a toxic, unfocused, dysfunctional culture at Ford. Within a year, he had galvanized more than 300,000 team members and aligned them around a shared vision.

~LEADER-FIRST SPOTLIGHT~
Organizational transformation is *possible during an organization's most merciless moments.*

When Mulally took the CEO job at Ford, the company was in a much different state. "Ford had become a house of brands. No one knew what the blue oval stood for anymore."[3] Executives would openly brag about driving cars other than Ford brands. Not a single Ford was parked in the executive garage when Mulally arrived. His executive team members didn't trust one another. There was no transparency. Each executive focused on self-preservation rather than fixing the flailing company. They mistakenly assumed that Mulally would quickly replace them with his own people. However, unlike most new executives, Mulally desired to preserve institutional knowledge—the history and the problems. Rather than lead with staffing cuts, he initially took the time to get to know team members. Mulally curiously navigated the company working to understand each person's unique value. Through his actions, he signaled to the executives the kind of culture he expected to build alongside them, then held them accountable to his expectations. Mulally knew he would not need to terminate anyone. Team members self-eliminated once they discovered they did not align with his new direction.[4]

As Mulally spent time getting to know team members throughout the organization, he recognized he would need to include those people most impacted by the company culture in creating a plan that would change it. He had an uncanny ability to see people and genuinely cared about hearing their voices. Early on, Mulally tapped Ford's brightest team members and then put them to work on creating a new direction for the company. Mulally called the plan *One Ford*, aligning stakeholders to work together across the company's vast global ecosystem. *One Ford* spelled out the expected behaviors necessary to achieve the company's vision (see *Figure 6.1*).

Mulally's messaging didn't emphasize improving the bottom line. He didn't push the team to innovate and create new products. Instead, Mulally developed the behavioral blueprint for how the team would courageously achieve those things together. *One Ford*'s behavioral expectations were not optional. Mulally led with the behaviors himself and expected them from the rest of his team. Over time, as Mulally and his

ONE FORD

F: Foster Functional and Technical Excellence

- Know and have a passion for our business and our customers.
- Demonstrate and build functional and technical excellence.
- Ensure process discipline.
- Have a continuous improvement philosophy and practice.

O: Own Working Together

- Believe in skilled and motivated people working together.
- Include everyone; respect, listen to, help, and appreciate others.
- Build strong relationships; be a team player; develop ourselves and others.
- Communicate clearly, concisely, and candidly.

R: Role Model Ford Values

- Show initiative, courage, integrity, and good corporate citizenship.
- Improve quality, safety, and sustainability.
- Have a can-do, find-a-way attitude and emotional resilience.
- Enjoy the journey and each other; have fun—never at others' expense.

D: Deliver Results

- Deal positively with our business realities; develop compelling and comprehensive plans while keeping an enterprise view.
- Set high expectations and inspire others.
- Make sound decisions using facts and data.
- Hold ourselves and others responsible and accountable for delivering results and satisfying our customers.

Figure 6.1: One Ford—Expected Behaviors

leadership team reinforced the right behaviors, they cultivated a culture where all team members could thrive and perform at their highest levels.

Some BL executives mistakenly assume that new products and services can solve systemic organizational failure. Internally toxic organizations suffocate innovation in two ways. First, if the organization *does* produce innovative products, implementation and customer delivery rarely flourish. Second, innovation fails to happen in the first place due to fear-induced risk aversion. Leaders must first prioritize untangling the toxic culture and rebuilding a healthy one. Healthy culture breathes life into innovation. Innovation at Ford happened organically. No one forced it. Mulally trusted team members to take risks, fail, and learn from failures. Eventually, what was happening on the inside started reflecting in Ford's external relations—and this time around, in the right way. Mulally's *One Ford* is widely known as the plan that returned Ford to a leadership position in the automobile industry.[4]

~LEADER-FIRST SPOTLIGHT~
Healthy culture breathes life into innovation.

I have often shared the Mulally/Ford story with teams of leaders when explaining how organizational systems work. However, talking about the turnaround doesn't always go far enough to show how the right leader behaviors lead to a healthy culture, and *then* healthy culture creates a breeding ground for high performance, innovation, commitment, and other desirable team member outcomes. Using the Mulally/Ford example, I want to show you how this works. Under section two of *One Ford*—Own Working Together—one of the behavioral expectations is to *"communicate clearly, concisely, and candidly."* The words weren't just written in a document and posted on a breakroom wall. Mulally said the words repeatedly (communication signal) and aligned his actions with his communications (action signal).

Early in Mulally's tenure, he could not get executive team members to talk to one another, least of all him. The *culture of fear* was deep, and no one was willing to share bad news. But knowing bad news quickly is critical in a failing organization. During his 7 am Thursday morning Business Plan Review (BPR) meetings, Mulally asked questions about how each division was doing. At every BPR meeting, his team members continued to say there were no problems. After repeatedly getting the same story, he changed his tactic.

Mulally implemented a color code system for the presentations executive team members used to report status updates during BPR meetings. The system was simple—green for no problems, yellow if problems existed but teams were actively dealing with the problem, and red if problems existed, but teams had not yet identified a solution.[4] It took some time, but Mulally overtly stating his expectation for candid communication, demonstrating it himself through his actions, and providing safety in the form of color-coded cards gave executive team members a small opening to trust Mulally's genuine desire for transparency.

Mark Fields, who would eventually succeed Mulally as CEO of Ford in 2014, was the first to show a red card during his presentation. Instead of admonishing him, Mulally gave him a round of applause and told Mark his report had great insight and visibility. This moment was pivotal for Ford. Mulally's applause and compliment signaled to Mark that *Integrity* and transparency were safe and highly valued. Although it was the first of many steps in untangling the *culture of fear*, it started the ripple that eventually built a *Culture of Trust* at Ford.

~Leader-First Leader Insight~

Lieutenant Colonel Kady Griffin
United States Air Force

"One of my leadership philosophy tenants is that bad news doesn't improve with age. When the leader visits parts of the organization, people are reluctant to tell the real story. Everything is always rainbows and unicorns. But we know this is not reality.

I encourage my team members to tell me that the emperor isn't wearing any clothes. Creating that level of trust environment is easier said than done, but that's what is necessary. As leaders, we must create safe environments where bad news is normalized. I tell my team to embrace the red because that is where we grow."

TOUCHSTONES—THE STANDARD-BEARER

I kicked off the Leader Touchstones part of the book with the story about Mulally because he showed us the best kind of leadership—he is one of the standard-bearers for other leaders to model. Suppose we had fifty more case studies like the Ford turnaround. We might have fewer companies failing, fewer team members leaving companies and the workforce altogether, and more dynamic, enduring organizations able to withstand the most challenging external forces.

The etymology of the touchstone dates back to the 1530s and represents a physical or metaphorical standard of value. In the physical sense, fine-grained quartz touchstones test the

quality of fine metals such as silver and gold. As a metaphor, it measures the merit of an idea or a concept. The nine Leader Touchstones collectively provide the standard of quality for LF Leadership. By naming them *touchstones*, I know this sets the bar high for LF Leaders, and intentionally so. I'm asking you to pursue a higher caliber, more intentional, and purposeful standard of leadership.

LF Leadership may be about excellence and the journey to pursue a higher purpose, but it is not about perfectionism. You should anticipate that you will have setbacks along the way. However, as you cultivate the Leader Touchstones, you'll have fewer setbacks, more success, and greater fulfillment in both leadership and life. The journey of leadership never ends. And sometimes, parts of the journey repeat. Each time you cultivate a touchstone, you grow as a leader, ever-untangling unhealthy culture dimensions and rebuilding thriving ones. Figure 6.2 distills the LF Leadership journey into four essential actions.

ESSENTIAL ACTION #1
Self-reflect and self-assess.

First, *self-reflect* on your competency in each touchstone. By purchasing this book, you have unlocked one *Leader Touchstones*™ *Assessment* (see *Appendix 6A* for instructions on

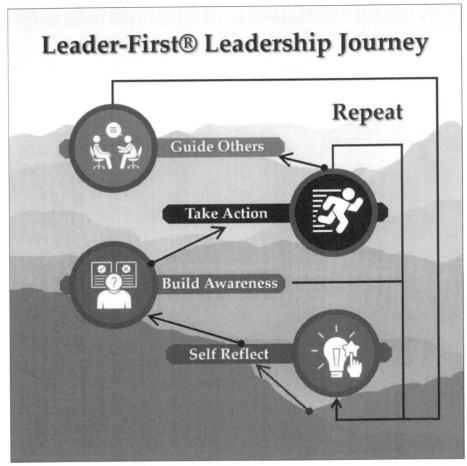

Figure 6.2: Leader-First Leadership Journey

how to access your complimentary assessment). The assessment and report can guide how you prioritize your cultivation of the Leader Touchstones. Do you have high *Emotional Intelligence* but score lower on *Courage*? Are you naturally *Curious* but struggling to focus on your *Resilience*? Taking the first step on your journey means acknowledging, without judgment, your starting point.

If you decide not to take advantage of the *Leader Touchstones*™ *Assessment*, engage in introspection that starts with asking yourself this question:

How comfortable in each touchstone am I?

In Leader Coaching sessions, when I ask this question of my clients, sometimes, they make excuses or tell me the stories *they want* to hear about where they are on their journey. The only way to truly grow in LF Leadership is to make a candid, initial self-assessment. When you do, you will make more significant strides over time. Once you feel comfortable with your starting point, spend some time deepening your understanding of how you demonstrate each touchstone. Detailed insight supports you in crafting a more meaningful cultivation plan.

ESSENTIAL ACTION #2
Build broader awareness.

If you believe you have a strong foundation in a particular touchstone or your Leader Touchstone Assessment indicates high proficiency, *build broader awareness* by asking this question:

What proof can I provide?

When you've built awareness about what areas you need to cultivate, don't hesitate to jump in right away to *take action* on what you know about yourself by creating a meaningful, action-oriented cultivation plan. Prioritize the Leader Touchstones where you need the most growth.

ESSENTIAL ACTION #3
Take action on what you know.

~KEY DEFINITION~

Touchstone Tai Chi is the disciplined practice of activating LF Leadership by cultivating the Leader Touchstones.

In each touchstone chapter, I will share some cultivation ideas called *Touchstone Tai Chi*. Integrating the essence of physical *Tai Chi*—disciplined and meditative movements practiced as a system of physical exercise—*Touchstone Tai Chi* shows you ways to build a disciplined practice of activating LF Leadership by cultivating the touchstones. Sometimes, along your journey, you'll want or need to repeat a step to continue growth. For instance, if you've worked hard to cultivate *Emotional Intelligence (EI)*, significant life changes can influence how you manage emotions. Life changes introduce new emotional triggers. When this happens, you need to step back and do the work again to step forward.

ESSENTIAL ACTION #4
Guide others.

The most important advice I can give you as you start the work is this—don't wait until you feel like you perfectly embody a touchstone before starting to *guide others* on your team. There are three reasons. First, the goal of LF Leadership is not perfection. Think of perfection as a destination. Remember that you never *arrive* in leadership. If you feel you have arrived, you have already started failing your organization and team members. Second, the very best leaders willingly and vulnerably share personal successes, failures, growth, and setbacks. When you humanize yourself to your team members in this way, you remind them that failure is a necessary part of growth. You also signal to them that success is possible after a setback.

~LEADER-FIRST SPOTLIGHT~

The very best leaders willingly and vulnerably share personal successes and failures, growth and setbacks.

Third, when you start infusing Leader Touchstones into the organizational system, you create a ripple that begins untangling unhealthy culture dimensions and tangling up healthy ones. Each new leader and team member demonstrating the touchstones creates a new ripple. The reinforcing LF succession environment grows in intensity and speed, and together, you build healthy, thriving culture exponentially faster. So, continue your personal growth, but start guiding your team members on their journeys as well.

Touchstone Tai Chi can serve your team members in cultivating the touchstones, but sometimes, you need to take specific actions first when team members feel unsafe or uncomfortable. Remember Mulally's executive team? If some barrier could potentially affect the cultivation of a particular touchstone, I've included a separate call-out box called *Leader Coaching Corner*. Think of *Leader Coaching Corner* as Mulally's color-coded card system. The recommendations in *Leader Coaching Corner* help you ready your team to cultivate certain touchstones.

INTRODUCING THE NINE LEADER TOUCHSTONES

I repeat the definitions of the touchstones three times throughout this book. You first learned about them in Chapter Two when I introduced you to the elements of the dynamic, enduring organization system. I include the definitions again here as a formal introduction and a reference point for how the rest of the book is structured. You may notice I opted for some widely-accepted definitions from fellow researchers and social scientists. However, some touchstone definitions intentionally deviate from the standard definition of the word. In each chapter, I'll explain any nuances to the touchstone definition and how you will use it to guide your cultivation. The definitions relate specifically to the LF Leadership model. Keep in mind that the nine Leader Touchstones fuel the dynamic, enduring organizational system. *How* you cultivate, exhibit, and guide the development of the touchstones can limit or enhance your effectiveness in reinforcing healthy culture dimensions.

Through my research, I discovered that cultivating some touchstones is more challenging, if not impossible, without some foundation of *The Big Three—Curiosity, EI, and Courage.* When I say these touchstones are foundational, I mean that *Curiosity, EI,* and *Courage* make the other six touchstones possible and reciprocally influence each other, intensifying their impact. If you're reading this book earnestly wanting to become a better leader, you already possess some level of these three touchstones. Although the four essential actions of the LF Leadership journey may seem simple, taking action on what you know and understand about yourself is some of the most challenging work you will do on your leadership trek. Therefore, I have organized the touchstone chapters starting with *The Big Three* in Seven, Eight, and Nine. Then we build on

~KEY DEFINITIONS—THE TOUCHSTONES~

Curiosity is the insatiable desire to know and understand unfamiliar things and then to put wonder into action.

Emotional Intelligence (EI) is the motivation to understand and the ability to apply emotional knowledge in a way that brings about positive outcomes for yourself and others.

Courage is acting on what is right, despite being afraid or uncomfortable, when facing situations involving pain, risk, opportunity, uncertainty, or intimidation.
(Definition adopted from Bill Treasurer)

Integrity is adhering consistently to morals, ethical principles, and values to do what is right, not expedient.

Authenticity is the daily practice of letting go of who you think you're supposed to be and embracing who you are through the interpretation and ownership of your life experiences.
(Part of the definition adopted from Brené Brown)

Rooted in sincere care for others' well-being, *Empathy* is the ability to understand and share someone else's emotions and perspectives.

Inclusivity is fostering an environment that values authentic contributions and empowers the full participation and acceptance of all people.

Gratitude is reflecting an appreciation for what brings meaning to your life and recognizing and expressing that the source of value falls outside of yourself.
(Part of the definition adopted from Robert Emmons)

Resilience is your capacity to overcome adversity by systematically renewing the four energy wellsprings—physical, emotional, mental, and spiritual.

The Big Three foundation. I cover *Curiosity* first because it is your learning touchstone. After reading about *Curiosity*, you will understand how your brain makes growing in all nine touchstones possible.

~LEADER-FIRST SPOTLIGHT~

Taking action on what you know and understand about yourself is some of the most challenging work you will do on your leadership trek.

Chapters Ten and Eleven independently explore *Integrity* and *Authenticity* but also examine the unique connection between the two touchstones. Both are central to leadership self-growth, but they have a synergistic relationship that changes the meaning of each when taken independently. We explore *Integrity* first since it is a foundational modifier to *Authenticity*. In fact, *Integrity* is the tool LF Leaders use to harness the ever-illusive *Authenticity*. On the other hand, by its standard definition, a person must not necessarily have *Integrity* to be authentic—think Adolph Hitler. Sadly, Hitler lived his manifesto, Mein Kampf, to the letter. But a life lived to brutalize, and murder other human beings is no life of *Integrity*. For LF Leadership, we only explore *Authenticity* through the lens of *Integrity*.

Chapter Twelve focuses on how your leadership approach directly influences your relationships with your team members through the *Team Three—Empathy, Inclusivity,* and *Gratitude.* Finally, in Chapter Thirteen, we will unlock the pièce de resistance—*Resilience.* While you can and should cultivate *Resilience* throughout this work, you make *Resilience* possible for your team members and your entire organization when you act on all the other touchstones first.

INEXTRICABLE LINK—BRAIN AND BODY SCIENCE

In each chapter, I will touch on some of the primary neurological and physiological touchstone drivers that might make you marvel and, at the same time, leave you exasperated. The part that might leave you exasperated is when you discover that you're hardwired to respond in ways counterintuitive to rationality. The part that might make you marvel (I know I do!) is when you discover the brain's capacity to learn and relearn across your lifetime and the body's remarkable ability to renew itself.

When I finally understood the brain and body science, I knew my original hypothesis, while correct, only told a small part of the story. You'll find the original hypothesis for each touchstone at the top of each touchstone research chart in Appendix 14A. I initially hypothesized that certain behaviors reinforce specific culture dimensions, resulting in particular outflows or results (similar to the linear diagram—Figure 2.1— that I shared with you in Chapter 2). For instance, initially, I expected *Courage* to reinforce the *Culture of Trust*, resulting in innovation and performance. Some leader behaviors do reliably and *primarily* reinforce specific culture dimensions. However, I discovered that each touchstone directly or indirectly strengthens *all four* culture dimensions. But that was not even the most exciting finding. The touchstones reinforce other touchstones, strengthening the touchstones themselves because of how the brain learns and grows! Exploring the beautiful brain science behind Leader Touchstones would take an entire book. Instead, I will demonstrate this by sharing a guiding example of how *EI* and *Courage* strengthen each other.

EI and the risk-taking behavior associated with courageous acts use the brain's emotional processing centers— the amygdala (located in the limbic system) and prefrontal cortex. Other brain structures and body systems are involved, but the amygdala and prefrontal cortex are the primary drivers. The amygdala processes and generates emotions, while the prefrontal cortex manages decision-making and impulse control. When you develop *EI*, you become more adept at recognizing and understanding your emotions and those of others. This heightened emotional awareness increases activation and connectivity between the amygdala and prefrontal cortex. As a result, you can better regulate your emotions and make informed decisions.

Engaging in risk-taking or courageous acts involves managing fear and taking calculated risks. *EI* increases your ability to navigate and regulate your emotional responses, particularly fear and anxiety, which may arise in the personal risk-taking necessary to act courageously. If you have high *EI*, you can better assess the potential risks and benefits of a given situation.

This barely scratches the surface. Table 6.1 shows a comprehensive menu of the brain structures and body systems involved in each touchstone's functioning, learning, and development. Since the definitions of each primary brain structure guided my research, I've included a complete list of descriptions in Appendix 6B. Some definitions will appear in the upcoming chapters. You'll find these in-text and in the *Key Definitions* section at the back of the book. Figure 6.3 shows all the possible Leader Touchstone reinforcing feedback loops based on how the brain processes information and learns. It's an elegant tangled up web of constructive behaviors. Just think how hard it would be to untangle your growth once you get started. By embracing LF Leadership and growing leaders

Leader Touchstones Brain and Body Science

Leader Touchstone	Primary Brain Structures and Systems Involved	Primary Neurochemicals	Primary Body Systems Involved
Curiosity	Prefrontal Cortex; Amygdala and Limbic System; Reward Circuitry; Basal Ganglia; Hippocampus; Mirror Neurons	Dopamine; Adrenaline	Autonomic Nervous: Sympathetic
Emotional Intelligence	Prefrontal Cortex; Amygdala and Limbic System; Basal Ganglia; Hippocampus; Anterior Cingulate Cortex; Anterior Insula; Mirror Neurons	Dopamine; Serotonin; Oxytocin; Adrenaline; Cortisol	Autonomic Nervous: Sympathetic and Parasympathetic; Cardiovascular; Endocrine; Immune; Musculoskeletal; Gut-Brain Axis: Digestive
Courage	Prefrontal Cortex; Amygdala and Limbic System; Hippocampus	Dopamine; Serotonin; Oxytocin; Adrenaline; Cortisol	Autonomic Nervous: Sympathetic and Parasympathetic; Cardiovascular; Endocrine; Immune; Gut-Brain Axis: Digestive
Integrity	Prefrontal Cortex; Amygdala and Limbic System; Anterior Insula; Hippocampus; Anterior Cingulate Cortex	Serotonin; Oxytocin	Autonomic Nervous: Parasympathetic; Immune; Gut-Brain Axis: Digestive
Authenticity	Prefrontal Cortex; Amygdala and Limbic System; Anterior Cingulate Cortex; Hippocampus; Anterior Insula	Dopamine; Serotonin	Autonomic Nervous: Parasympathetic; Immune; Musculoskeletal; Gut-Brain Axis: Digestive
Empathy	Prefrontal Cortex; Amygdala and Limbic System; Anterior Cingulate Cortex; Anterior Insula; Hippocampus; Mirror Neurons	Serotonin; Oxytocin	Immune; Musculoskeletal; Gut-Brain Axis: Digestive
Inclusivity	Prefrontal Cortex; Amygdala and Limbic System; Anterior Cingulate Cortex; Anterior Insula; Hippocampus; Mirror Neurons	Dopamine; Oxytocin	Immune; Musculoskeletal; Gut-Brain Axis: Digestive
Gratitude	Prefrontal Cortex; Amygdala and Limbic System; Anterior Cingulate Cortex; Anterior Insula; Hippocampus; Reward Circuitry	Dopamine; Serotonin; Oxytocin	Immune; Gut-Brain Axis: Digestive
Resilience	Prefrontal Cortex; Amygdala and Limbic System; Anterior Cingulate Cortex; Anterior Insula; Reward Circuitry; Hippocampus; Basal Ganglia	Dopamine; Serotonin; Oxytocin; Adrenaline; Cortisol	Autonomic Nervous: Sympathetic; Hypothalamic-Pituitary-Adrenal Axis; Cardiovascular; Endocrine; Immune; Musculoskeletal; Gut-Brain Axis: Digestive

Table 6.1: Leader Touchstones Brain and Body Science

Figure 6.3: Leader Touchstones Reinforcing Environment

who embody the touchstones, you create the mechanism that breaks down unhealthy culture dimensions and reinforces thriving ones. Indirectly, cultivating touchstones in yourself signals a model of behavior for your team members to follow. Directly, when you guide your team members to develop the touchstones, reinforcement of thriving culture dimensions intensifies. This creates the conditions to unleash your team's unique potential and deliver sustainable results. You generate a natural, reinforcing LF succession environment, making it possible to build dynamic, enduring organizations.

CHAPTER SEVEN
Be Annoyingly Curious

*At a child's birth, if a mother could ask a fairy godmother to
endow it with the most useful gift, that gift would be curiosity.*
~Eleanor Roosevelt

Leading up to Madi's first birthday, she was already showing signs of walking. Entirely emblematic of her personality, she waited until her first birthday party in a room filled with people, then stood up and took three wobbly steps. As family members and friends cheered, she raised her arms in accomplishment. Her smile and laughter melted the room. From that moment, her voyage of self-discovery and exploration began. She was so curious to understand the world around her. I'd like to say that Madi gets her *Curiosity* from me. I have always been curious—sometimes to the point of being annoying. "Be annoyingly curious," the title of this chapter, is one of Crescent Leadership's five Living Value Statements, and for good reason. But truthfully, Madi didn't get it from me. *Curiosity* is fundamental to evolution, not just as a species, but as individual humans. Everyone starts with a baseline level of *Curiosity*. During the first few years of life, *Curiosity* naturally and aggressively aids in cognitive development. *Curiosity* makes you discover and learn over your lifetime.

As my self-awareness has grown, how I express my *Curiosity* has changed, but it has never faded. Every great leader I've ever known is afflicted with the *Curiosity* bug. *Curiosity* is a powerful motivator. Albert Einstein said, "I have no special talent. I am only passionately curious." Imagine that—*Curiosity* getting cred for some of the world's most important scientific discoveries. *Curiosity* catalyzes intellectual growth, artistic expression, and technological innovation. It inspires you to question, challenge assumptions, and explore new perspectives. *Curiosity* stimulates your desire to learn in your personal life and profession and motivates you to seek new experiences.

The Leader-First (LF) Leadership Model defines *Curiosity* as the insatiable desire to know and understand unfamiliar things and then to put wonder into action. While my family members probably bought this book because they love me, your *Curiosity* had a hand in you making that decision. Maybe the brightly colored stones on the cover stirred you to pick the book. Perhaps you frequently seek out new leadership insights, and the title intrigued you. Maybe you heard me speak or attended a seminar I facilitated. Perhaps you are one of my former students or team members. Regardless of what sparked your *Curiosity* about 9 *Leader Touchstones*, I'm thrilled

~KEY DEFINITION~
Curiosity is the insatiable desire to know and understand unfamiliar things and then to put wonder into action.

you're here for the journey. The fourth line of the LF Leadership Manifesto reads, "Leaders are naturally curious and know that their leadership journey never ends." If you've made it this far in the book, your continued commitment to *Curiosity* will only deepen your LF Leadership progress.

CURIOSITY—THE BRAIN SCIENCE

Your brain continuously adapts and reorganizes itself throughout your lifetime. *Neuroplasticity* modifies the brain's structure and function in response to experiences, learning, and environmental changes. Learning triggers changes in neural

~KEY DEFINITION~
Neuroplasticity modifies the brain's structure and function in response to experiences, learning, and environmental changes by triggering changes in neural pathways, forming new connections, and strengthening existing ones.

pathways, forming new connections and strengthening existing ones. For instance, practicing a musical instrument can change the structure of brain regions involved in motor control and auditory processing. This improves musical abilities. Similarly, working to improve the Leader Touchstones can change the brain structures related to each one (see Table 6.1 and Appendix 6B for more details on Leader Touchstones and corresponding brain structures).

During the first few years of life, our brain's plasticity is strongest, making it easy for neural connections to form. At birth, a baby's brain is only a quarter of the size of a fully developed adult brain. By 18 months, no additional neurons form. At three years old, the brain grows to 80%. By five, the brain grows to 90%. Don't worry. The brain contains approximately 100 billion neurons and roughly 100 trillion neural connections. Your brain cells evolve and change based on how you put your brain to work. "Scientists can now actually see and measure how these cells thicken with use. The more a neuron or neural pathway is used, the stronger it becomes, much like our bicep muscle does when we work out."[2]

If you stop challenging yourself, particularly later in life, your brain starts to atrophy. When you feed *Curiosity*, your hippocampus creates rich, detailed representations of your experiences. Then the brain releases dopamine creating a pleasurable sensation that fuels happiness, motivation, productivity, and focus. My father-in-law, Dick DeShields, still goes to the office every day. While my brother-in-law, Harold, primarily runs the day-to-day operations of the family business, Dick engages with customers, pays bills, and lends a hand where he can. A lifelong learning enthusiast, he regularly reads and often sends me articles on leadership and business. At 90 years old, he still puts his brain to work, and in return, his brain serves him well. Just like getting and staying healthy is a choice and requires motivation, so does learning and growing your brain. Specifically, motivation plays a significant role in determining how much effort you put into learning and how effectively you acquire new knowledge and skills.

~LEADER-FIRST SPOTLIGHT~

"The more a neuron or neural pathway is used, the stronger it becomes, much like our bicep muscle does when we work out." ~Britt Andreatta

Motivation can be intrinsic or extrinsic. Intrinsic motivation comes from inside you, driven by your personal interests, enjoyment, or *Curiosity*. Extrinsic motivation, on the other hand, comes from external factors such as rewards, punishments, or social pressure. While extrinsic motivation can create short-term outcomes, intrinsic motivation promotes long-term learning and engagement more effectively. However, both drive dopamine release through your brain's reward system. Dopamine's pleasurable sensations reinforce behaviors and support goal achievement. As I'm writing this paragraph, it's 4:15 am, and yet I feel excited and motivated to finish the book so you have the chance to read it. My brain is firing on all cylinders and rapidly releasing dopamine. When you engage in experiences that involve *Curiosity* and exploration, the hippocampus and dopamine system work together to create a rich and rewarding learning experience.

Motivation drives the exploration of new learning but also affects the quality of learning. When motivated, you will more likely engage in deep learning, creating connections between new and existing knowledge. This activates your desire to analyze information more thoroughly and apply it to new situations. Deep learning improves knowledge retention and supports knowledge transfer to new situations and other people. When you choose to expand your knowledge, it starts with an exploration based on *Curiosity*. For instance, obtaining a terminal degree is not typically necessary to survive in a competitive marketplace. Although reasons vary for achieving this goal, motivation drives the need for self-actualization.

In the next section, I'm returning to an older case study—the fall of Enron Corporation. While you've likely read the case study or, at a minimum, have a baseline exposure to the details, here I explore the unraveling of Enron through the lens of faux *Curiosity*.

FAUX *CURIOSITY* AND THE FALL OF ENRON

It's been over 20 years since Enron, named by Fortune as "America's Most Innovative Company" from 1996 to 2001, fell from grace with the discovery of dubious accounting practices that sent the company spiraling into bankruptcy.[3] Sometimes, it feels like it was yesterday. Indeed, it must feel that way to the individuals and families destroyed by the scandal. Before things started devolving, I had just graduated from Texas A&M University. An ambitious graduate, I applied to some of Texas's largest, most reputable organizations. I feel lucky Enron didn't want me, and after graduation, I took a job in Houston with Eaton Corporation.

I would come home to the *Legendary Penwaugh Marina*, my family's business, anytime I could steal away. Beth and Harry Dehtan, the owners of Penwaugh Marina, had taken me in just before I turned 16 years old. I loved traveling up Highway 59 on my way to the marina. The further I got away from the city, and the closer I got to the lake, a sense of peace would build inside me. The people who find their way to Penwaugh Marina are special. It felt good to be a part of such a close-knit community. From an outsider's perspective, the Penwaugh Marina store looked nothing special. It was just your standard fishing store filled with tackle, some snacks, a tank with live minnows, and worn, comfy couches and recliners arranged in a big circle in the middle of the store. These chairs were where the magic happened. At Penwaugh Marina, some of the most brilliant minds of the city would check their egos and pretenses at the door and sit for hours talking about life, fishing, golf, and, yes, business. Soaking up their conversations about what was happening and… what was coming sparked my own *Curiosity*.

No doubt, David Wilson was my favorite Penwaugh "groupie." I count David among the most ingenious people I've had the honor of knowing. He always asked me hard questions to make me think about the world in new ways. I still covet the books he gave me over the years and cherish that he cared about my future. David died suddenly and unexpectedly in 2013, leaving an untarnished legacy in the oil and gas industry where he was known as the "gas guru." His career spanned 47 years as a leader and consultant in various companies. In 2000, at the time of his retirement, he led Price Waterhouse Cooper's Energy Strategic Advisory Services Group. Even after his retirement, he continued to serve on the boards of oil and gas businesses. In 2002, he was named as an expert witness in trials related to the fallout of Enron's collapse.

David was larger than life, but to us, he was just David. From when I was seventeen years old, when I first met him, until my thirties, when he passed away, David passionately shared his shrewd wisdom whenever we talked. It was like he needed me to internalize insight that did not translate easily in the world he frequented. Since those days at the Penwaugh store, learning from David's stories of organizational successes and failures fueled my *Curiosity* to understand why some companies, positioned to do so much good, go a different way—either gradually declining or quickly imploding, leaving devastation in their wake.

I especially remember our vivid conversations about Enron, Wall Street's once darling. The bull market of the nineties and the dotcom boom provided a breeding ground for Enron's stratospheric growth. For Enron, the numbers were everything. The company was fixated on its stock price. Plastered to the elevator doors at 1400 Smith Street in Houston, Texas, formerly Enron complex, employees were surrounded by this singular measure of success. Ken Lay's *ready-aim-fire* and *get-big-fast* approaches to business and Jeff Skilling's *Darwinist* slant on success shaped a culture focused on a single outcome—increasing the bottom line at any cost.

Half-Baked Innovation

Skilling joined Enron in 1990. He was widely considered an innovation mastermind. However, Skilling had a blind spot. He lacked the basic understanding of the fundamental tenets of innovation—an idea and the execution of an idea are two very different things, and *both* are necessary to achieve innovation. This is where problems really started for Enron. Skilling's energy trading innovation had flaws—lots of them. Instead of asking "why" things weren't working and attempting to fix the problems, Skilling and his team started hiding them. The full realization of innovative pursuits requires *Curiosity*. Without *Curiosity*, revolutionary ideas never graduate to the classification of innovation.

~BOTTOM-LINE EXECUTIVE BEHAVIOR~

The full realization of innovative pursuits requires Curiosity. *Without* Curiosity, *revolutionary ideas never graduate to the classification of innovation.*

When Skilling was promoted to COO in 1997, Lay shifted his sights outside the organization. Lay relied too heavily on Skilling and took his eyes off what was happening inside the organization.[3] After nearly a decade of perceived growth, things started to unravel. Increased competition threatened Enron's once-monopolized energy trading space. In response, shareholders increased pressure to perform. Enron had made its investors millions of dollars, and they were uninterested in seeing that end. That pressure flowed throughout the organization.

Skilling's SEC-approved use of mark-to-market accounting—recognizing unrealized future gains to current income statements—once seemed like a disruptive way to recognize innovation. One of the most notable demonstrations of this faulty practice was Enron's launch into broadband with its revolutionary Blockbuster deal to stream video nationwide. Enron booked $53 million to its books for future earnings. Unfortunately, the deal fell through because engineers couldn't make the technology work. The entire venture never made a dime. It was revolutionary but never converted to innovation. Skilling's mark-to-market accounting became an outlet to overinflate earnings, please Wall Street investors, and ultimately improve the bottom line. Layered onto that, Andy Fastow used and abused special purpose entities (SPEs). This gave Enron a place to move troubled assets off its books.

When Bethany McLean of Fortune Magazine started digging into the numbers, the financials simply didn't make sense. In 2001, she published the article, *Is Enron Overpriced?*[4] While she couldn't prove that Enron was engaging in illegal activity, hers were the first real questions publicly raised about how Enron was making money. And it was enough to start making others question the magical money-making of Enron. When Skilling took over as CEO in February 2001, the company was riddled with problems, many of which he and his team had created.

Enron Execs — Victims of Their Own Behaviors

During his Senate testimony, Lay maintained that he had nothing to do with the corruption that led to Enron's demise. Instead, he laid blame 100% at the feet of CFO Andrew Fastow, who had stolen millions of dollars from Enron through his SPEs.[5] At no time did Lay publicly take responsibility for bankrupting Enron. Ultimately, his staunch position of ignorance had little effect, and a grand jury convicted him on ten counts of securities fraud. Lay died of a heart attack three months before sentencing, resulting in a vacated judgment.

Skilling remained adamant that he abruptly resigned as Enron's CEO in August 2001 for personal reasons and thought the company was in stellar financial health upon his departure. Like Lay, he was unwilling to accept any personal responsibility for Enron's collapse. During a Senate hearing, Skilling tried to position Enron as the victim of a brutal cycle of business and media embellishment.[6] He was convicted and sentenced to 24 years in prison, reduced later to 14 years, and served 12. Skilling was released in 2019, and in 2020, he started fundraising to launch an online oil and gas trading platform called Veld, LLC.[7] Here's to hoping his prison time gave him space to realize that the value of *Curiosity* only comes with iteration, reflection, learning, and action based on new knowledge.

Results in Ruins

The results of not asking the right questions or caring about the answers came at a catastrophic price. In 2000, Enron's highest valuation was around $70 billion, with its shares trading at $90.75, making it the seventh largest publicly traded company. But that success was built on a house of cards. Not only did more than 20,000 people lose their jobs, livelihood, and health insurance, but by the end of 2001, Enron's share price had dropped to under $1. The scandal revealed cracks in the US business system and financial markets. It exposed the complicity of auditors, analysts, regulators, banks, and credit agencies. Arthur Anderson, the country's oldest accounting firm, collapsed after being investigated by the Department of Justice. 85,000 of the firm's partners and staff members lost their jobs. The conviction was later reversed, but it was too late for the organization to recover.

Enron employees felt the wave of corruption more intensely than any business entity or group of people. When the share price was around $32, Enron froze employee retirement accounts, squashing any hope employees had to try to salvage what was left of their life savings. During that time, executives were selling their shares. Enron did not reopen retirement accounts until the share price was $9. The scandal wiped out over $1.2 billion in retirement funds, and retirees lost $2 billion in pensions.[7]

Throughout *9 Leader Touchstones*, I've shared with you the damaging impact of focusing on outcomes or results instead of infusing the right behaviors into the organization. Too many companies place innovation at the top of their list of strategies. *Curiosity* is what drives innovation. If you desire innovative organizations, and I'm guessing that for most leaders, the answer to that question is "yes," you must first cultivate *Curiosity* in yourself and then make *Curiosity* possible for your team members.

Before showing you how *Curiosity* builds healthy organizational culture, take a look at the Leader-First Story contributed by Crescent Leadership Collaborator Shefali Chudgar on how *Curiosity* drives success in healthcare through the lens of Lean Leadership.

A LEADER-FIRST STORY

***Curiosity* and Lean Leadership in Healthcare**

~Contributed by Shefali Chudgar, MHA, CLSSBB~
Crescent Leadership Collaborator
System Director of Ambulatory Ventures,
Bon Secours Mercy Health

"Humble inquiry is not a checklist to follow or a set of prewritten questions—it is behavior that comes out of respect, genuine curiosity, and the desire to improve the quality of the conversation." ~Edgar Schein

The old saying "*Curiosity* killed the cat" does not apply to Leader-First Leadership. *Annoying Curiosity* is needed more than ever across organizations, especially in the healthcare sector. As a performance improvement leader in a Catholic healthcare system for twelve years, I have observed firsthand how leaders encourage or BL executives stifle *Curiosity* in team members. Depending on which one, it can build or break the *Culture of Trust*.

Curiosity is a non-negotiable for organizations that need to evolve constantly. The great news is this—*Curiosity* can be honed through the art of humble inquiry. In his groundbreaking book, Edgar Schein defines humble inquiry as "the fine art of drawing someone out, of asking questions to which you do not already know the answer, and of building a relationship based on *Curiosity* and interest in the other person."[9]

Humble inquiry is fundamental in developing a *Lean* culture. Lean principles originated in the Japanese manufacturing industry, and the philosophy is derived primarily from the Toyota Production System starting in the 1970s. Lean is an outcome-focused methodology that seeks to deliver value to the customer by eliminating waste. Waste can be anything that adds cost without adding value. In healthcare organizations, Lean leadership flips the script of traditional care delivery by forcing the needs of the patients and families to dictate business decisions. The frontline staff know the customers and processes best and are empowered to lead problem-solving. Through humble inquiry and annoying *Curiosity*, leaders guide, empower, and hold their teams accountable.

Lean was adopted in healthcare about 30 years after revolutionizing the manufacturing industry. One of the first adopters was Virginia Mason Medical Center (VMMC), based in Seattle, WA. Based on an initial case study, in the first two years of Lean transformation, VMMC conducted 175 process improvement events that resulted in the following:

⇒ *Reduced inventory cost by 53% ($1.35M)*

⇒ *Improved productivity by 36% (158 FTEs redeployed)*

⇒ *Reduced risk/safety investigation turnaround time by 98% (3 months)*

⇒ *Reduced process lead time by 44% (23,082 hours)*[10]

The gains continued to be significant after seven years:

⇒ *Reduced liability insurance expense by 38%*

⇒ *Improved operating margin by 5.9%*

⇒ *Reduced Operating Room patient Length of Stay (LOS) by 25% (27 hours)*

⇒ *Reduced wait to see primary care physician by 63%*[10]

In Chapter Two, Jes introduced a systems model that shows leaders how to use their behavioral influence to untangle a toxic system and build a thriving one. Humble inquiry and *Curiosity* provide the first tools to untangle an unhealthy system, reinforcing *Trust* between leaders and their team members. In his book, Schein confirms that humble inquiry aims to build *Trust*-based relationships, which inevitably improves communication and collaboration.[9]

One of the principles that Toyota implemented was going to the *Gemba*—the Japanese word for "where the work gets done." It encourages leaders to walk the line, interact with their teams, and empower frontline workers to "stop the line" if they see a safety or quality issue. Through *Curiosity* and humble inquiry, the culture shifted to one where teams felt empowered to solve problems, ask questions, and make decisions. Rather than the traditional command-and-control leadership model, Toyota transformed into a Lean organization that valued *Curiosity*, *Trust*, and relationships to drive continuous improvement, safety, quality, and reliability.

When Lean concepts entered the healthcare space, initially, leaders struggled to adopt them. They were often too busy to ask questions because they were "putting out fires." The fundamental problem is that we tend to value task accomplishment more than the relationship-building it takes to see the bigger picture.[1] In an industry like healthcare, often the problems are life-or-death. Leaders must build relationships with their teams through *Curiosity*, humble inquiry, and *Trust* so the "fires" become manageable or get snuffed out before going ablaze.

CURIOSITY AND CULTURING

As a curious leader, you build dynamic, enduring organizations by approaching problems with an open mind and exploring multiple solutions instead of continually navigating to the same old way of doing things. In an interview, Eric Schmidt, the former CEO of Google, said, "We run this company on questions, not answers." Demonstrating *Curiosity* reinforces the *Culture of Trust* by encouraging your team members to consider unconventional ideas and approaches.

When you ask questions and make it acceptable and desirable for your team members to ask them, you stimulate creativity and innovation. Innovation and team member engagement organically grow by creating a safe space for collaborative experimentation and risk-taking. *Curiosity* promotes personal growth in your team members and helps them to develop *Courage* by challenging them to step outside their comfort zones and try new things. *Curiosity* also helps you and your team members develop critical thinking skills essential for making informed decisions and solving complex problems. As you and your team members identify your

Integrity-baseline (more on this in Chapter Ten) and move closer to *Authenticity*, you reinforce the *Culture of Belonging*.

Your commitment to *Curiosity* and the development of *Curiosity* in your team members builds confidence and self-esteem throughout the organization. This aids in mental energy renewal, strengthening *Resilience* and reinforcing the *Culture of Vitality*. *Curiosity* builds the *Culture of Vitality* through *Gratitude* as well. *Curiosity* motivates you to seek knowledge and explore new ideas, whereas, *Gratitude* promotes a sense of contentment and appreciation for what you already have. When combined, *Curiosity* and *Gratitude* create a feedback loop—*Curiosity* drives you to seek new experiences and knowledge, while *Gratitude* helps you acknowledge and value the lessons and opportunities you encounter along the way.

You reinforce the *Culture of Purpose* by encouraging your team members to explore their interests and passions. *Curiosity* sparks a genuine interest in understanding your team members' unique gifts. This intensifies their intrinsic motivation, deepening not only their learning but also their commitment to the organization.

To wrap up this section on *Curiosity* and culturing, take a look at the Leader Coaching Corner at the top of page 158. These are a few actions you need to take to build safety for your team members before they will fully embrace *Curiosity*.

TOUCHSTONE TAI CHI—*CURIOSITY*

To personally cultivate *Curiosity*, you must look at life and leadership with the desire to explore what you don't yet know about yourself, others, and your surroundings. You need to ask questions—lots of them and seek answers instead of always giving them. When you do this in the workplace, you also spark *Curiosity* in your team members.

LEADER COACHING CORNER
Cultivating *Curiosity* in Your Team Members

✓ Model intellectual humility.
✓ Foster continuous learning by encouraging exploration, safe risk-taking, and smart failure.
✓ Celebrate *Curiosity* and learning achievements.
✓ Implement Ideas Programs.
✓ Allocate resources (time and budget) to support *Curiosity*-driven projects.
✓ Mine for healthy ideological conflict.
✓ Build psychological safety.
✓ Facilitate cross-functional collaboration.
✓ Create inclusive mentorship programs.

Ask questions. Seek answers.

Be open to looking for new ways of doing things. When faced with a new idea or a situation you did not expect, ask questions to learn more and gain a deeper understanding. Don't interrogate or engage in what Michael Bungay Stanier calls "drive-by questioning."[11] Care enough about the answer to ask only one question at a time, listen, and observe. As Stephen Covey said, "seek first to understand, then to be understood."

Embrace smart failure.

The taboo surrounding failure has conditioned us to strive for perfectionism. However, the greatest successes and innovative discoveries started with failure. Shift your mindset about failure and then design an environment where *smart failure* thrives. *Smart failure*, first introduced in 2002 by Diane Coutu, author and former editor of Harvard Business Review, is a constructive, strategic approach of intentionally pursuing ideas or endeavors that carry a risk of failure but to gain valuable insights, learning, and improving future outcomes. It involves taking calculated risks, experimenting, and pushing the boundaries of existing knowledge to foster innovation and continuous improvement.

> **~KEY DEFINITION~**
> *Smart failure* is a constructive, strategic approach of intentionally pursuing ideas or endeavors that carry a risk of failure but to gain valuable insights, learning, and improving future outcomes.

Before embracing "smart failure" as a strategy, you must first build psychological safety by demonstrating that failure is necessary for learning and evolution. Implement consistent methodologies for detecting and analyzing failures and then iterating and adapting based on what the team learns. Mulally's BPR meeting color code system helped him to detect failure early once his team finally started talking. Keep in mind that failure is just failure unless you and the team learn from it.

It's a natural human tendency to avoid failure at all costs. This leads to teams taking too long to abandon failing plans and mediocre ideas, ultimately costing more money in the long run.

~KEY DEFINITION~

The *sunk cost fallacy* refers to a cognitive bias where individuals, teams, or organizations continue to invest in a project or decision even when it is no longer rational because they have already invested significant resources, such as time, money, or effort, into it.

This cognitive bias is called the *sunk cost fallacy* where individuals, teams, or organizations continue to invest in a project or decision even when it is no longer rational because they have already invested significant resources, such as time, money, or effort, into it. In other words, past investments—sunk costs—influence future decisions, even when those decisions are no longer in their best interest.[12] Embrace failure, learn from it, and move forward.

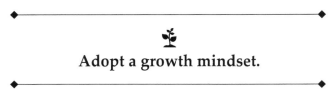

Adopt a growth mindset.

A growth mindset means that you believe in the power of personal development and that you can accomplish anything through hard work and dedication. You willingly learn from mistakes, admit when you "don't know," and value multi-directional feedback. You challenge, test, learn, and adapt. When you fall off track, you persevere through grit and determination.

Make time to explore and experiment.

Exploration sparks *Curiosity* by opening your mind to new points of view. This can happen through new experiences, trying something different that you might not normally try, reading books, or listening to blogs, especially those that challenge your beliefs. On that note, I'm going to wrap up Chapter Seven by sharing a powerful Leader-First Story contributed by Crescent Leadership Collaborator James Lovaas on reading to develop you as a leader.

A LEADER-FIRST STORY
Reading to Develop the Leader
~Contributed by James Lovaas, MBA, FCA~
Crescent Leadership Collaborator; Owner, Freefall Consulting;
Director of DTC Operations, Korbel Champagne Cellars

*"The man who does not read has no advantage
over the man who cannot read."*
~Mark Twain

Each morning I like to start my day outside, enjoying the beauty and the exhilaration of a morning workout. For some, this is a solitary time. Others enjoy working out with a community of people and get energized by the fellowship. While I read books, too, audiobooks have allowed me to share my runs with respected leaders, artists, or entrepreneurs. I've learned so much simply from listening to the voices of these great thinkers.

We all want to see our teams develop and grow. We all want to see our companies and teams succeed. The question is, how? That varies from team to team and individual to individual. But it is the leader who makes the differentiation. Great leaders have the vision and skills to inspire their teams to exceed goals and take organizations to new heights. What we need to remember, however, is that leaders don't start out with these skills when they are born. Their leadership acumen develops over the course of their lives. And it does not end when they earn a degree or get a specific job or title. Learning continues for a lifetime.

Most of us would only seek fitness coaching from an individual in shape. We would seek life coaching from someone that inspires us with their messaging and approach. We look to those in a place we want to be—to those who have gone where we want to go. While many companies offer a variety of continuing education opportunities, good leaders seek meaningful development. In the article, *Good Leaders are Good Learners*, the authors tell us that "leaders who are in learning mode develop stronger leadership skills than their peers."[13]

Many organizations have limited resources for training and development. There is never as much money or time as training seminars, conferences, online courses, and college programs. Accordingly, we all have to make choices and pass on many opportunities. The pandemic made it even more challenging to connect with meaningful development opportunities. For nearly 18 months, almost all in-person opportunities vanished. We were overcome by changing priorities and unforeseen obstacles. Many fought to stay employed, while others reconsidered new careers entirely.

One opportunity that remains constant for all of us is the chance to read. Years ago, President Harry Truman said, "Not all readers are leaders, but all leaders are readers." In previous eras, reading was considered a luxury for the wealthy, the privileged, and the aristocracy—those with the time and resources. Today, we all have access to thousands of books, articles, and blogs in our modern society. Yet, the evidence indicates that Americans are reading less and less. In 2015 the Pew Research Center found that the average American read a single book. That number exponentially increases if we include avid readers jumping to 12 books a year.[14] Countries such as

India, Thailand, and China read significantly more. College graduates read even more. Women read more as well. CEO's? Overall, they read substantially more, with some indications that many read four to five books per month. Steve Siebold interviewed 1200 of the world's wealthiest individuals over thirty years and found that they all read to self-educate.[15]

Reading activates our *Curiosity* through exposure to new concepts, ideas, renewal, and growth. We avail ourselves of many thinkers and leaders across cultures and nations. Jeremy Kingsley, an author and speaker, says there are *at least* four reasons good leaders are readers.[16] When we read, it reminds us of important concepts we've already learned, and it allows us to use that knowledge again. We also come face-to-face with new thoughts that might otherwise be outside our purview. Reading can provide a distinct advantage in a competitive world filled with people who believe they are too busy to read. The writings of others offer new context that encourages better decision-making. These benefits, and more, are available to those that read liberally.

Earlier, I talked about sharing my runs with great thinkers. I spend every morning with luminaries like Tim Grover, Brené Brown, and Paul Stanley. These people, and many others, make their books available to us in various formats. As I run, I can listen to Brené talk about the *Courage* it takes to be vulnerable. John Moe describes overcoming depression, and Jamie Kern Lima talks about faith, family, and building a billion-dollar business. My morning runs are so important because I get to spend time with people I may never meet in person but who make their lives available to us through their words. Reading (or listening) allows us to access some of the greatest minds of our time. We can feed our *Curiosity*, feel inspired, and experience adventure, all through the writings of others.

CHAPTER EIGHT
Shape the Game—Emotional Intelligence

Anybody can become angry—that is easy. But to be angry with the right person and to the right degree and at the right time and for the right purpose, and in the right way—that is not within everybody's power and is not easy.
~Aristotle

In the Introduction of this book, I told you the story of Leo from Company XYZ. During my exploratory interviews his former team members provided detailed accounts of Leo's destructive behavior. During one encounter with the leadership team, a team leader described a time when Leo got angry after listening to a quarterly report from a department manager. He lashed out suddenly and aggressively at the manager responsible for the department. The team member described the moment in vivid detail. She told me she had been wearing a striped white and blue collared shirt that her mom had given her for her birthday. She remembered because she stared at the stripes for nearly twenty minutes during Leo's rant, afraid to lift her eyes.

Leo cared about one thing—results. He could not see beyond the bottom line and certainly could not see himself reflected in his actions. His emotional explosions not only affected the team member he targeted. It affected every team member, starting while they were still sitting in the room. When team members returned to their desks after meetings, they continued to feel his wrath, often preoccupied with wondering when they would become the target of one of his explosions.

While I never met Leo in person, judging from my conversations with his team, I presumed he had low *Emotional Intelligence* overall and very little self-awareness.

At Crescent Leadership, when we work with leaders, most come to us with a basic understanding of *Emotional Intelligence*. But with *Emotional Intelligence*, it doesn't matter what you know. What matters is how you *use* what you know. When I refer to *Emotional Intelligence*, EQ and *EI* are not interchangeable. Like an IQ test, EQ is an inventory designed to measure your capacity for recognizing and understanding how your emotions operate.

> **~KEY DEFINITION~**
> *Emotional Intelligence (EI) is the motivation to understand and the ability to apply emotional knowledge in a way that brings about positive outcomes for yourself and others.*

Applying what you know about your emotions is altogether different. Successful application of emotional knowledge is the realization of *Emotional Intelligence*. The Leader-First (LF) Leadership model defines *Emotional Intelligence (EI)* as the motivation to understand and the ability to apply emotional knowledge in a way that brings about positive outcomes for yourself and others.

EI—THE BRAIN SCIENCE

Human brains are hardwired to perceive experiences emotionally before perceiving those same experiences rationally. Our prehistoric ancestors encountered danger around every corner. Threats to life and safety were constant. Instead of evolving, the human stress and fear response—fight-or-flight—optimized for the long-term survival of our species. Fight-or-flight helped our ancestors stave off death by avoiding poisonous plants, falling off cliffs, and outrunning woolly mammoths.

One of the least evolved areas of the brain, the amygdala, still drives a critical function that ensures our survival. Unfortunately, sometimes the amygdala overreaches. Something as seemingly simple as presenting in front of peers can evoke the same physiological fear response as turning a corner and coming face-to-face with a woolly mammoth. When you encounter something that your brain perceives as a threat—that scary presentation, conflict with a team member, or a snake on your hiking path—regardless of the difference in the level of threat to safety, an identical process takes place in your brain.

> **~KEY DEFINITION~**
>
> The *amygdala*, a key component of the limbic system, regulates emotions, particularly fear and aggression. It evaluates the emotional significance of incoming stimuli allowing for a rapid and automatic response to potential threats or dangers in the environment. The amygdala plays a role in the function and development of every Leader Touchstone.

Typically, sensory signals first get routed through the cortex. The cortex houses rational thought, consciousness, and interpretation of facts. However, in the case of *dangerous* stimuli, your senses bypass the cortex and send the messages straight to the amygdala. The amygdala gets "hijacked" when we feel stress or fear.[1] The limbic region (emotional brain) overrides the cortex (thinking brain), even when no real danger exists.[2] The amygdala interprets these messages as a threat and triggers the fight-or-flight response before the cortex can determine whether or not the danger is real (see Figure 8.1).

When the amygdala activates your survival mechanism, it gears up your body for immediate reaction. The amygdala triggers a distress signal to the hypothalamus, which stimulates

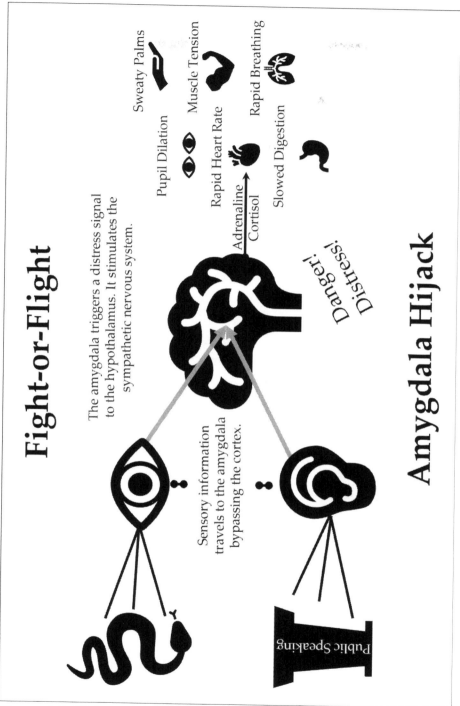

Figure 8.1: Fight-or-Flight and the Amygdala Hijack

the sympathetic nervous system. The sympathetic nervous system activates the adrenal glands and causes the release of adrenaline and cortisol. In this state, your body goes into a chain of physiological responses—pupil dilation, rapid breathing and heart rate, muscle tension, slowed digestion, and sweating palms.

You feel numb, rigid, and out of control. The experience is like hovering above yourself, looking down at the situation below, helpless to stop your exaggerated response from happening. Only after the perceived threat has passed does the parasympathetic nervous system start to calm the body back to a state of rest. Now for the good news—just as we can train the limbic system to overcome fear and increase *Courage* (more on that in Chapter Nine), we can also teach it to grow in *EI*. In fact, the exact mechanism is in play.

If presenting in front of the entire organization makes you fearful, you will likely experience the physiological effects of an amygdala hijack. However, to build *Courage*, you must push through just to the other side of fear, possibly by doing a smaller presentation to your team first or practicing several times with your family. With each small step forward, *Courage* increases, and you become more aware of how you respond emotionally. Once your awareness grows, you can employ strategies to help regulate your emotional response. This explains the mutually reinforcing relationship between *EI* and *Courage*. Growing in *EI* brings *Courage* into closer reach, and when you activate *Courage,* you simultaneously grow in *EI*. This creates a powerful reinforcing feedback loop. The limbic system learns and evolves best through motivation, practice, and feedback. Motivation is a key determinant in whether or not a person can grow in *EI* in the same way that it drives *Curiosity* and meaningful learning. I brought back the story of Leo to demonstrate this point—a person unmotivated to improve *EI* will remain stuck on a never-ending, emotional seesaw.

~BOTTOM-LINE EXECUTIVE BEHAVIOR~

Motivation is a key determinant in whether or not a person can grow in EI in the same way that it drives Curiosity and meaningful learning. A person unmotivated to improve EI will remain stuck on a never-ending, emotional seesaw.

EI—THE FOUR PROGRESSIONS

The four *EI* skills are progressive.[3] While you can grow in each domain independently, the progressions are inherently linked. You must achieve a basic level of competency in each progression before you can sustainably grow in the next (see Figure 8.2). Self-awareness is the first skill and serves as the foundation of *EI*. Regulation of emotions, the second skill, focuses on self-management. The third skill, social awareness, includes *Empathy* and the discernment of other people's emotions. Relationship management, the fourth skill, uses emotional knowledge to facilitate performance and navigate social complexity.[4]

SELF-AWARENESS. If you have high self-awareness, you understand your emotions as they happen, and you express them naturally. You also detect how your emotions affect other people. You know and can name your natural advantages,

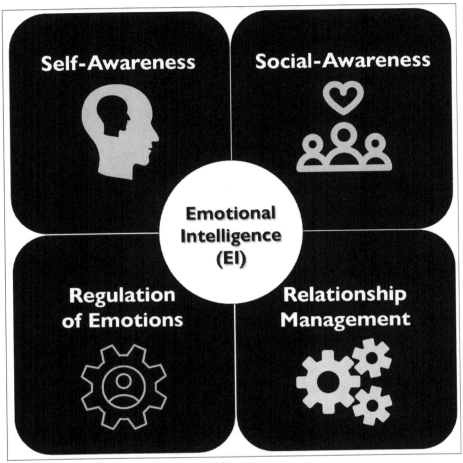

Figure 8.2: The Four EI Progressions

personality pitfalls, values, and motives. You are aware of thoughts and physiological sensations related to your emotions and can accurately label them. Not fully understanding yourself makes it difficult, if not impossible, to understand and respond appropriately to the emotions of others. That's why building self-awareness is an essential precursor to growing in social awareness.

A Harvard Business Review study revealed a gap between research and the practice of self-awareness. Of 3,600 leaders who participated in the study, researchers found that

95% overvalued their self-awareness, compared to 10% to 15% of leaders who actually exhibited self-awareness.[5] I have coached some bottom-line (BL) executives who stop progressing in *EI* at self-awareness. They understand their emotions and the impact their emotions have on their team members. They say things like, "I know I am difficult," "I know I don't take feedback well," or "I know I don't follow through at what I say I am going to do." This signals false vulnerability and creates a false sense of security in others. BL executives weaponize self-awareness by not taking action to grow, even when they understand the harmful effect their emotions have on others.

~BOTTOM-LINE EXECUTIVE BEHAVIOR~

BL executives weaponize self-awareness by not taking action to grow, even when they understand the harmful effect their emotions have on others.

Self-awareness is not *EI*. It is simply the first step to becoming more emotionally intelligent. You must also commit to making the necessary changes to continue growing in *EI*. Motivation to improve moves you from awareness to using what you know about your emotions to better regulate them.

REGULATION OF EMOTIONS. Regulation of emotions is about self-management. Emotional self-management means staying in control. If you effectively regulate your emotions, you separate emotion from logic, choose how to respond to emotions, and think before acting. You can prevent your emotions from automatically influencing your behavior. Leaders who demonstrate high regulation of emotions take initiative and navigate constantly changing environments adeptly.

In the LF Leadership program, I facilitate a session called *Be the Anchor. Take the Risk.* This session introduces the symbiotic relationship between *EI* and *Courage* that I discussed earlier in this chapter. During challenging or high-stress situations, leaders with high emotional regulation will think clearly, communicate transparently and thoughtfully, and make rational decisions, even when those decisions require the leader to summon *Courage*.

SOCIAL AWARENESS. High social awareness enables you to sense and understand other people's emotions and needs. When you have heightened social awareness, you express *Empathy* and sincere concern for your team's well-being. You read emotional signs and discern genuine versus forced engagement from verbal and non-verbal cues like body language and facial expressions.

Socially aware leaders use *Reframing* as a tool to reconceptualize a problem to see it from a different perspective.

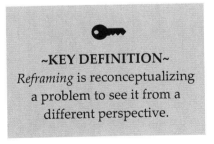

~KEY DEFINITION~
Reframing is reconceptualizing a problem to see it from a different perspective.

You build *Trust* by valuing diversity of thought, intentionally communicating, demonstrating *Gratitude*, and leading by example. When you achieve the state of *EI* social awareness, you activate the touchstones of *Empathy, Inclusivity, and Gratitude. EI* social awareness and relationship management significantly affect your ability to coach your team members and help them grow in touchstones.

RELATIONSHIP MANAGEMENT. Relationship management is about using what you know about your emotions and the emotions of others to facilitate positive outcomes. You direct emotions toward constructive activities. A highly skilled leader in this area successfully manages team conflict, navigates challenging situations, and cultivates personal and team member *Resilience*. You take the time to understand your team members' unique gifts and work with them to unleash their fullest potential. You foster collaboration, share leadership, and build a thriving organizational culture.

~ LEADER-FIRST SPOTLIGHT~

By understanding your team members' unique gifts, you unleash their fullest potential.

Some research has shown that emotionally intelligent people have the capacity to use their power of persuasion and high relationship management expertise to manipulate others.[3] Typically regarded as a positive skill, the unethical pursuit of goals necessitates a stricter LF Leadership definition of the *EI* Touchstone. The LF Leadership model includes these words in the *EI* definition—*in a way that brings about a positive outcome for yourself and others*—to intentionally guide leaders in its use.

EI AND CULTURING

Leaders high in EI possess a significant advantage. *EI* reinforces *Cultures of Trust, Belonging, Vitality*, and *Purpose*, as well as every other touchstone. Studies have repeatedly established links between high *EI* and increased productivity, job performance, *Resilience*, team member satisfaction, and commitment. A TalentSmart study tested 34 workplace skills and found that *EI* is the strongest predictor *of* performance.[6] In all job categories, *EI* explains 58% of success. Further, 90% of high performers rated high in *EI*. In the public sector, team members with heightened self-awareness have less burnout and improved job satisfaction.[7] A Gallup study of 2 million team members across 700 companies found that at companies with high *EI* leaders, employees were four times less likely to leave their organizations.[8]

Research has also demonstrated a dangerous link between low *EI* and disease susceptibility. Stress, anxiety, and depression suppress the immune system.[9] Suppression occurs when neuropeptides send messages between the immune system and your emotions.[10] Stress signals the brain to shift focus away from fighting disease, making your body more vulnerable to other illnesses and more difficult to recover. The effects of high-stress, low-*EI* workplaces increase team members' absenteeism and, ultimately, decrease productivity.

~BOTTOM-LINE EXECUTIVE BEHAVIOR~
*The effects of high-stress, low-EI workplaces
increase team members' absenteeism and,
ultimately, decrease productivity.*

Daniel Goleman, whose research popularized *EI* in the 1990s, said, "The interest in emotional intelligence in the workplace stems from the widespread recognition that these abilities—self-awareness, self-management, *Empathy*, and social skill—separate the most successful workers and leaders from the average. This is especially true in professional roles like those with higher-level executives, where everyone is about as smart as everyone else, and how people manage themselves and their relationships gives the best an edge."[11]

To build a *Culture of Trust*, self-awareness is a prerequisite. By committing to personal development, you signal to your team that you care about how you lead them. You deepen *Trust* with your team members through the regulation of your emotion. Instead of exploding when things go wrong, you explore why problems happen, speak transparently and respectfully about consequences, highlight what gets learned from the experience, and develop solutions in partnership with team members.[12] You know that for multi-directional feedback to thrive, you must first make it safe. Emotionally intelligent leaders understand that *Trust* is the foundation of strong relationships and high-performing teams. Through your demonstration of social awareness, team members *Trust* that you understand and genuinely care about their opinions and needs.

~LEADER-FIRST SPOTLIGHT~

Instead of exploding when things go wrong, leaders explore why problems happen, speak transparently and respectfully about consequences, highlight what gets learned from the experience, and develop solutions in partnership with team members.

Simultaneously acting on self-awareness and social awareness reinforces the *Culture of Belonging*. This starts with embracing your natural advantages and exploring your gaps and blind spots. From there, you move to facilitate performance through two actions. First, you surround yourself with team members who complement you. Then you empower them to do the work where they shine. This allows your team members to showcase *their* unique advantages. In *Wired to Connect*, Britt Andreatta said, "The best teams, the highest-performing ones, create a cohesive unit through honoring each member's unique contributions and making them feel included and valued for who they are as individuals. It turns out there is an *I* in team."[13] When team members feel valued and included, they engage fully and contribute their best work. High-*EI* leaders know this and work to create inclusive environments that celebrate diversity, promote equal opportunities, and address bias promptly and effectively.

~LEADER-FIRST SPOTLIGHT~
"It turns out there is an I *in team."*
~Britt Andreatta

To create a *Culture of Purpose*, an emotionally intelligent leader aligns team members to shared goals and an aspirational vision. Leaders skilled in relationship management actively participate in achieving goals, share accountability for the outcomes, celebrate successes, and promote respect among team members. You reinforce the *Culture of Purpose* by helping team members find meaning in their work. Team members take ownership of their contribution when they feel they can fully invest their distinct value in achieving the organization's purpose.

Leaders use *Empathy* as a gateway to reinforce the *Culture of Vitality*. *Empathy* and *EI* mutually strengthen each other. Social awareness drives you to want to understand the needs of those around you. You set boundaries, promote self-care practices, encourage open discussions about health, and provide resources and support for personal well-being. Your *EI* positively influences health outcomes for your team members through the reduction of stress.[14] Emotional energy renewal strengthens your immune system, protecting you from disease.[15] When you protect your well-being and care about the well-being of your team members, you reinforce the *Culture of Vitality*. Team members have complex lives with differing needs. You demonstrate social awareness and relationship management by encouraging team members to work smarter instead of harder.

TOUCHSTONE TAI CHI—*EI*

Cultivating *EI* requires you to engage in a disciplined practice of each progression, depending on where you start in each progression. I've divided the Touchstone Tai Chi section by each of the four *EI* progressions. In each section, I've included lists of strategies to help you cultivate each of the four *EI* skills in yourself and your team members. We've used these strategies with our clients, and I've used these with my own teams for years to cultivate *EI*. While the lists are not comprehensive, they will help you start to develop an action plan. In each progression, brainstorm about how you can actively work to improve each area. If you prefer, start at self-awareness (or the domain where you need the most growth) and consistently work there. Next, select at least two to three actions you can commit to work on over the next three to six months.

SELF-AWARENESS TAI CHI

Track your emotions through journaling or an emotions tracker app. Use these four steps to guide your practice:
- ✓ Step One: Identify the emotion.
- ✓ Step Two: Rate the emotion between 1 (very unpleasant) and 10 (very pleasant).
- ✓ Step Three: Rate your energy between 1 (low energy) to 10 (high energy).
- ✓ Step Four: Reflect on the experience.

Name and describe your emotional triggers. Who triggers you? What situations trigger you? What physiological reactions do you detect when there is a change in your emotional control? Take the time to feel emotions and responses until you understand them.

Write down your unique advantages and areas for growth. Actively seek collaboration with team members that complement you rather than think like you.

Take a pause to ensure your emotions are in check before making decisions or commitments.

Treat every situation as an isolated incident, and don't beat yourself up if you make a mistake.

Complete the core values exercise found in the *Integrity* touchstone chapter. Name your personal core values. Start using these as a guide for your decision-making and action.

Seek feedback from an accountability partner or your team members. Listen to what they say and ask clarifying questions to understand their feedback better.

Hire a professional coach to support your journey.

READING RECOMMENDATIONS

⇒ Read *How the World Sees You*[16] by Sally Hogshead. Take the Fascinate® Test to learn your distinct advantages.
⇒ Read *Presence*[17] by Amy Cuddy to understand *Authenticity*.
⇒ Read *The Gifts of Imperfection*[18] by Brené Brown to better understand self-reflection and processing deep emotions.
⇒ Read *Self-Awareness (HBR Emotional Intelligence Series)*.[19]

REGULATION OF EMOTIONS TAI CHI

Take 5 to 10 deep breaths before responding when you feel you are on the verge of being triggered. If you are already triggered, **walk away from the situation** until your physiological reactions return to a normal state.

Identify and practice respectful ways to **gently decline requests**. Remember, "no" is a complete sentence.

Overcome the impulse to pursue perfectionism by applying the *Pareto Principle*, also known as the 80/20 rule. 80% of the results come from 20% of the effort. When you've put in 20% of the time, you're already 8/10's of the way done.[20]

Celebrate accomplishments without comparison to others, and don't allow others' opinions to impact your joy.

If needed, **set aside a challenging emotion** to deal with at a planned time.

Choose battles wisely to preserve emotional energy.

Relieve stress by identifying a hobby that brings you joy and renews energy.

Get up and move frequently throughout the day. When engaging in deep work, use the **Pomodoro Technique**.[21]

Set aside a block of time in your day for **problem-solving and carefully consider all alternatives** before making major decisions.

READING RECOMMENDATIONS

⇒ Read *Credibility*[22] by James Kouzes and Barry Posner to understand how to build and maintain credibility through smart choices and actions.

⇒ Read *Deep Work*[23] by Cal Newport to understand how to complete important work more efficiently and preserve mental energy, thus protecting emotional energy.

⇒ Read *Essentialism*[24] by Greg McKeown to gain insight into prioritization and *Resilience*.

⇒ Read *Thrive*[25] by Ariana Huffington to gain insight into personal *Resilience* and renewal.

SOCIAL AWARENESS TAI CHI

Make it a habit to **get to know people in your sphere** and **greet them by name** when you see them.

Familiarize yourself with body language and pay attention to body language when interacting with people.

Identify and name diverse norms, including those that are unjust.

Pay attention to and acknowledge how others contribute.

Regularly praise work by peers and team members.

Pay attention during meetings. Refrain from taking notes or reading emails. Absorb what is happening in the moment.

See if you can go through an entire meeting with your colleagues **without offering information or solutions unless asked**. Listen intently to everything that is said.

List the potential outcomes of a decision you must make to understand how it affects your team members.

Recognize input and feedback from team members and thank them for contributing their voices.

Prioritize your health and emotional energy to help you be more compassionate to others.

Reframe situations to see them from another perspective.

Substitute screen time with *people* time.

Spend out-of-work time getting to know your colleagues. Go to a networking event together or plan gatherings.

READING RECOMMENDATIONS

⇒ Read *Presence*[17] by Amy Cuddy to learn about how to read body language.

⇒ Read *Atlas of the Heart*[26] by Brené Brown to learn more about the distinction between emotions and to build your emotions vocabulary.

⇒ Read *Talking to Strangers*[27] by Malcolm Gladwell to understand others better.

RELATIONSHIP MANAGEMENT TAI CHI

Listen to all feedback, and do not judge or react negatively to it. Take it as constructive and determine what you can learn from it.

Deepen your relationships through small acts of kindness or gestures, demonstrating that you genuinely care for those in your sphere.

Demonstrate respect and *Gratitude* for your team members.

Practice speaking in front of people you trust to give you constructive feedback. Don't judge, but rather, acknowledge what you hear.

Delegate problem-solving.

Demonstrate vulnerability during team member interactions.

Make yourself available and approachable.

Identify your unconscious biases. Actively work on resisting bias and stereotypes.

Be an active listener. Ask probing questions to gain a deeper understanding.

Transparently explain your decisions.

Tackle hard conversations and situations expeditiously instead of avoiding or delaying them.

READING RECOMMENDATIONS

⇒ Read *Crucial Accountability*[28], *Crucial Confrontations*[29], and *Crucial Conversations*[30] by Kerry Patterson et al. All three books build insight into effectively communicating with your team members and holding them accountable.

⇒ Read *How to Be an Inclusive Leader*[31] by Jennifer Brown to become an open, accepting, and inclusive leader.

⇒ Read *The 5 Languages of Appreciation*[32] by Gary Chapman and Paul White to learn how to care for your team and extend *Gratitude*.

⇒ Read *The Fearless Organization*[33] by Amy Edmondson to build a psychologically safe organization.

CHAPTER NINE
Take the Risk—Everyday Courage

Courage is grace under pressure.
~Ernest Hemingway

About twelve years ago, I decided to put my fear in check and jump out of a perfectly good airplane. Around that time, I started recognizing that the effects of fear had held me back for much of my life. I missed out on having new experiences, making the right decisions for my health and wellness, and embracing new opportunities. Skydiving was not

 necessarily on my "bucket list." But it was something I thought I would never be bold enough to do. So, on August 22, 2011, I decided to jump out of fear...and a *plane.* Let me repeat... I jumped out of an

airplane! Although I pushed my fear aside just long enough to jump, my physical reaction to fear showed up vindictively on cue.

The body's physiological response to fear and stress is well-documented. Waiting anxiously in my seat aboard the tiny puddle jumper, as we gained altitude, I experienced all of the responses I expected. My sympathetic nervous system kicked into overdrive, and my heart rate began to rise. My breathing accelerated. My hands were cool and clammy. I was hypersensitive to my surroundings. I watched as one... two... three people poured out the open door strapped to their tandem skydiving instructor. Mostly, they were smiling. I could not, for the life of me, understand why. And then, it was my turn. Within milliseconds, my body flooded with cortisol and adrenaline. I kept telling myself, "Don't look down... don't look down." Then I felt weightless and free.

I am introducing you to the topic of *Courage* by sharing this story, not because jumping out of a plane takes *Courage*. But because accessing *Courage* requires you to walk through things that scare you. Many mistakenly assign fearlessness to *Courage*, but *Courage* is the exact opposite. Merriam-Webster defines *Courage* as "the mental or moral strength to venture, persevere, and withstand danger, fear, or difficulty." The theoretically and empirically supported definition of *Courage* came from a team of researchers in 2007. They defined *Courage* as "a willful, intentional act, executed after mindful deliberation, involving substantial objective risk to the actor, primarily motivated to bring about a noble good or worthy end."[1]

My experiences of accessing everyday *Courage* are less "noble" but get their drive from seeking a worthy end. The sensation of *Courage* feels a lot like jumping out of a plane. My physiological reactions show up on cue. These continue until I make myself move through the fear. Then, in a semi-euphoric haze, I push through to the other side of the action that required me to summon my *Courage*. Typically, the push lasts about ten seconds, *ten seconds of insane Courage*. Then, just on the other side, I almost immediately start to feel weightless and free.

So much of what I have learned about *Courage*-building in the workplace started with seeds planted by my longtime friend and colleague, Bill Treasurer. I first met Bill when we served on a nonprofit board in Asheville, NC. Since then, I have absorbed his teachings on *Courage* like a sponge. Bill is *the* authority on building *Courage* in yourself and guiding others to build their *Courage*.

In his book, *Courage Goes to Work*,[2] Bill defines *Courage* as "acting on what is right, despite being afraid or uncomfortable, when facing situations involving pain, risk, opportunity, uncertainty, or intimidation." I've adopted Bill's definition for the Leader-First (LF) Leadership model because no other more succinctly captures the challenges leaders wrestle with daily. *Courage* is not only necessary to lead people well. It is essential. To live and lead courageously, you must push through fear and get comfortable with vulnerability. To cultivate *Courage* in team members, you must help them move through fear as well.

~KEY DEFINITION~

Courage is "acting on what is right, despite being afraid or uncomfortable, when facing situations involving pain, risk, opportunity, uncertainty, or intimidation." ~*Bill Treasurer*

COURAGE—THE BRAIN SCIENCE

Contrary to common misperception, *Courage* is not isolated to bold acts of heroism. In fact, everyday *Courage* happens all around us. Sometimes in small decisions that affect a single person or large ones that affect others, acts of *Courage* move people, teams, and organizations forward, regardless of the outcome. When made through the lens of *Curiosity*, a courageous decision that results in a failed attempt can create an invaluable learning opportunity that shapes the next iteration. When a courageous decision leads to a successful outcome, it sparks more *Curiosity* and reinforces future courageous acts.

Depending on effort and practice, you can learn to become more courageous and nurture *Courage* in others.[3] With each new challenge, neuroplasticity reorganizes and reshapes neural pathways and brain regions associated with *Courage*. This remodeling process makes the brain more resilient, flexible, and better equipped to confront future threats that require you to summon *Courage*. To understand the function of cultivating *Courage*, it is crucial first to understand that our brain chemistry plays a part in determining who might be more predisposed to risk-taking and who might be more risk averse. Returning to our definition, risk plays a central part in demonstrating *Courage*.

When I started writing and speaking about *Courage* as an essential Leader Touchstone, the brain science finally clicked for me one day while traveling to a client engagement. I took advantage of some inflight entertainment and found *Free Solo* in the line-up.[4] The documentary features Alex Honnold, largely considered the best free-solo rock climber in the world, as he attempts to conquer the first free solo climb of Yosemite National Park's El Capitan. Climbing free solo means ascending without protective equipment of any kind. Considered the purest way to climb, it is also perilous and, some would say, suicidal. Just watching Honnold's ascent launched my sympathetic nervous system into overdrive. He is fearless — quite literally.

The documentary features a brilliant segment between Honnold and Dr. Jane Joseph, a professor of neuroscience at MUSC (Medical University of South Carolina). Dr. Joseph explained how Honnold's brain works differently than the average human's brain. Again, as with *EI*, it all comes down to the amygdala. Chapter Eight explored the amygdala's function of housing emotional response and regulation, including fear conditioning and emotional memory.[5]

Fear conditioning and emotional memory function symbiotically as a protection mechanism. I'll give you an example of how it works. Several years ago, I walked onto my condo porch and heard a loud symphony of buzzing. Within seconds I felt the sensation of getting stabbed by a thousand red-hot needles. I had not noticed the hornet nest tucked away from sight on my porch eave. This experience conditioned me to fear the sound of buzzing. I jokingly tell people I have an irrational fear of "buzzy things." Any time I hear buzzing, the emotional memory of that day sends me into fight-or-flight mode—racing heart, clenched fists, tensed muscles, rapid breathing... and running away really fast like I'm competing in the 100-meter dash.

Returning to Honnold's story, Dr. Joseph conducted an MRI to measure his amygdala activity. By doing this, she could judge the likelihood of risk-seeking and risk-aversion based on Honnold's amygdala response to a range of images—everyday items like furniture to more disturbing images like stabbing and ships sinking. Honnold was twice as risk-seeking as the average person measured by his amygdala stimulation compared to control subjects. His body doesn't react to fear stimuli in the same way as the average person. Honnold is undoubtedly an extreme example. However, the way his brain works shows us why some people are more predisposed to seeking out sensation or risk-seeking behavior. People with fewer dopamine receptors need higher levels of stimulation to feel satisfaction and may be more likely to take risks to achieve it.

TOUCHSTONE TAI CHI—*COURAGE*

This touchstone chapter is laid out differently than the last two. I've integrated Touchstone Tai Chi as a part of our continuing exploration of the general nature of *Courage*. How you cultivate *Courage* also exposes the relationship between *Courage*, risk-taking, and fear.

Understanding the brain science behind risk-taking can modify how you build *Courage*, but keep in mind that having a higher predisposition to risk-taking *does not* necessarily mean you will act courageously. Brain science shows that a person with lower risk aversion (fewer dopamine receptors) would experience a less significant physiological response—fear sensation and anxiety—when engaging in acts that involve risk. You might willingly take risks, such as skydiving, that do not lead to a courageous act. Unless, of course, you are chasing after a person who accidentally forgot to strap on a parachute before jumping out of the plane! However, you cannot summon *Courage* without also assuming risk.

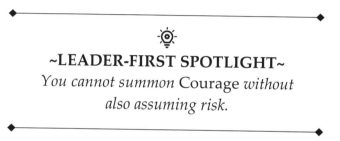

~LEADER-FIRST SPOTLIGHT~
You cannot summon Courage *without also assuming risk.*

Courageousness is inevitably linked to risk-taking because *Courage* requires action that puts you in a position of vulnerability. *Courage* involves acting on what is right anyway, *despite* the risk.[6] Brain science helps us understand why someone with higher risk aversion would experience a more intense physiological response when faced with the choice to act courageously or not. Yet, because the limbic system can learn, in the same way that you train yourself to regulate your emotions and improve your *EI*, building *Courage* is possible for any determined person. The limbic system evolves best through motivation, practice, and feedback. Therefore, increasing *Courage* requires an individualized approach, effort, and application.

Move just beyond your comfort zone.

Each day, when I look at my daily commitment list, I decide what makes me most nervous or even scares me a little. Whether calling to talk to a client who provided negative feedback about an experience, creating a video message (something I really, *really* dislike doing), or sharing difficult feedback with a team member, I challenge myself to prioritize these more difficult items first. I have found that when I start the day doing something that makes me draw on my *Courage*, usually, the situation is less scary than I expected.

When I clear the tough things first, I no longer occupy the brain power and emotional energy needed to hold onto fear or anxiety. Completing them not only makes me more productive the rest of the day but I also get rewarded with the boosted energy that comes from building confidence. It also reinforces my desire to do the hard things again. Repetitive action, in small doses, has increased my everyday *Courage* throughout my career. I rarely put off tough things these days. I've trained myself to know that moving through fear has far greater rewards, and holding onto fear comes at a far greater cost to my health and well-being.

Skydiving strengthened my conviction to push through fearful situations. However, jumping out of an airplane riddled with fear is incomparable to reducing fear in small increments. I probably lost a few years of my life that day because of the level of anxiety I experienced. *Courage*-building sustains when you take small steps just outside your comfort zone to try something you might not ordinarily try. When you operate inside your *comfort zone,* you use a limited set of skills to deliver steady performance in an anxiety-neutral, risk-free space.[7]

The area far outside the comfort zone has been called many things—the danger zone, the discomfort zone, the stress zone, or the panic zone. Most often referred to as *the danger zone,* in this space, you experience fear and anxiety. The body's response to the danger zone exposes why the use of fear to drive performance is highly misunderstood. A *culture of fear* can increase performance but only to a certain point. Bottom-Line (BL) executives can scare team members into performing by threatening their jobs, humiliating them in front of their peers, limiting their growth opportunities, and making errors a death sentence. However, fear causes diminishing performance returns.[7] Any results yielded in the danger zone are short-term and unsustainable. So, the cost is high for the organization but even higher for team members. In Chapter Thirteen, I'll show you just how high. Chronic anxiety and stress increase fatigue, apathy, and even mortality.[8]

~BOTTOM-LINE EXECUTIVE BEHAVIOR~
*Any results yielded in the danger zone
are short-term and unsustainable.*

Anxiety *does* start to increase in the area just outside the comfort zone—the *Courage* zone. However, a manageable stress level, intentionally applied, can actually improve performance and lead to development. This is where you unleash your team's unique potential. Figure 9.1 shows how each zone contributes to performance and how each relates to stress, anxiety, and fear. Consistent, small actions amplify the *Courage-*

building experience. A skosh of *Courage* regularly practiced goes a long way to filling your reservoir over time. In the *Courage* zone, you and your team members produce sustainable high performance.

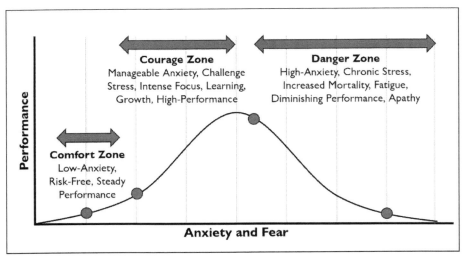

Figure 9.1: Comfort, Courage, and Danger Zones

Induce challenge stress.

Challenge stress takes place in the *Courage* Zone. It is a unique form of stress, distinct from other forms, such as chronic stress or distress, typically associated with negative outcomes. Challenge stress has positive effects on cognitive, emotional, and physical well-being. If you *perceive* demanding situations as opportunities for growth and achievement, it enhances your performance. When you appraise a demanding situation as a challenge rather than a threat, you will more likely experience positive effects associated with stress, anxiety, and even fear.[9]

This is a form of cognitive reframing. You shift your mindset, perceiving stressors as opportunities for professional or personal development.

~LEADER-FIRST SPOTLIGHT~

If you perceive *demanding situations as opportunities for growth and achievement, it enhances your performance.*

As a leader, when you induce challenge stress by exposing team members to new opportunities or stretch assignments, the brain releases oxytocin.[10] Oxytocin is called the love hormone and for good reason. It makes you feel warm and fuzzy, AKA happy. Oxytocin also intensifies focus and collaboration by modulating increases in *Trust, Empathy,* and relationship-building. Challenge stress happens in the *Courage* zone. It evokes the physiology of excitement like the body's threat response evokes the physiology of fear. However, the brain produces nearly the same reaction in both situations. Cortisol gives you an energy boost, your heart rate increases, and adrenaline courses through your body, but your mind interprets these experiences differently.[10] You experience challenge stress as pleasurable and a threat as unpleasurable. Converting anxiety to excitement involves training your brain.

~KEY DEFINITION~
Challenge stress is a unique form of stress that has positive effects on cognitive, emotional, and physical well-being. When a person perceives demanding situations as opportunities for growth and achievement, it enhances their performance.

Challenge stress is a beautiful thing. However, it only aids in *Courage*-building if you provide concrete guidelines and set attainable goals. I've worked with BL executives who claim to give their team members growth opportunities but set them up for failure. When team members fail, the failure often stems from challenges shrouded in vagueness with impossible-to-reach goals.

Convert anxiety using protective frames.

Converting anxiety to constructive emotion requires you to use protective frames. This mechanism gives you and your team members time to modulate fear while building *Courage*.[2] In his book, *The Dangerous Edge: The Psychology of Excitement*, Dr. Michael Apter revealed how protective frames could decrease the strength of anxiety or diminish it completely.[11]

To convert anxiety and build *Courage* using the *detachment frame,* you participate only as an observer, such as in shadowing assignments. This gives you or your team member time to understand the challenge better without exposure to risk. Especially in high-stakes situations, using the detachment frame is a practical first step. Observational learning allows you to get an objective image without the impact of fear and stress.

Protected by the *safe-fail frame,* you create a space where your team members feel stress-free and safe to explore learning through transparent communication and smart failure. In *The Fearless Organization*, Amy Edmondson defined psychological safety as "the belief that the work environment is safe for interpersonal risk-taking... feeling able to speak up with relevant ideas, questions, or concerns."[13] Creating safety starts with the simple act of telling your team that you want them to be honest and engage in multi-directional feedback. Then you have to tell them you want them to take smart risks and demonstrate that you're willing to take risks too.

Strengthening the safe-fail and confidence frames pushes your team members further into their *Courage* zones, but using them together as tools to convert fear yields the most significant growth. Increasing confidence requires a more profound commitment from you to coach and guide. Strengthening the *confidence frame* involves experiential learning that happens in small doses. You provide the safe-fail frame by assuming the risk as your team member learns.

In Chapter Three, I shared a story about my work with a company that hired me to help their leadership team break through challenging team dynamics. I told you that by the end of the second day, they had built enough *Trust* to give multi-directional feedback to one another. This particular exercise is one of the most challenging experiences I have created for leadership teams. Giving feedback to peers, leaders, and even team

~KEY DEFINITION~
Psychological safety is the belief that the work environment is safe for interpersonal risk-taking, where you can speak up with relevant ideas, questions, or concerns. ~Amy Edmondson

members can evoke the same physiological response as facing down a rattlesnake while hiking through the woods. To increase their confidence in giving feedback to one another when I am no longer in the room, I provide a safe-fail frame where they practice with me as their guide. This practice strengthens their confidence frame and reduces the stress they feel when engaging in multi-directional feedback during real-life situations.

Strong protective frames make acts of risk-taking, small and large, possible. Even fearless Alex Honnold strengthens his protective frame before diving into a risky free solo challenge. Before taking on El Capitan, he practiced and prepared for nearly seven years, rehearsing moves, meticulously taking and studying notes, and doing the route repeatedly with safety gear. Yes, brain chemistry plays a part in how well we manage risk. But that's just a starting point. Building *Courage* is possible for anyone with the patience and motivation to practice consistently.

THE COURAGE TO SHARE LEADERSHIP

I first met Elizabeth Gilbert at Texas A&M University in 1998. We became fast friends and supported each other as we transitioned into the early part of our careers. Right out of college, Elizabeth took a job working for a prestigious landscape architecture firm in Houston, Texas. Over the past four decades, the firm has transformed the outdoor environment of the 4th largest metro in the United States.

A few years after college, we drifted apart. Nearly fifteen years later, Elizabeth ended up taking one of my classes in Cornell's Executive Leadership program. We had the chance to reconnect over my favorite topics—leadership and organizational change. Elizabeth and other organizational leaders found themselves uniquely positioned to buy the company where they'd collectively invested nearly 60 years of their lives. I was honored to work with them and their team through the ownership transition.

Early on, these leaders recognized that the power of the organization's brand came from their team members' collective, unique talents. While our work started with developing a succession plan and a shared leadership model to carry them into the future, our more recent work has focused on how to unleash the potential of their team. These leaders also understand the importance of well-planned succession and know it starts with sharing knowledge and leadership throughout the organization. Sharing knowledge and leadership takes *Courage*.

Every time you give a team member the chance to learn something new and lead something you would typically lead you activate your *Courage*. At the same time, you infuse *Courage* into that team member. In theory, this sounds like a no brainer, but sometimes, even small steps into the *Courage* zone prove challenging for you, and for your team members. That's why moving just beyond the comfort zone, inducing challenge stress, and strengthening protective frames can make team members feel safe to learn new skills and take risks that help them, *and you*, grow.

COURAGE AND CULTURING

From the moment you opened this book, when I shared Robert Frost's poem, *The Road Not Taken*, I told you the LF Leadership journey would challenge you. The act of choosing to do this work requires you to summon *Courage*. However, as challenging as it has been or will be, you will reap the pervasive benefits of your continued *Courage* inside the enduring organizational system. Infusing *Courage* creates a profound ripple effect yielding quicker returns because it reinforces every culture dimension and every other Leader Touchstone. Of the six generally accepted categories of *Courage*, leaders will primarily use five in the workplace to untangle toxic culture dimensions and reinforce healthy ones—Physical, Social, Intellectual, Moral, and Emotional (see Table 9.1).[13]

Types of *Courage* Used by LF Leaders to Reinforce the Dynamic, Enduring Organization System			
Type	**Definition**	**Culture Dimension(s)**	**Touchstone(s)**
Physical	Developing your strength, *Resilience*, and awareness	Vitality	Resilience
Social	Acting at the risk of social embarrassment or exclusion, rejection, or unpopularity	Trust Belonging	Integrity Authenticity Inclusivity
Intellectual	Challenging ideas, questioning your thinking, risk-taking, and making mistakes for the sake of growth	Trust Belonging Purpose Vitality	Curiosity Inclusivity Resilience
Moral	Doing the right thing even when difficult, unpopular, or uncomfortable	Vitality Belonging	Integrity Resilience Inclusivity Curiosity Empathy
Emotional	Embracing emotions, even uncomfortable ones	Vitality Trust Belonging	EI Inclusivity Resilience Empathy Gratitude

Table 9.1: Types of Courage and Systems Connections

Cultures of Trust and *Purpose* get huge boosts when you demonstrate intellectual *Courage*. Cultivating *Courage* in your team members creates an environment where multi-directional feedback flourishes. Team members feel safe to challenge ideas and take ownership in helping the organization realize its reason for existence. For this to work, you must willingly let go of control and understand that your way of doing things is not the only way to accomplish organizational goals.

Trust and *Courage* create a powerful reinforcing loop that intensifies each time you delegate opportunities to your team members. When you create safe-fail zones that strengthen the protective frame, you instill *Courage* in your team members to take risks and explore *Curiosity*.[12] When they either succeed or learn through smart failure, it reinforces your *Courage* to give them more opportunities.

Your emotional *Courage* and *EI* have a symbiotic relationship. Both build *Cultures of Trust* and *Belonging* through your willingness to embrace vulnerability and *Empathy*.[6] Vulnerability signals to team members that you value *Authenticity* and diversity. Your *Empathy* creates an environment where inclusion and human connection thrive, and you untangle the *culture of isolation* in the process. By courageously demonstrating authentic leadership, you create a reinforcing loop that strengthens with each iteration. Moral and social *Courage* reinforce the *Culture of Belonging* and are foundational to the touchstones of *Inclusivity* and *Integrity*. However, *Inclusivity* can only build a *Culture of Belonging* after a strong foundation of *Trust* and psychological safety exists.

The *Culture of Vitality* gets reinforced when you use four kinds of *Courage*—physical, intellectual, moral, and emotional. Each type aligns with the four wellsprings of renewable energy.[14] Focus on energy renewal intensifies *Resilience*. Emotional *Courage* gives you the foundation to be grateful and express *Gratitude* to your team members, reinforcing the *Culture of Vitality*.

To wrap up this chapter on *Courage*, I want to go back to the story about Elizabeth. As she and the other leadership team members navigate their new terrain, they know that they must first create the right conditions inside the organization to unleash their team's unique potential. A significant step for these leaders is demonstrating the *Courage* to let go of the work they've expertly led for decades. They continue to patiently and consistently create a healthy organizational culture so that when they extend opportunities, team members feel safe and confident to courageously embrace the moments where they will experience their most significant growth.

CHAPTER TEN
Establish Your Moral Center—*Integrity*

When the whole world is silent, even one voice becomes powerful.
~Malala Yousafzai

My first teaching gig was at a local community college in North Carolina. At the time, I worked in the nonprofit industry but taught night classes as a side hustle. I moved to Asheville, North Carolina, from Houston, Texas, mere months before the SEC began its investigation into Enron's accounting practices. By the time I started teaching Business Ethics to motivated yet inexperienced business students, Congress had passed the Sarbanes-Oxley Act (SOX) with bipartisan support. Enron is likely the most recognizable offender, but Congress's rush to pass SOX in 2002 resulted from a series of egregious corporate abuses and ethics violations at the turn of the century. SOX was one of the first of its kind—a federal law established to protect investors and whistleblowers through sweeping auditing and financial regulations. Teaching business ethics in the shadow of SOX gave us some thought-provoking class discussions about the intersection of laws, *Integrity*, and morality.

One night my student, Emma, asked, *"If I act unethically, am I breaking the law?"* My short answer was, *"No, not always."* Two dilemmas at the intersection of ethics and law make it tricky to answer the question well. Ethics are principles and values held by individuals or societal groups. They represent the highest standard of behavior. By guiding behavior, ethics help us discern right from wrong and inform morally responsible actions. On the other hand, laws are structured rules that governments create and represent the minimum standard of behavior. Laws differ from country to country and change at a dizzying pace.

The first dilemma happens when laws have never represented or no longer represent the principles of a society. Morally-motivated laws are designed to protect citizens, such as those against rape, murder, and theft. However, some politically-motivated laws get created that don't align with generally held moral principles. Further, because ethics evolve as society progresses, some outdated laws that have not changed with progress might be deemed unethical today. The second dilemma arises because the expanse of law does not cover all unethical activity. Since laws *should* cover the minimum standard of behavior and ethics define the maximum measure of behavior, there is a gap between them. This is called the *ethical crevice*.

Lawmakers create laws when individuals or groups of people exploit commonly accepted ethical practices. Laws can stop the widening of ethical crevices, but often the damage is already done. I have repeatedly debated with my colleagues and students whether Enron actually broke the law or just exploited an ethical crevice. The other side of the argument holds that Enron executives gamed a system full of crevices not yet covered by the expanse of law, and they did that because they believed their actions were in the best interest of their shareholders. That may have been true as it was happening. However, when Enron failed suddenly and disastrously, it destroyed shareholder value *and* the lives of its broader group of stakeholders.

~KEY DEFINITION~
An *ethical crevice* is the gap between a minimum standard of behavior defined by an established law and the highest standard of ethical behavior.

Let's go back to the discussion during my Business Ethics class. Next, Emma asked, *"If breaking an undefined code of ethics is not yet covered by the law, what can we use to guide our behavior?"* Every business school in the country teaches business ethics to help students answer this exact question, but unfortunately, most business ethics courses miss the mark.

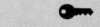

~KEY DEFINITION~
Integrity is adhering consistently to morals, ethical principles, and values to do what is right, not expedient.

These programs often teach theory but fail to teach students how to navigate ethical crevices when laws fail. This is where *Integrity* comes in. *Integrity* is the practical application of ethics — the manifestation of ethical behavior in real-life situations.

Action-oriented application is the starting point in defining *Integrity* for the Leader-First (LF) Leadership model. Borrowing from the LF Leadership Manifesto, *Integrity* is adhering consistently to morals, ethical principles, and values *to do what is right, not expedient.*

When you have *Integrity,* you consistently demonstrate ethical conduct and ensure that decisions and behaviors align with the direction of your moral center (your *Integrity*-baseline). Understanding the theory of ethics is one thing. However, acting on morally-challenging situations in the face of intense pressure is altogether different. Enron executives did what was *expedient,* not what was *right.* Decades later, the debate continues about whether they acted illegally. However, there is no question as to whether or not they acted with *Integrity.* In the next section, I will explore Dieselgate — Volkswagen's emissions scandal. The Volkswagen scandal rocked the automobile industry and consumer trust. In this case study, there is no question. It reveals both legal *and* ethical lapses in an organization fueled by a culture focused on results at any cost and a systematic lack of *Integrity*.

DIESELGATE—VOLKSWAGEN'S MORALITY MOMENT

Volkswagen has a long history of unbridled ambition. In 2011, the company was the second-largest automobile manufacturer in the world, outranked only by Toyota. But Volkswagen's executives desired the company to become the preeminent car manufacturer. CEO Martin Winterkorn stood on stage in Chattanooga, Tennessee's new Volkswagen manufacturing facility, and to a crowd of dignitaries, he said, "By 2018, we want to take our group to the very top of the global car industry."[1] Volkswagen's bottom-line (BL) executives knew that would not be possible without increasing the company's interest in the US market. Their singular focus on dominating the market through increased US sales created unbearable pressure to perform inside the company.

In the 1970s, the newly created Environmental Protection Agency (EPA) was charged with administering the Clean Air Act, designed to reverse the growing air pollution caused by motor vehicles and industries. Due to the severe impact of emissions, the EPA established stringent standards for carbon monoxide, hydrocarbons, nitrogen oxides, and particulate matter. Of these, nitrogen oxide, or NO_x, causes nutrient pollution in coastal waters and interacts with atmospheric chemicals to form acid rain. NO_x has a particularly harmful effect on the human respiratory system triggering asthma and bronchitis, respiratory infections, cancer, cardiovascular diseases, and premature death. NO_x primarily gets into the air through the exhaust created by burning fuel at high temperatures.[2]

While diesel engines have better fuel economy with lower emissions of global warming gases like carbon dioxide, they can produce as much as 20 times the amount of NO_x. Catalytic converters have successfully reduced NO_x in petroleum engines, but because of the high oxygen content of diesel exhaust, they cannot efficiently reduce NO_x in diesel engines.[3] Over time, as the EPA has toughened emissions regulations, manufacturers of diesel cars have struggled to meet them. To have diesel efficiency and reduce NO_x emissions to a level that would meet the EPA's US emission thresholds, manufacturers had to develop NOx traps that would catch and burn it before it escaped into the atmosphere. NOx trap parts are expensive and wear out quickly, requiring replacements every few thousand miles.

If You Can't Beat Them—Cheat

Wolfgang Hatz, the head of Volkswagen engines and transmission development, was at the center of an internal struggle to address the requirements. He had spoken out publicly about what he considered unrealistic US emissions standards. Hatz was set on finding a less expensive diesel emissions technology. Working within a restrictive budget and against a challenging timeline, engineers could not produce a solution that complied with the NO_x emissions standards *and* lower fuel consumption.[4] So, instead of reporting their concerns and resisting the pressure to cheat the system, the engineers proactively and systematically engineered an illegal defeat device. They designed the device to cheat emission tests inside a test environment. Outside the test environment, its diesel cars would produce dangerously high NOx levels, up to 40 times more than allowed.

Working with three students from West Virginia University, John German of the International Council on Clean Transportation decided to do routine testing primarily out of interest in how Volkswagen's US-manufactured diesel cars were clean but those in Europe were not. The goal was to gather data that could be returned to Europe for development. German's team was not trying to prove that the diesel cars were unclean and were surprised to discover the result.[5] They revealed their findings at an academic conference in San Diego. The California Air Resources Board (CARB) took an interest and decided to do some tests of its own. CARB confirmed German's results. Even after Volkswagen was exposed, the company only superficially took responsibility for emissions irregularities, but not for cheating the test.

When You Get Caught—Cheat More

Over the next several months, company executives methodically stalled, deflected, misled, and worked to smokescreen the scandal—yes, unethical, but also very much illegal. Oliver Schmidt, head of Emissions Compliance for the US, was at the center of the cover-up. In December 2014, Volkswagen executives authorized a recall for the nearly 500,000 affected US vehicles under the guise of fixing the emissions problem. Instead, they attempted to *fix* the defeat device to further cheat customers and regulators. After this was discovered, CARB and the EPA took action against Volkswagen, telling the company that if they refused to submit to requests for transparency, no 2016 cars would be certified in California and, ultimately, the US—even petroleum-based vehicles.[5]

The Price Tag for a Human Life

Finally complying, Volkswagen ultimately recalled 11 million diesel vehicles worldwide involved in the falsified emissions test results. The company pled guilty to three felonies—conspiracy to defraud the United States, to commit wire fraud, and to violate the Clean Air Act.[6] Six Volkswagen executives were indicted on criminal charges. Since the scandal became public in 2015, Volkswagen has paid more than $35 billion in legal fees, sanctions, and settlements.

Steven Barrett and a team of researchers at MIT developed a model to quantify the impact of excess admissions on human health and associated costs. The tangible cost of more than 482,000 emissions-cheating diesel vehicles sold in the US between 2008 and 2015 is estimated to be between 59 to 140 premature deaths. Other projections include $450 to $910 million in health and social expenses.[7]

PUT *INTEGRITY* TO WORK—THE ETHICS CHECK-IN

At the beginning of this book, I told you that the nine Leader Touchstones are the compass that guides you on your journey to build enduring organizations. Think of *Integrity* as the moral center of that compass. The Volkswagen case study demonstrates what people are capable of doing when moral judgment fails. It is one thing to know and understand ethics. It is another thing to put your morals to work. *Integrity* is personal to you, but it gets tested and tempted by external influences at every turn. You will inevitably face decisions that push the boundaries of your ethics. These decisions might come with a situation that exists in a crevice yet to be covered by the law or by a law that exists but has yet to evolve with the morality of society. The most challenging dilemmas might present when you're pressured to break the law *and* your ethical code. However, I will offer this. By intentionally establishing your *Integrity*-baseline, your compass will signal you when you've fallen off your path or face an ethically challenging decision. You can read this book and learn how to strengthen your moral center, but only you have the power to listen and summon the *Courage* to act.

Emma's last question was the most important one. She asked, *"How do we know if we are following our moral center?"* The answer is more straightforward if you've worked to establish your *Integrity*-baseline (covered later in this chapter). I told her to start with doing an *Ethics Check-in* (see Table 10.1) by answering the questions honestly in all six areas (the *Ethics Check-in* list has evolved since this conversation took place). If

ETHICS CHECK-IN	
THE GUT CHECK	
✓	*Is my stomach turning as I make this decision? Does it make me physically ill? Will I resent this later? Do I resent this now?*
THE VALUES CHECK	
✓	*Does this violate my core values?*
THE DÉJÀ VU CHECK	
✗	*I think this has happened before. Do I feel the same way then as I do now?*
THE FRONT-PAGE CHECK	
✓	*How would I feel in my decisions ended up on the front page of the New York Times?*
THE SOCIAL MEDIA CHECK	
✓	*How would I feel in my decision went viral?*
THE GRANDMA CHECK	
✓	*What would my grandma think about my decision?*

Table 10.1: The Ethics Check-in

you take an action that fails any of these tests, you are likely letting outside pressure guide your decisions, not your personal ethics. This seems simple enough. Unfortunately, so many forces are working outside of your control. Sometimes a violation of your code of ethics may be clear to you and obscure to others. While generally accepted moral principles exist, your *Integrity* is personal and specific to you.

☀ ~LEADER-FIRST SPOTLIGHT~

By intentionally establishing your Integrity-baseline, your compass will signal you when you've fallen off your path or face an ethically challenging decision.

Years ago, I faced a moral dilemma. BL executives at my organization set a direction that would have damaging long-term impacts on our company. I could choose to go in the same direction and keep the peace (and my job), or I could voice my concerns and demonstrate why the decision would negatively impact us. I mustered my *Courage* and expressed my concerns to the executive team. I explained that the proposed direction would give us a short-term boost but ultimately have long-term negative ramifications for our organization. They disagreed. They focused solely on performance that would lead to quick results. In doing so, they signaled that short-term wins were more important than long-term harm.

In this situation, my ethical code failed three tests—*The Gut Test, The Values Test,* and *The Front-Page Test.* My brain told me we were about to take a short-sighted, damaging approach. When I elevated my concerns to the Board, and my recommendations to change direction fell on deaf ears, my gut told me the decision was at odds with my code of ethics and personal values. Knowing the long-term effects would damage, if not destroy, our business, I did not want my name or reputation connected to this decision that was not mine to make. It was not easy, but given the option to break my code of ethics or leave the company, I resigned.

Thankfully, I was able to line up another opportunity quickly, so my family did not suffer as a result of my resignation. When I think back to my work with Company XYZ and my conversations with the team members there, I know they felt like they had no choice. A clear misalignment existed between their code of ethics and the actions they took. In many situations, team members were left with unthinkable choices. They could choose to follow Leo's direction or decide not to feed their families.

When you face morally-challenging decisions, at a minimum, ethical check-ins bring concerns to the top of your awareness. So, if you act unethically, you have done it conscientiously. If you fail to do the ethical check-ins altogether, you can fall victim to *ethical fading* (introduced in Chapter Four). At Volkswagen, the high-pressure environment created the conditions for ethical fading. The engineers focused solely on performing and achieving the result at any cost. In doing so, they lost sight of the bigger picture—the human cost. Regardless of scope, all decisions are susceptible to ethical fading and unethical decision-making. That's why it's vital to take the time to establish your *Integrity*-baseline.

INTEGRITY AND CULTURING

It's easy to say, "I have *Integrity*." But until you find yourself in the middle of a challenging and morally questionable situation, you won't really know. If you've not done the work to establish your moral center—your *Integrity*-baseline—*Integrity* is just an intangible idea. Leaders make *Integrity* tangible through three imperatives. Each imperative builds on the other, and all three are necessary to activate the four healthy culture dimensions. Your *Integrity*-baseline also helps you harness the illusive *Authenticity* (more to come in Chapter Eleven). The three imperatives help you grow in *Integrity* and signal a model of behavior for your team members to follow. Following this section, Touchstone Tai Chi provides tangible tools to aid you in initially establishing your *Integrity*-baseline, and then to help you continue the process of nurturing *Integrity*.

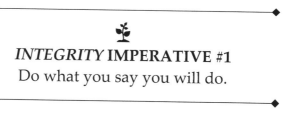

INTEGRITY IMPERATIVE #1
Do what you say you will do.

Early in my consulting career, I worked in a team environment. Our team consisted of organizational and leadership generalists, like myself, and several specialists who served as experts in key knowledge areas. I had a teammate in one of these specialized roles that really knew his stuff. Initially, I raved about his brilliance. His knowledge outshined nearly everyone on the team. He also exhibited compassion and deeply cherished our work. Despite these valuable contributions, he often missed deadlines. He frequently told clients he would follow up with information for them. Weeks and even months later, he did not follow through with his promises. His inaction and lack of follow-through often irreparably damaged relationships and derailed critical projects. Exasperated clients would come to me as the project lead, and I would ultimately do the work myself. He always had "a good excuse," but I lost faith in his credibility over time. I hesitated and sometimes refused to partner with him on projects. I stopped entrusting him with important client relationships. His brilliance was not enough to outshine the fact that he rarely did what he said he would do. Credibility eclipses competence every time. I lost respect for this person, and eventually, his lack of credibility led me to question his *Integrity* and distrust everything he said.

~LEADER-FIRST SPOTLIGHT~
Credibility eclipses competence every time.

Conceptually, *Trust* and *Integrity* go hand in hand. To *Trust* is to believe that a person is honest and credible. To reinforce the *Culture of Trust,* use *Integrity* to build credibility through transparency. Once you establish credibility with your team, you can increase psychological safety. Team members in a high-*Trust* environment feel safe to hold each other accountable and engage in healthy, ideological conflict, ultimately driving innovation and performance.

I teach an executive leadership course that focuses on building credibility. Of all the courses I teach, this one, in particular, stretches leaders. It pushes them to reflect deeply on how their actions and behaviors build or break down credibility and *Integrity*. In the first days of the course, leaders seek feedback from peers, team members, and even family members through a credibility survey. The outcome either quickly affirms or drastically disrupts their perspectives on their credibility. This gives us a starting point to dig deeper into the reasons behind their results. Our discussions help them make needed adjustments to grow in credibility or fix the damage they have caused along the way.

I tell my students that this imperative—*do what you say you will do*—represents one of the easiest ways to maintain credibility. You and your team build a *Culture of Purpose* through multi-directional accountability by following through on shared commitments. Your example encourages team members to act ethically and honestly when they make responsible decisions that align with the organization's values. It fosters a sense of ownership when team members understand the impact their actions have on the organization and its stakeholders.[9] Self and peer accountability enhances performance and mitigates risks, ensuring compliance with laws, regulations, and ethical standards.

Sometimes forces outside your control, and sometimes inside your control but outside your awareness, cause you to fail at keeping your commitments. Failing to meet the commitments you make can negatively impact your *Integrity*. Understanding these potential forces helps you limit situations where you or your team members might face them. It also safeguards your credibility and *Integrity* and helps your team members do the same. Table 10.2 lists and describes common reasons for failed commitments.

Failing to meet a commitment is not an end in itself. To further reinforce a *Culture of Purpose*, leaders demonstrate *Integrity* by taking responsibility for mistakes and calling them out as learning moments. Your accountability and ownership models accountability and ownership for team members. Transparent communication is your go-to tool to salvage credibility and alleviates the impact of overcommitting and underdelivering. When you communicate what has happened without placing blame, transparent communication itself can build *Integrity* and reinforce *Cultures of Trust* and *Purpose*.

WHY COMMITMENTS FAIL
OVERCONFIDENCE
You commit because you are confident you can deliver, only to find out later that you can't because you don't have the skills, resources, information, or bandwidth you need.
COMMITMENT DEPENDS ON OTHERS
You commit, but other people have a bearing on whether or not you can deliver on your commitments.
PLANNING FALLACY BIAS
You're prone to take on too much, and the pressure to achieve helps you move big projects or initiatives across the finish line. You look at the finish line optimistically rather than fully accounting for worst-case scenarios.
TOO MANY COMPETING PRIORITIES
You have too many competing priorities without a sound system to manage requests.
POOR VETTING
You don't take the time to thoroughly vet projects or requests before committing and find out later that the commitment entails more than you can handle.

Table 10.2: Common Reasons for Failed Commitments

INTEGRITY **IMPERATIVE #2**
Name your *North Stars.*

Integrity means being your whole self and letting your values uncompromisingly guide you. Team members are encouraged to lean into their *Authenticity* and showcase their unique advantages in a *Culture of Belonging*. When you demonstrate *Integrity*, you create an internal environment where diversity thrives. You signal to your team members that you celebrate difference and welcome all perspectives. When you act with *Integrity*, you put the best interests of all the organization's stakeholders first, including your team members. In doing so, you reinforce the *Culture of Belonging*.

I first introduced The North Stars as tools to help you reinforce the *Culture of Purpose* in Chapter Two. However, values and purpose shepherd you as an individual as well. Your purpose represents your *why*—your reason for existence and the driving force behind your actions and decisions. Your values shape *how* you deliver on your why. Your North Stars are tangible manifestations of your life experiences and are core to your most authentic self. These powerful yet practical tools ground, guide, and lift you. In the LF Leadership program, most leaders come to us at different places on their leadership journeys. We work with owners and founders, CEOs and presidents, C-suite members, and mid-level managers. At the beginning of our work together, I ask the leaders in the room this question:

Why do you think knowing your values and purpose is important?

At the start of our program, less than 5% of leaders can state their core values. Less than 1% can tell us their purpose. I ask this question because, as a leader of people, you must be able to articulate your purpose and your values—to say them out loud. Saying them out loud is the first step to internalizing them in a way that makes them central to your decision-making process. Although many of our participants have completed some type of core values exercise at their organizations to develop a list of organizational values, most have never identified their personal core values. So, we take them through a two-part exercise that accomplishes two things. First, you identify the words that best represent your core values. Then you convert those words into *Living Value Statements*. Living Value Statements are action-oriented versions of your core values based on your specific experience and definition of the word. By putting action to core values, eliminating ambiguity, and making them meaningful, they become tangible tools for you, a crucial part of your *Integrity*-baseline. Living Value Statements provide a clear guide for your behavior.

After establishing Living Value Statements, our LF Leaders spend time in small groups sharing stories about key experiences that have shaped their lives. We have the leaders source these stories to hone in on their personal life purpose. Knowing your values and purpose is the starting point. However, being able to state them out loud doesn't go far enough to signal *Integrity* to your team

~KEY DEFINITION~
Living Value Statements are meaningful, action-oriented core values. These tangible tools are a crucial part of the *Integrity*-baseline and provide a clear guide for behavior.

members. Words are important, but as we have already established, actions speak louder than words.

INTEGRITY **IMPERATIVE #3**
Align *North Stars* to action.

Aligning your values and actions directly serves you by activating your *Integrity*. It also signals to your team members that you can be trusted. During a one-on-one Leader Coaching session with a client, a C-Suite member told me a story about his Chief Executive Officer. My client's experience was similar to others that I hear often. When an executive's stated values misalign with their actions, it damages their credibility and builds mistrust with their team members:

> *"It's hard to put my finger on it. But have you ever met someone that says all the right things and posts all the right things on social media but then shows up and acts like a completely different person? That's what it feels like to work for my CEO. Last week on LinkedIn, she posted a John Maxwell quote—*Leaders become great not because of their power but because of their ability to empower others. *She always kicks off leadership team meetings with quotes like this and talks about how she trusts us to do our work. But at every turn, she micromanages us to the point of suffocation. As members of her senior leadership team, we are not even trusted to make hiring decisions or to complete performance evaluations for our team members. It undermines our ability to connect with our team members and hold them accountable. It also makes it impossible to coach and support their development. I just don't trust her. Her actions don't match up to the words she spins."*

This is a powerful demonstration of how *Integrity* suffers when there is a misalignment between values and actions. *Integrity* is not just about being honest with others but about being honest with yourself. As a leader, you know you cannot do this work alone, empowering others to help you and the organization and then expressing *Gratitude* to those who help you reinforces the *Cultures of Vitality* and *Trust*.

    Integrity positively impacts organizational performance and the bottom line. A study of 6,800 employees across 120 hotel properties established that demonstrating leader *Integrity* led to higher profitability and improved customer experience scores.[8] Higher profitability and improved customer experience represent some of the outcomes teams need to achieve so they can build enduring organizations. However, *Integrity* is not the direct cause. When team members felt their leaders credibly kept promises and lived by the core values they described, they *trusted* their leaders more. When team members *trusted* their leaders, they demonstrated a more profound emotional commitment to the organization. When team members had a more profound emotional commitment to the organization, they were likelier to remain in their jobs and perform above and beyond expectations to drive organizational growth. By demonstrating *Integrity* through the alignment of values and action, you reinforce the *Culture of Trust*, creating the right conditions for your team members to innovate and perform at their highest levels.

TOUCHSTONE TAI CHI—*INTEGRITY*

Integrity is a commanding driver of thriving cultures. However, sometimes, as a leader, you might get so busy that you become unaware of how you show up for your teams and for the people you care about most. In the following few pages, I have included additional tools to build awareness and grow in *Integrity*.

Use the *Integrity*-based decision maker.

To safeguard your credibility, I have included the *Integrity*-Based Decision Maker (see Figure 10.1). This tool can support decision-making depending on the unique circumstances of the situation. It guides you to fulfill

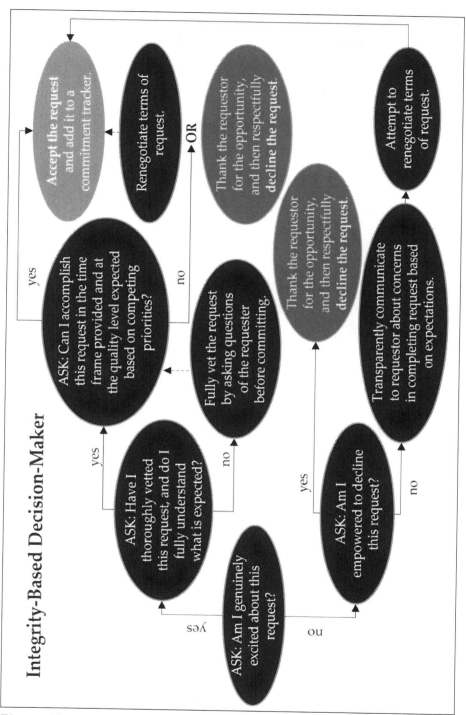

Figure 10.1: Integrity-Based Decision Maker

commitments in a way that helps you maintain credibility throughout the process of deciding which commitments to take on, and which ones to decline. It also gives you some guidance for handling situations where the decision to act falls outside your control.

Do an *Integrity* self-check.

Leaders, to determine if your perception of your credibility aligns with the views of others, start with an *Integrity* self-check. Ask yourself honest questions about how you show up for your team members, peers, business partners, family members, and other close relationships. Table 10.3 includes some questions I recommend to get you started.

INTEGRITY SELF-CHECK
Do I do what I say I will do? *What evidence do I have?*
Can I be trusted with high-stakes projects? *What evidence do I have?*
Do I know my core values and my purpose? *Take a moment to write them down.*
Do my actions align with my values and purpose? *What evidence do I have?*

Table 10.3: Integrity Self-Check

Conduct an *Integrity* pulse survey.

Conduct a pulse survey with people you trust to be honest with you about how you demonstrate credibility. You may not like the results, but this can give you real-time insight into how you show up for others. Listen to what they tell you. Even if you find that only one person you survey has an opinion that doesn't align with your perception, ask yourself why you show up differently for this person.

For the most pervasive insight into your credibility, include mentors, supervisors, peers, team members, family members, and friends. Sometimes you will find that you are showing up well in one area of your life but not in all areas. Keep the pulse survey simple to increase response. Use the questions in Table 10.4 as a starting point for your survey.

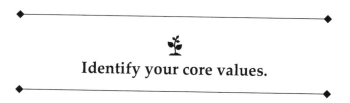

Identify your core values.

Using the list in Figure 10.2, follow the process to narrow the list down to the most important values to you. The list is not comprehensive, but it is extensive. If there is a value important to you that you don't see in the list, write it down and carry it forward as you go. This process should go quickly. Responses should be based on gut reaction. When you overthink this process, you open yourself up to identifying values based on what you assume other people expect you to value versus what you truly value.

- **STEP ONE** (2 minutes): Narrow the list to 10 values.
- **STEP TWO** (1 minute): Narrow the list of 10 to 5 values.
- **STEP THREE** (30 seconds): Narrow the list of 5 to 3 values.
- **STEP FOUR** (15 seconds): Narrow the list of 3 to 1 value.

When I do this exercise with teams, I stop between each transition and ask them to describe how it feels to narrow the list further and further. During an engagement with a group of airmen at Dover Air Force Base, an airman wearily raised his hand and said, "It feels weird to mark through *family* and keep *community*, but that is what my gut is telling me to do." I explained to him that the resulting list of core values serves as a guide to how you live your life. Just because you value community does not mean you do not value family. It simply means that if you allow your value of community to guide you, you will work to improve the community through your actions and decisions. Ultimately that positively impacts your family.

INTEGRITY PULSE SURVEY
How often (% of the time) do I do what I say I will do?   *If less than 100% of the time, please provide a specific example that helps me to understand your response.*
Would you trust me with a high-stakes project?   *Why or why not?*
How often (% of time) do I communicate clearly and transparently—say what I mean, do what I say?   *If less than 100% of the time, please provide a specific example that helps me to understand your response.*
How often (% of time) do I act according to my values?   *If less than 100% of the time, please provide a specific example that helps me to understand your response.*

Table 10.4: Integrity Pulse Survey

List of Core Values

Authenticity	Inner Harmony
Achievement	Innovation
Advance	Integrity
Adventure	Intelligence
Authority	Justice
Autonomy	Kindness
Balance	Knowledge
Beauty	Leadership
Boldness	Learning
Building	Love
Compassion	Loyalty
Challenge	Meaningful Work
Change	Openness
Citizenship	Optimism
Community	Passion
Competency	Peace
Conscientiousness	Pleasure
Contribution	Poise
Courageousness	Popularity
Creativity	Progress
Curiosity	Recognition
Determination	Religion
Fairness	Reputation
Faith	Respect
Family	Responsibility
Friendships	Security
Fun	Self-Respect
Grace	Service
Growth	Stability
Happiness	Status
Health	Success
Honesty	Sustainability
Humanity	Teamwork
Humor	Trustworthiness
Inclusiveness	Wealth
Influence	Wisdom

Figure 10.2: List of Core Values

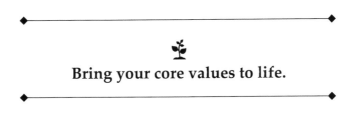

Bring your core values to life.

I will be the first to say that the values listed on the previous page are all lovely words. But unfortunately, if I were to take the word "fun" and ask five people what "fun" means to them, I would get five different definitions of the word. These words are too broad to guide meaningful action. So, let's bring them to life! Follow the process in Table 10.5 to write your Living Value Statements.

INTEGRITY AND THE LONG GAME

Integrity is essential for leaders who wish to play the long game. *Integrity* attracts and retains high-performing employees who share the organization's values. When team members align with the values and actions of an organization, they feel a strong sense of purpose and commitment. *Integrity* also contributes to stakeholder confidence. Customers, investors, and partners have increasingly emphasized the importance of ethical behavior and corporate social responsibility because of the abuses of the past few decades. Organizations prioritizing *Integrity* gain a competitive edge by establishing trust with external stakeholders. Customers are likelier to remain loyal to organizations that demonstrate *Integrity* in their products, services, and interactions. Similarly, investors and partners prefer to work with organizations that uphold high ethical standards, reducing the risk of reputational damage and legal liabilities.

LIVING VALUE STATEMENTS EXERCISE

STEP ONE: Review your top three to five core values:

My Core Values: Love, Learning, Health, Happiness, and Courage

STEP TWO: Create your *Values Dream Team.* Name one person to represent each of your top values and write a brief statement on why they embody this value. This person should embody the value to you. I've included my Values Dream Team as an example:

My Values Dream Team:
- ⇒ **Love** – My dear friend, Laresa
- ⇒ **Learning** – My brother, Anthony
- ⇒ **Health** – My husband, Brian
- ⇒ **Happiness** – My dear friend, Heather
- ⇒ **Courageousness** – My mentor and friend, Kerry

STEP THREE: Use rich detail to explain *why* you chose your team. It is important to use specific words when describing each person. I'll share one example of my five to give you an idea of how this looks:

Learning: (My brother, Anthony)—Anthony is the smartest person I know. When he was in high school, he made a perfect score on his ACT. Instead of "Ask Google," our family says, "Ask Anthony." It's maddening to play Jeopardy with him. Forget about winning. It may sound like I'm jealous, but I'm actually proud to know someone like him that constantly expands his knowledge. He's a huge nerd, and I LOVE IT!

STEP FOUR: Develop an overarching Living Value Statement for each value. Be sure that each statement starts with a verb. The statement does not need to include the single-word value but can, if the other words fully embody what the value means to you and how you put it into action in your daily life. These two elements give your values action orientation. Try to limit each statement to just a few words. Short is better to help make them memorable. Stay away from cliches. This helps to make them meaningful and authentic. I have included my personal Living Value Statements here as an example:

- ⇒ **Love**: Love first… period.
- ⇒ **Learning**: Be annoyingly curious. Own my nerd.
- ⇒ **Health**: Protect health like my life depends on it.
- ⇒ **Happiness** – Laugh-cry more.
- ⇒ **Courageousness**: Live just beyond my comfort zone.

STEP FIVE: Share with someone you trust to get feedback and make edits.

Table 10.5: Living Value Statements

I will wrap up Chapter Ten by sharing a powerful Leader-First Story contributed by Crescent Leadership Collaborator Maryann Dwyer on the inextricable link between *Integrity* and *Trust*.

·ıl|ı·ıı·

A LEADER-FIRST STORY
Look First to Self in Building the *Trust* Culture
~Contributed by Maryann Dwyer, FCA, RP®~
Crescent Leadership Collaborator

"What you do has far greater impact than what you say."
~Stephen Covey, Author, Leader, and Speaker

Early in my career, I purchased Bert Decker's book, *You've Got to Be Believed to Be Heard.*[10] I hoped that it would assist me in my role as an internal consultant for a national non-profit organization. My job was collaborating with individuals and small and large groups of people to persuade them to... well... do things they were not currently doing but should be.

I had a clear vision of the results I wanted to achieve in this role, and I assumed that the best way to accomplish them was to become a better communicator and improve my presentation skills. I researched the literature on communication and determined that Decker's book might hold some answers. The book's premise is this—to be successful as a communicator, you must be able to reach *"it."*

"It" refers to the First Brain, the most basic part of the brain. It is real, it is physical, and it is powerful; the seat of our emotions, the place where *Trust* is established, where our

gut response to others occurs. To have a personal impact, to truly persuade other people to listen to your message, you must win their emotional *Trust* before any meaningful verbal communication can take place."[11]

Despite this powerful statement about *Trust*, a sizable portion of the book was focused on communication. However, I had a different takeaway from the book. Communication, in and of itself, was not the solution. Building *Trust* was the solution. At Crescent Leadership, we often talk about creating a *Culture of Trust* with our clients. It is one of the four culture dimensions necessary to build an enduring organization.

Arguably, *Trust* is the first that must be established before the other three are possible. Personally, it has been fundamental to my leadership development and critical to supporting the leaders I have worked with over the years. Sometimes the epiphany a reader has when reading a book or article is not what the author intended. The book's title was my takeaway, not the techniques outlined in its pages. *You've Got to Be Believed to Be Heard* became a guiding principle for all the work I have done in my career. It led me to resources focused on active listening, authentic leadership, leading by example, and collaboration.

Trust—gaining it and keeping it—is essential to leadership.

As a leader, you can learn various techniques and practice. However, *Authenticity*, honesty, transparency, adherence to ethical standards, and *Empathy* are behaviors.

If, as a leader, you do not embrace and cultivate these attributes, your long-term results will reflect it.

I have had numerous experiences with poor leadership. Although it may not have felt like it at the moment, they were invaluable lessons. They honed my skills in managing up, communicating, and building commitment among my peers. These experiences allowed me to solidify and practice my values, and shaped my approach to working with other leaders.

Consider these two scenarios. It was the first staff meeting with our new CEO. The new CEO was known to the team from the community and had a stellar reputation. The meeting began with standard introductions and status reports. It ended with a few remarks from the CEO regarding her goals, her open-door policy, her consensus-building style of leadership, and her hope that we could work together as a team for years to come. Lovely. Good sentiments. But her closing statement has stuck with me over the years. To paraphrase it, "Please know that if you speak poorly of me in this office or in the community, I will know it, and there will be consequences." Despite her initial assertions, this statement negated everything she had said prior.

From that moment, we no longer believed that honest and transparent communication was possible. This was a crucial moment for her to build a *Trust* culture. Instead, an entire sub-culture emerged—a *culture of fear*. We questioned every directive, request, and compliment bestowed upon a staff member. In the next 12 months, 75% of senior staff left the organization, and the impact of the culture was evident in its declining results.

Contrast this with another scenario. Despite having a shorter tenure than many team members, a peer was promoted to lead her former team. This situation presented challenges for both the leader and the team. Although she had the expertise and direct knowledge of people and processes, she needed to demonstrate her credibility in the role, which started with demonstrating *Integrity*. She knew she had to figure out how to navigate the altered relationships with colleagues and new expectations from the organization's executives.

Her first act was to gather information from each individual. Next, she crafted a summary with recommendations, shared it with the team for feedback, incorporated their insight and suggestions, and then held a team meeting. The meeting focused on implementing changes, addressing questions regarding those items not implemented, and exploring the impact the changes would have on the team. It was clear to the team that their input had been thoughtfully considered.

Without speaking to her leadership style, she demonstrated her values and intended way of working through her actions, a crucial first step in establishing a *Trust* culture. This team stayed together for nearly five years, producing exceptional results for the organization. These scenarios demonstrate how every action and interaction is an opportunity to build or break *Trust*.

CHAPTER ELEVEN
Harness the Unicorn—Authenticity

No one is you, and that is your superpower.
~Elyse Santilli

I spent the entirety of my childhood and young adult life trying to fight my way out of the vicious cycle of poverty. I grew up surrounded by addiction in all its forms, but I found a haven inside books and in school. When Beth and Harry opened their home to me the summer before my junior year of high school, the damage was done. *I did inherit addiction.* My addiction was perfectionism and achievement. At the time, it didn't seem like a big deal. I like to succeed. That is a good thing, right? I like to stay busy. I thrive in freneticism. I would not fully understand my addiction's harmful and damaging effects until years later.

Even though I don't remember this, Harry tells me stories about how I would push myself to the edge of complete fatigue. Between AP classes, working on the weekend, sports, and clubs, I would flop into bed sometimes at 2 or 3 am. There were days when the exhaustion was so overwhelming that I couldn't go to school. By the time I graduated high school with perfect grades and my scholarship to Texas A&M University, frankly, I was tired. I don't mean the kind of tiredness that makes you not want to get out of bed in the morning. My mind was tired. It was like I couldn't breathe. I was suffocating under my self-inflicted pressure.

So, I stopped trying.

Midway through my freshman year, I started going to parties nearly every night. Half the time, I was hungover and didn't make it to class. By the middle of my second semester, I was flunking two of my five classes. I got placed on academic probation, and by the end of the semester, it was clear I would lose my scholarship. Then I entered a dark room I'd never experienced before. *Failure.*

I've learned that in the consequential moments when we make decisions that change the trajectory of our lives, we rarely forget the details. During finals, at 3 am on a Wednesday, I was leaning on a pillow against my bed, desperately trying to cram four months of U.S. History lessons into a single night. There was no way I was passing that final exam. Then, my phone rang. My sister's voice was on the other end of the line calling me from Italy.

~LEADER-FIRST SPOTLIGHT~

In the consequential moments when we make decisions that change the trajectory of our lives, we rarely forget the details.

She had been stationed at Aviano Air Base for over a year, and she had just found out she was pregnant with my niece, Jordan. I could tell she was scared. She was young and alone in a foreign country, and now she was going to have a baby. At that moment, I instinctively knew. I just knew. I had to get the hell out of College Station, Texas, and as far away from my past as possible. I was about to experience my first *crescendo.* I blurted out, "I'll come to Italy." The next day—after failing my history exam—I walked out of that dark room and straight into the passport office.

Transformational experiences create identifying markers in personality development. Personality markers bear influence on how you live your life. Transformational experiences that shape you can happen in an instant, or they can build in intensity over time until the moment arrives when you must make a shift, despite the circumstances or potential outcomes. I call these moments *crescendos*. Crescendos arise when you have made enough minor, seemingly insignificant decisions that drive you off course. When you repeatedly face expectations that fall outside your values or purpose, each moment builds in intensity. Your internal compass screams that something is wrong and you need to reorient. During the build-up of these moments, you may feel like you are wading through quicksand. Sometimes you may feel like you are in a dark room with no windows and can't find the light switch.

~KEY DEFINITION~

A *crescendo* is a transformational life experience that happens as a result of pressure building in intensity when you repeatedly face expectations that fall outside of your values or purpose. Your internal compass screams that something is wrong and you need to reorient. When the intensity becomes so significant, a moment arrives when you must make a shift, despite the circumstances or potential outcomes.

Embracing crescendos requires you to walk through fear and the unknown. Crescendos require *Courage*. Crescendos require you to give up control in exchange for faith. Pay attention to these moments and the decisions that follow them. When you summon the *Courage* to embrace a crescendo, you purposefully choose to move into discomfort and find your way back onto the path you were meant to travel. You reclaim *Integrity* that may have been lost along the way, and you move closer to *Authenticity*.

AUTHENTICITY-*INTEGRITY* LINK

Put simply, *Authenticity* is real, not imitation. Then why does living authentically feel out of reach for so many people? During a Leader-First (LF) Leadership workshop session, a participant said, "*Authenticity* is about as easy as chasing a damn unicorn!" I laugh out loud every time I think about that moment. I'm not sure anyone had ever summed it up so succinctly yet described the challenge of achieving it so thoroughly. Authenticity can feel mystical or idealistic. Brené Brown says, "The idea that we can choose authenticity makes most of us feel both hopeful and exhausted."[1] It certainly changes our awareness.

~ LEADER-FIRST SPOTLIGHT~
Authenticity is about as easy as chasing a damn unicorn!

For me personally, as I've conscientiously moved toward living authentically, the exhaustion comes when I know I'm not showing up as my true self. The hope comes when I make progress toward weaving it into the fabric of my everyday life. Because *Authenticity* is an active choice, I integrated Brené's description, "the daily practice of letting go of who we think we're supposed to be and embracing who we are," into the LF Leadership model definition. This part reminds leaders that *Authenticity* is not a foregone conclusion and requires consistent focus. But I included one important addition. Daily practice only moves you closer to *Authenticity* when you embrace who you are *by interpreting and owning your life experiences.*

In Chapter One, I told you that we are a reflection of our life experiences—the good ones and the hard ones. I also told you that how our stories mold and guide us has less to do with whether the experiences are good or bad and more about how we interpret them. Recalling your stories, interpreting versus judging them against your current reality, and owning how they have shaped you are all

~KEY DEFINITION~

Authenticity is the daily practice of letting go of who you think you're supposed to be and embracing who you are by interpreting and owning your life experiences.

important steps to strengthen your *Integrity*-baseline and move you closer to *Authenticity*.

Independently, *Authenticity* and *Integrity* are formidable Leader Touchstones. Authentic leaders build purpose-driven organizations that operate beyond the bottom line. Leaders with *Integrity* stand up for what is right, even if that means standing alone or coming at a personal cost. But together, these touchstones have an irrefutable, synergistic relationship adept at untangling the most chaotic, toxic culture dimensions.

~ LEADER-FIRST SPOTLIGHT~

Leaders with Integrity *stand up for what is right, even if that means standing alone or coming at a personal cost.*

In Chapter Six, I used the Hitler example to show how *Integrity* and *Authenticity* modify each other. A person of *Integrity* is inherently authentic because *Authenticity* entails being true to who you are and what you believe. However, you can be true to who you are but not act with *Integrity*. Hitler is an extreme but not uncommon example. For LF Leadership, this makes both touchstones necessary to reinforce healthy culture dimensions. Even though *Integrity* is not foundational to *Authenticity*, it augments how *Authenticity* shapes that system by rooting it in morality. Establishing your *Integrity*-baseline makes *Authenticity* more accessible to you. Interpreting and owning your stories exhumes your deepest-held beliefs, values, and personal principles.[2] By converting these to tangible tools (see *Integrity* Touchstone Tai Chi in Chapter Ten), *Integrity* becomes the harness you need to seize the *Authenticity* unicorn.

Having *Integrity* and living authentically are conscientious choices. It starts when you build self-awareness and then act on new knowledge about yourself. It's not easy, and it takes consistent practice. When you *live* and *lead* with *Integrity* and *Authenticity*, you seek to understand and interpret your story. When you own it, you allow your most authentic self to be seen. Living abroad in Italy opened my mind to a new way of life. I unearthed some drivers of my unhealthy addiction to achievement and perfectionism. Every step I had taken until that point was about pleasing someone besides myself. I was trying so hard to be the person I assumed everyone wanted me to be that by the age of 20, I had already become a full-fledged imposter in my own life. I felt like I had to prove myself over and over again. It would take me decades—with lots of introspection and hard work—to deprogram the person I thought I was supposed to be and become the person I am today… the person I have actually been all along.

TOUCHSTONE TAI CHI—*AUTHENTICITY*

A few years ago, during a team coaching workshop with a client, a CEO at an organization with over 11,000 team members shared a story in a raw and unexpected moment of vulnerability. When he was in his teens and throughout college, those closest to him expected him to become a champion swimmer. The pressure had built to such intensity that he chose to cheat during an important race to win. No one ever knew of his deception until he shared his story during our session.

The CEO affirmed two important lessons for his team in this powerful moment. First, allowing others to shape your identity can have consequences beyond living inauthentically. It can unintentionally come at the cost of your *Integrity*. Second, failure is not an end. Cheating was a crescendo for this leader. When he listened to it, that moment ultimately shaped his life for the better. When he stepped away from the failure and interpreted the situation without judgment, he knew he was not acting in accordance with his values and had ended up on the wrong path. The crescendo catapulted the life change that brought him closer to his authentic self.

We started this chapter looking at crescendos. Crescendos only move you closer to *Authenticity* when you listen to them like this CEO did. They also don't scream as loudly when you've not taken the time to establish your moral compass or *Integrity*-baseline. Cultivating *Authenticity* aligns with how you develop *Integrity* because your *Integrity-baseline is your unicorn harness*. In the following few sections, we'll go deeper into this work while simultaneously exploring how *Authenticity* builds thriving organizational culture.

Deprogram Self-Image

Last year, Madelyn Ridgeway, my colleague, and I were co-facilitating a discussion series on Executive Presence (EP). Our discussion kept coming back to the struggle with *Authenticity* when EP gets misused and weaponized by executives who believe team members should act, dress, talk, and walk in a prescribed way. The essence of EP—*the ability to inspire confidence*—gets lost. EP is intuition, not pantyhose and high heels, a tie, or a perfectly groomed haircut. During one of our many discussions, Madelyn asked something profound that has stuck with me. She asked the group, "Who were you before the world told you who you were?"

◆————————————————————————◆

-👁️-

~LEADER-FIRST SPOTLIGHT~

"Who were you before the world told you who you were?" ~ Madelyn Ridgeway

◆————————————————————————◆

Every day, messages from our environment cunningly program us. Our experiences shape us. Our parents shape us. What we watch on television shapes us. What we read shapes us. It's really easy to become the person the world tells us to be. Although programming is surface-level, without intervention, either from ourselves through growth in self-awareness or by others who give us meaningful feedback, it seeps deeper into our identity, surreptitiously constructing our new reality. Even to this day, I still work to interpret my history with the hope that it keeps moving me closer to *Authenticity*.

During my time in Italy, I started the process of deprogramming my destructive self-image. After my *Italian fling*, as I like to call it, I returned to Texas A&M and worked hard to win back my scholarship. I got my grades up and graduated with a 2.98. It certainly wasn't what I envisioned when I started. Countless times I had imagined the day I would walk across the stage, top of my class. But when I started, I wasn't attending college for myself or my future aspirations. I was going for everyone else who, I assumed, expected me to go.

Instead, I walked proudly across that stage bunched in with about 1,700 other students as the first person in my family to graduate from college. It was also the first time I felt like I'd succeeded at something for myself. That was the more significant accomplishment. Instead of staying at Texas A&M and pursuing master's and doctorate degrees in Psychology (again, what I thought was expected of me), I took my bachelor's degree in Psychology to Houston and got a job. Fourteen years later, I would earn my doctorate, but I did it on my terms, inspired by what I was starting to realize was my life's purpose.

Reprogram Self

At Crescent Leadership, we use the *Fascinate®* System to support our work with clients. Created by world-class branding expert Sally Hogshead, the *Fascinate®* Test uses branding principles to help you identify what makes you different but also what makes you most valuable. These are your natural advantages versus strengths or weaknesses. When communicating using these advantages, leaders and team members become more influential, persuasive, and successful.[3]

I took the *Fascinate®* Test ten years ago after seeing Sally give a keynote presentation at a conference. It was a game-changer for me. Her quote, "Different is better than better," has stuck with me. My awareness of my unique value grew simply from taking the test and listening to her that day. Fascinate® encouraged me to actively embrace those parts of my personality I had previously suppressed.

When I understood that this test could shape how people own their distinct value, I started using the system with my own teams and then with our clients when I launched Crescent Leadership. We use the Fascinate® Test instead of other personality assessments to enhance our team and leader coaching work. As a tool, it pushes leaders and their team members to embrace their *Authenticity*—one of our primary goals. When leaders demonstrate *Authenticity* and truly desire their team members to do the same, they reinforce the *Culture of Belonging*. Only when this happens can organizations realize their most significant competitive advantage—the power of the team.

~SPOTLIGHT~

"Different is better than better."
~Sally Hogshead

AUTHENTICITY AND CULTURING

Authenticity reinforces all four culture dimensions of *Trust, Belonging, Vitality*, and *Purpose. Curiosity, EI, and Courage* are foundational touchstones for *Authenticity* and create reinforcing feedback loops. Nurturing the big three is requisite to realizing *Authenticity*. These Leader Touchstones expose places in yourself you might not have willingly traveled in the past. These places are important because they help you make sense of the experiences that have shaped you throughout your lifetime. *Curiosity* drives the intrinsic need to understand what you don't know about yourself. Emotional self-awareness *deprograms* the doubts and misconceptions that shroud your *Authenticity. Courage* gives you the strength to peel back your layers so you can *reprogram.* But fully reprogramming isn't possible without first establishing your *Integrity*-baseline or your moral center—bringing you closer to your authentic self.

Authenticity and *Integrity* create a reinforcing feedback loop when you embrace your *Authenticity*. A strong sense of ethics and morality guides authentic leaders. When *Integrity* grows, it moves you closer to *Authenticity*. Authentic leaders are honest and transparent in interactions with team members. By sharing information freely and not hiding your intentions or motives, you encourage your team members to do this as well. Your transparency creates an environment of openness where everyone feels comfortable to share ideas and concerns.

Prioritizing Your Energy and the Culture of Vitality

Authenticity is a foundational touchstone for *Resilience*. Authentic leaders honestly and openly set personal boundaries. In doing so, you reinforce the *Culture of Vitality*. When you have energy, you are likelier to engage in healthy behaviors such as exercise, healthy eating, and protecting sleep. You're honest when you need time to renew to prevent burnout. You also make it safe for others to express their needs for energy renewal. Authentic leaders change the narrative about *Vitality* and *Resilience* by lifting them up as strategies. You see the direct link between energy renewal and high performance and work to cultivate it in yourself and in your team members. Through *Resilience*, authentic leaders reinforce the *Culture of Vitality* and create organizations better equipped to cope with adversity.

Personal Values and a Culture of Purpose

I have found no leadership development more challenging or rewarding than embracing personal *Authenticity* and empowering others to embrace *Authenticity* as well. Living and leading authentically takes active practice pushing you into a space of vulnerability that may cause discomfort. While

Authenticity is a conscientious choice, it's a necessary one for leaders who want to lead well and play the long game. You may be asking yourself this question. Why would I conscientiously choose to get uncomfortable? Virginia Rometty, the former CEO of IBM, said, "Growth and comfort don't coexist."

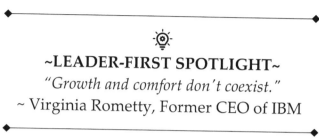

~LEADER-FIRST SPOTLIGHT~

"Growth and comfort don't coexist."
~ Virginia Rometty, Former CEO of IBM

I can attest that I've never felt comfortable in the moments of my life when I've experienced the most growth. But once you move through the discomfort with active practice, on the other side, you realize a freedom you could have never imagined possible. As an authentic leader, you reinforce the *Culture of Purpose* because you intuitively understand that finding purpose and living according to your values is impossible without *Authenticity*. When you lead authentically, you do your work without compromising your values.

When I do values work with my students and clients, a huge light-bulb moment happens for them when I say, "You do not have two sets of core values—those you have at work and those you have at home. Core values are just that. They are core to who you are." Some of them will argue this point with me incessantly, but I have research on my side. Studies have shown that when leaders and team members are encouraged to embrace their core values and identity at work, it reduces anxiety and improves performance.[4]

One study used the fear of public speaking and a well-established stress test to measure the impact of personal values on performance. Before I get into the study and its findings, I want to provide some context about why public speaking is a powerful research tool. Glossophobia—the fear of public speaking—affects 76% of the population to some degree. It is more common than the fear of death, heights, and spiders. You heard me correctly. People fear talking in front of a group more than *ceasing to exist*. Speaking in front of people evokes such an intense fight-or-flight response that researchers can reliably use it to determine what conditions improve or impair performance.

◆────────────────────────────────◆

-☼-

~LEADER-FIRST SPOTLIGHT~

You do not have two sets of core values—those you have at work and those you have at home. Core values are just that. They are core to who you are.

◆────────────────────────────────◆

In this particular study, researchers instructed participants to prepare and deliver a speech to a panel of judges about why they would be a good candidate for a well-known and competitive position.[4] To induce more significant stress, judges harassed participants by yelling—*Go faster!*—every minute during the speech. Participants were also instructed to count aloud backward from 2083 by thirteens for the five minutes following their speeches.

Before receiving instructions, researchers randomly assigned participants to a control or value-affirmation condition. Both groups completed a values questionnaire, much like the one I provided for you in the *Integrity* touchstone chapter of this book. The values-affirmation group wrote about the value most central to their core identity. The control group wrote about a value not crucial to their core identity.

In Chapter Eight on the *EI* touchstone, I shared how the body releases cortisol in response to threats and anxiety. During this state, cortisol slows bodily functions and impairs mental processing. After their speeches, participants submitted a saliva sample to test their cortisol levels. The researchers found that participants from the values affirmation group who had written about a value that was core to their identities had significantly lower cortisol levels than the control group. This study affirms that identifying and using your core values as a filter can buffer stress. This prevents anxiety and improves your performance.

Core Identity and Cultures of Purpose and Trust

Amy Cuddy talks about the concept of *Authenticity* through the power of personal stories in her book, *Presence*.[5] Cuddy says, "When we don't believe our stories, we are inauthentic, we are deceiving, in a way, both to ourselves and others. And this self-deception is, it turns out, observable to others as our confidence wanes and our verbal and nonverbal behaviors become dissonant. It's not like people are thinking he's a liar; it's that people are thinking something feels off. I can't completely invest my confidence in this person." When you demonstrate *Authenticity* and your credibility grows, another natural consequence coincides. You signal to your team members that *Authenticity* is not only safe, but valued. Team members start to trust that they can do their work without compromising their core identity.

When team members feel they can bring their authentic selves to work and share vulnerably, it unleashes the distinct value of each person and the collective ingenuity of the team. You are more willing to take creative risks and allow your team members to take risks as well. When you are grounded in *Authenticity*, you feel a sense of agency and ownership over your life and work. In *Cultures of Trust* and *Purpose*, authentic leaders encourage passions and interests through personal development. When team members feel they can meaningfully contribute, they pursue shared goals with vigor because they understand their part in realizing the organization's purpose.

No matter how hard we may try, not everyone is or will ever be exceptional at everything. Team members and leaders have to get comfortable being exposed to one another, where they feel safe to say things like "You're better than I am at that," "I was wrong," "I made a mistake," and "I need help." It takes *Courage* to be vulnerable enough to embrace imperfection and set personal boundaries. It takes *Courage* to say, "I'm not good at that," and "Someone else on that team can achieve a better outcome." It takes *Courage* to say, "I have too much on my plate," and "I'm worried I'm going to drop the ball." Sometimes, it even takes *Courage* to say, "I am good at this—give me a chance to try."

Most organizations attempt to socialize team members in congruence with organizational norms and values. However, when leaders and team members take the time to truly understand the core identities and unique gifts of each person on the team, they create team euphoria. When teams achieve euphoria, it generates a rare competitive advantage that few teams have the fortitude to clench. Researchers have sought to demonstrate the bottom-line impact of teams built on a foundation of authentic expression. In one study, call center team members participated in various experiences of a new-employee onboarding.[6] All study participants attended a ½ day orientation. Researchers assigned team members to one of three groups. The first group focused on individual identity. The second group focused on organizational identity. The third group served as the control group.

The control group underwent the company's standard orientation process focused on necessary skills and general awareness. The identity groups received the same information as the control group. In addition, the individual identity group gave participants the chance to reflect on and then share the unique gifts they brought to the organization. Each participant received fleece sweatshirts and badges inscribed with their names. In the organizational identity group, participants had the opportunity to learn about the company's achievements and culture and think about what made them proud to join the organization. They also received fleece sweatshirts and badges but their badges were inscribed with the company's name. In both identity conditions, team members outperformed the control group. However, team members who had the opportunity to express their unique identities and *Authenticity* outperformed the organizational identity group and the control group in customer satisfaction ratings, employee retention, and overall job satisfaction.

Being True to Yourself while Building Belonging

In the past, the relationship between *Authenticity* and *Belonging* has been complex. *Authenticity* focuses on being true to oneself, and *Belonging* focuses on building connections in a larger community. Often, connections start with identifying shared beliefs and values.

I anticipated this divergent complexity for the LF Leadership model when I defined a *Culture of Belonging*. A *Culture of Belonging* is an environment where human connection thrives, diversity is valued, and team members are encouraged to lean into their *Authenticity* by showcasing their unique advantages. Authentic leaders build a *Culture of Belonging* by creating psychologically safe work environments where team members feel welcome to be themselves and use their gifts to advance the organization. When you demonstrate *Authenticity*, you treat others with respect and dignity, regardless of differences.

Normalizing *Authenticity* has a bottom-line impact, but it also balances the sometimes-unintentional scapegoat effect of adaptive leadership. When leaders use adaptive leadership as Fiedler's Contingency Model first intended, they use evolving information to inform decisions and actions in real-time. However, when I work with leaders, especially women, people of color, or anyone with a discernable difference, some feel they need to *adapt* so significantly that it masks their *Authenticity* in the workplace. These are the real voices of our clients, and it represents a fraction of what I hear daily:

·ıl|ı·ı·

~LEADER-FIRST WOMEN SPEAK OUT~

"I don't feel like I can fully bring myself to work if I desire to be taken seriously and respected. What suppresses my authenticity is stereotypes—being too young and emotional or an entitled millennial. These are common phrases used at my workplace."

"The messages are so mixed for me. As a woman of color, I deal with so many conflicting messages. These are some of the messages I hear: Be positive; Don't be too over-the-top. Be real; Don't be too open about who you are personally. Be hard; Be more caring. Most of the time, I struggle to know what will set me back and what will carry me forward."

"Throughout my career, I have felt the need to be overly personable, overly agreeable, and over-delivering to demonstrate that I am capable. I don't show emotion or vulnerability. I always come in with a smile and a cheery disposition, even if I felt the complete opposite. Honestly, I'm just exhausted."

There is a nuanced difference between adjusting your identity and adapting to situations. Leaders must adapt to the unique forces of an environment and meet their team members where they are. It becomes problematic when those adaptations shift you away from your core identity. Situational leadership and *Authenticity* can only coexist when personal values guide leaders.

CHAPTER TWELVE
Love Your Team—Empathy, Inclusivity, Gratitude

*To increase revenue, improve customer experience, and
develop higher-performing teams, it's time for leaders to
stop looking for quick fixes to complex business problems
and start building a culture of love. Yes, love.*
~Mohammad Anwar

We all have moments that change the ebb and flow of
our leadership journey. For me, these go back to experiences as
early as high school. Some moments, however, completely
change our trajectory. One moment, in particular, not only
changed how I lead, it has shaped how I coach other leaders to
lead their people. I can trace it back to the action of a single
leader in my life and someone I still consider a mentor.

When Kerry Connolly asked me to join her Consulting
Team, my confidence had hit the lowest point of my life. At the
time, I was going through a painful divorce. The divorce and
the experiences leading up to the decision to leave had
obliterated my ability to trust and annihilated my self-
confidence. I was a problem-solver and a good one. But after
nearly a decade of trying to fix the broken relationship with my
then-husband, I couldn't figure out how to pull my marriage
from the depths of hopelessness. It rocked me. My years of
experience, education, and accomplishments did not feel as big
as the shadow of my divorce. I felt like a failure.

No matter my state of mind, I had to think about Madi,
who had just turned four when I decided to leave my marriage.
I was going to be a single mom now. The job Kerry offered me
would provide security and flexibility. Being a devoted, present

mom, these were non-negotiables for me. No matter how big my career grew, I committed never to let it overshadow my relationship with my daughter. Even though, at the time, Kerry didn't know all I was going through, she intuitively sensed what I needed.

As our relationship grew, she asked questions at appropriate times so that she could better understand my circumstances. After years of working together, I know now that she has a strong sense of *Empathy*. Once she understood me and my situation, she adjusted to my needs. During our relationship, she never asked me to put the job before motherhood or other aspects of life that hit me when I least expected it. From our first meeting, her actions told me I could trust her. I didn't take advantage of her *Empathy* or flexibility. Instead, it fueled my desire to do my best work. I did not want to let her down.

While there are three generally accepted types of *Empathy* (defined later in this chapter), the Leader-First (LF) Leadership definition focuses heavily on Compassionate *Empathy* because it extends from the cultivation of two Leader Touchstones—*Curiosity* and the third progression of EI—Social Awareness.[1] Rooted in sincere care for others' well-being, *Empathy* is the ability to understand and share someone else's emotions and perspectives.

~KEY DEFINITION~
Rooted in sincere care for others' well-being, *Empathy* is the ability to understand and share someone else's emotions and perspectives.

One month into the job, she called me and said, "We want you to do a workshop for around a hundred CEOs on transformational leadership. I know you have this expertise. We've never addressed the concept of leadership directly at this conference. When we get face time with these CEOs, we primarily focus on business challenges, product roll-outs, and initiatives—more tactical, tangible topics they can implement immediately. This is a significant departure from what we have done in the past. Not everyone supports it. But you and I both know leadership is everything. None of these other initiatives have a chance to succeed without a solid foundation of leadership."

She was right. I 100% agreed. I was honored to be asked. But damn, I was terrified. As a lifelong purveyor of leadership, these stakes were high. I had one chance to make this experience matter enough to open up future dialogue about shifting focus to leadership as a key growth strategy. I thought to myself, "It's OK. Kerry is going to help me with this." To say I was mistaken about that is inaccurate. Kerry did help me. But she didn't help me in any of the ways I expected.

The first time we met to discuss the workshop, I came prepared to ask 50 questions about the content. However, she, ever so gracefully, explained, "I hired you for your expertise. I'm not going to develop the workshop for you. I need your brain on this. I'm going to focus on making sure we keep the door open for this workshop so that you get the audience you need in the room. When we meet again, I want you to tell me how you're going to solve this problem, and then we can build from your ideas."

Then she let me go. No, I don't mean she hung up on me. I mean, she nudged me out of the nest. She let me test my wings. She signaled to me that my expertise was valuable to her, to the project, and to the organization. And along the way, she removed barriers that might have derailed me. It did not matter that I was new to the team or unproven in a workshop of this magnitude. Kerry trusted me. Before she hired me, she thoroughly vetted me. She knew what she was getting when she offered me a job, so she put my capabilities to work without hesitation. Throughout our work together, I watched her repeatedly remove barriers for our team members—first by understanding our needs, then by understanding our distinct value, and then by involving us in decision-making and strategy. She didn't care about our race, gender, religion, age, or sexual orientation—she cared about unleashing each team member's unique contributions.

~LEADER-FIRST SPOTLIGHT~

She nudged me out of the nest. She let me test my wings. She signaled to me that my expertise was valuable to her, to the project, and to the organization.

The value of the *Inclusivity* touchstone cannot be overstated. Of late, anything related to DEI has been overtly or latently attacked. A common problem is that DEI efforts are fragmented or flawed, leading to confusion about the intent and function. DEI work gets minimized to a "this is what we're supposed to do" initiative, instead of a "this is the wisest investment I can make to give my organization a competitive edge." If you're not already at the latter, my goal is to shift your thinking and help you understand *Inclusivity's* bottom-line, positive impact. So, let's start by defining how it propels growth in dynamic, enduring organization. The LF Leadership model definition of *Inclusivity* is fostering an environment that values authentic contributions

~KEY DEFINITION~
Inclusivity is fostering an environment that values authentic contributions and empowers the full participation and acceptance of all people.

and empowers the full participation and acceptance of all people. Before we unravel this enigma, let's look at the final *Team Three* touchstone.

When the workshop was done, Kerry continued to fuel my confidence, extend *Trust*, and open doors for me. She didn't take credit for my success, but rather, she showered me with a genuine appreciation for my work. Leaders know that *Gratitude* brings a robust ROI to the organization. But that value only materializes through genuine demonstration without expecting something in return. For those reasons, I adopted the essence of Robert Emmons's definition of *Gratitude* for the LF Leadership model.[2] *Gratitude* is reflecting an appreciation for what brings meaning to your life and recognizing and expressing that the source of value falls outside of yourself. Leaders don't need to waste time taking credit for their team members' contributions. Team success is a natural reflection of good leadership.

~KEY DEFINITION~
Gratitude is reflecting an appreciation for what brings meaning to your life and recognizing and expressing that the source of value falls outside of yourself.

In Chapter Two, when I first introduced you to the four healthy culture dimensions, I told you that "the surest way to extinguish the passion of a highly-motivated and competent employee is to signal to them that their expertise and knowledge have no value to you as a leader." Throughout our relationship, Kerry did just the opposite. She was empathetic and demonstrated *EI* by seeking to understand the unique circumstances of my situation and meeting me where I was at the time. She showed *Courage* by entrusting me with a project of high stakes and one where she bore the ultimate accountability. In doing so, her empowerment profoundly boosted my self-confidence. That experience reminded me that I already had everything I needed. I just had to tap into my own *Courage*.

Kerry exhibited *Inclusivity* by removing barriers to my success and giving lift to my unique contributions. Because of that, I knew that my truest self, my authentic self, was not only enough but highly valued. She had the *Integrity* to let me shine for my contributions and expressed genuine *Gratitude* each time I was successful. I found my voice again. I remembered why I had earned that job. Under Kerry's leadership, over and over again, her actions reinforced *Cultures of Trust, Belonging, Purpose,* and *Vitality*. Because of the culture she created, she unleashed my unique potential, and I performed at my highest level.

During the first days of the LF Leadership program, we focus heavily on helping leaders understand how to cultivate the touchstones that require deep introspection. On the last day of the program, we shift focus to their teams and entire organizations. I ask participants this question:

Do you genuinely care about your team members?

They almost always unanimously say, "Yes." Then I ask them if their team members would answer that question the same way and what evidence they would provide. This question gets them to stop and think. I have found that for some leaders, expressing sincere care for their team members feels uncomfortable and even foreign. Some associate showing compassion and care with demonstrating vulnerability. They are not the same, but both are vital in signaling *Trust* and *Belonging* to your team members.

LEADING WITH THE TEAM THREE

I started this chapter with the story about Kerry because our work together demonstrated the influential relationship among The Team Three—*Empathy, Inclusivity,* and *Gratitude.* Figure 12.1 shows The Team Three functions of understanding, involving, and appreciating your team members using these team investment touchstones.

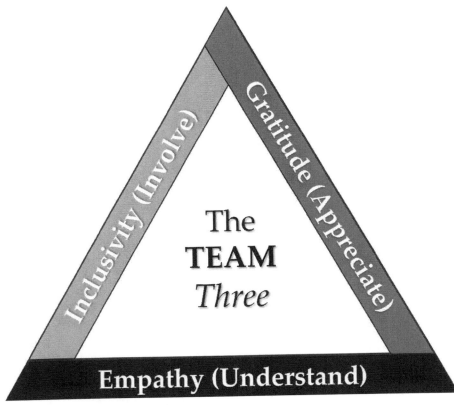

Figure 12.1: The Team Three

I don't want to convey that these three touchstones are less important than the other six because they didn't get their own chapters. Instead, I will show you how they synergistically work together to unleash your team members. Just like any of the touchstones, you have to actively work to cultivate each. All three have positive outcomes for you as a leader and as a human being. But taken together, they yield the most precipitous, pervasive impact on your team members' individual and collective success.

Empathy—More Than Caring, Understanding

The essence of the *Empathy* Touchstone comes from compassionate *Empathy*. Compassionate *Empathy*, also known as empathic concern or "feeling with" *Empathy*, combines elements from cognitive *Empathy* and emotional *Empathy*.[3] Cognitive *Empathy* is perspective-taking or thinking *Empathy*. Driven by *Curiosity*, cognitively empathetic people seek to understand another person's emotions and point of view. It involves an intellectual process of analyzing and imagining yourself in another person's situation and, therefore, gaining insight into their feelings and thoughts.

Cognitive *Empathy* has a reciprocal relationship with *Inclusivity*. You can recognize and appreciate that other people have unique perspectives that may differ from yours. It requires you to imagine yourself in another person's shoes to understand their thoughts, intentions, and emotions. You make a cognitive shift from your perspective to that of another person, allowing for a deeper understanding of their mental and emotional state. If you have high cognitive *Empathy*, you will successfully attribute mental states to your team members, peers, and stakeholders, allowing you to understand and predict behavior, anticipate needs, and respond empathetically.

Emotional or affective *Empathy* differs from cognitive because emotional *Empathy* involves experiencing and sharing the emotional experiences of others. You vicariously feel another person's joy, sadness, fear, or pain. While emotional

Empathy can help leaders connect more deeply, it can also lead to emotional overload. When this happens during stressful or high-pressure situations you risk burning out and experiencing decision-making fatigue. Emotional *Empathy* can also inadvertently open the gateway to bias and favoritism if you have deeper emotional attachments with some team members.

When you use compassionate *Empathy*, you understand your team members' perspectives (cognitive) *and* experience their emotions (affective) but do so without overreaching. Compassionate *Empathy* is action-oriented. It motivates you to take action by providing support.[3]

At the heart of empathetic leadership is active listening and open communication. When they need you, give your team members undivided attention, maintain eye contact, and seek to genuinely understand their viewpoints and unique contributions. These actions foster *Cultures of Trust* and *Belonging*. You deepen both culture dimensions by creating a safe space where team members feel heard and valued. Cultivate a *Culture of Purpose* by providing your team members opportunities for growth, nurturing their talents, and promoting their ownership in achieving the organization's shared goals.

~KEY DEFINITIONS~

Cognitive Empathy is also known as perspective-taking Empathy or "thinking" Empathy. It means to understand another person's emotions and point of view.

Emotional or *Affective Empathy* means to experience and share the emotional experiences of others.

Compassionate Empathy means to understand another's perspective and share their emotions, motivating you to take action and provide support.

As an empathetic leader, you model well-being and acknowledge its importance to your team members. You recognize they have responsibilities beyond the workplace and reinforce the *Culture of Vitality* by promoting flexible schedules, encouraging self-care practices, and showing compassion during challenging times.

INCLUSIVITY—A BOTTOM-LINE IMPERATIVE

The Peterson Institute for International Economics found that companies with at least 30% female leaders earn 6% more profits than those without female leadership.[4] A recent study showed that companies with above-average diversity on their leadership teams reported 19% higher innovation revenue than companies with below-average leadership diversity.[5] In a study of 366 organizations in the top quartile for racial and ethnic diversity, McKinsey found that they were 35% more likely to have financial returns above the national average.[6] A Gallup study of two companies found that the most gender-diverse of 800 business units had average revenues 14% higher.[7]

~LEADER-FIRST SPOTLIGHT~

Organizations in the top quarter for racial and ethnic diversity are 35% more likely to have financial returns above the national average.

We typically discuss *Inclusivity* in the context of social justice and moral obligations. When organizations politicize and fight *Inclusivity* because it gets touted as an ESG (environmental, social, governance) issue and nothing more, they leave money on the table. We rarely discuss the positive, bottom-line impact of *Inclusivity*. *Inclusivity* is a necessary, strategic imperative if leaders want to play the long game.

As an inclusive leader, you recognize and appreciate the unique value, perspectives, backgrounds, and experiences each team member contributes to the organization. Actively seeking out individuals from different cultures, races, genders, ages, abilities, and backgrounds and you remove barriers to their active participation and involvement. A diverse workforce fosters innovation, creativity, and a broader range of ideas that can lead to better outcomes.

Inclusive leaders encourage team members to bring their authentic selves to work, strengthening psychological safety and engagement. When team members feel respected, they will more likely contribute unique perspectives. *Inclusivity* reinforces all four culture dimensions to unleash innovation, problem-solving, better decision-making processes, and increased productivity. These culture dimensions reduce costly employee turnover and absenteeism. Inclusive leaders save their organizations substantial recruitment and training costs while enhancing overall operational efficiency.

When you embrace *Inclusivity,* your team can tap into previously underserved markets and demographics. Diverse and inclusive workforces understand an increasingly diverse customer base. Expanded markets increase revenue, build competitive advantage, and improve customer loyalty. Team members from diverse backgrounds that collaborate unlock a rich tapestry of perspectives, ideas, and experiences. Diversity of thought challenges conventional thinking, stimulates creativity, and encourages the exploration of new approaches and solutions.

Inclusivity is not just a profitable thing to do. It represents a core principle of social responsibility. As an inclusive leader, when you commit to fairness, equity, and equal opportunities, you contribute to building a more equitable society and addressing systemic inequalities. These actions enhance your organization's reputation and generate positive public perception. By championing *Inclusivity*, you gain a competitive edge because you can attract top talent, loyal customers, and long-term partnerships—all of which grows the bottom line.

~LEADER-FIRST SPOTLIGHT~

As an inclusive leader, when you commit to fairness, equity, and equal opportunities, you contribute to building a more equitable society and addressing systemic inequalities.

GRATITUDE—THE POWER OF THANKS

Each night before bed, I have a fairly standard routine. I brush my teeth, wash my face, have a sip of water, and just before I turn off the lights, I review my daily WHOOP insights. My husband was hooked on his, so last year, he convinced me to join the bandwagon. The WHOOP goes further than other fitness and health wearable that I have used in the past. Instead of simply tracking things like activity, nutrition, and sleep, WHOOP provides me with daily feedback on what to do with the insights so that I can build healthier, more sustainable habits. I also complete a quick daily journal that I customized at the beginning of my WHOOP subscription. WHOOP tracks those entries to identify which daily practices support improved sleep and recovery.[8]

While overall health and fitness are important to me, my most significant challenge has always been sleeping. I have never been a great sleeper. For decades I ran my body and mind into the ground and slept only 3 to 4 hours a night. It took my research on the impact that health has on a person's ability to lead people well before I realized that I was trying to convince leaders to do something I was not doing myself. So, I begrudgingly purchased yet another wearable because my husband assured me *this* was the one. It was not until three months after purchasing it that my WHOOP insight made my jaw drop, and I knew he was right. It said:

After reporting gratitude (10x in the past 90 days), your REM Duration typically increased by 7.0%.

Let me start by saying that the essence of this insight was not new news to me. In fact, at the time, I was working on research for *9 Leader Touchstones* (one of which is *Gratitude*), and understanding the power of *Gratitude* is the exact reason I added this to my daily WHOOP journal. I wanted to see *Gratitude* in action. Decades of research by Psychologists and Mental Health experts have demonstrated a robust connection between *Gratitude* and health. Related to sleep, "hypothalamic regulation triggered by gratitude helps us get deeper and healthier sleep naturally every day."[9] I get it. But there it was, staring back at me—the outcome I knew was possible through years of research had finally, meaningfully impacted me personally. At that moment, the intangible power of *Gratitude* became tangible for me. That WHOOP insight doesn't even begin to tell me how my expressions of *Gratitude* positively impacted the recipients.

Grateful leaders are positive catalysts. When you demonstrate *Gratitude*, you increase connection and loyalty with your team members by reinforcing *Cultures* of *Trust*, *Purpose*, and *Belonging*. By expressing *Gratitude*, you untangle fear and build psychological safety. Team members feel valued and motivated. Acts of *Gratitude* are powerful tools that inspire your team members and connect them to the organization's greater purpose.

During the LF Leadership program and one-on-one Leader Coaching, we talk to leaders about the power that *Gratitude* has in reinforcing the *Culture of Vitality* and untangling the *culture of fatigue*. Our research has overwhelmingly confirmed the results of reinforcing this culture dimension— higher team member productivity and increased engagement, among other things. Studies on *Gratitude* and appreciation have shown "that when employees feel valued, they have high job satisfaction, are willing to work longer hours, engage in productive relationships with co-workers and supervisors, are motivated to do their best and work towards achieving the company's goals."[10]

~LEADER-FIRST SPOTLIGHT~
Grateful leaders are positive catalysts.

As a retired professional fundraiser, during the early days of my career I witnessed the power of the word *thanks*. Recently I reviewed an article that established gratitude's effect on team members, specifically for professional thankers (also known as fundraisers). Researchers at the Wharton School of the University of Pennsylvania found that leaders who expressed *Gratitude* to their team members increased team member motivation, leading to higher productivity.[11] In the study, fundraisers were randomly assigned to two groups. The first group made typical solicitation calls to alums to ask for donations. The second group met with the Director of Annual

Giving on a different day. During the meeting, she told them she was grateful for their efforts. The following week, team members from the second group made 50% more solicitation calls than their counterparts from the first group. Even fundraisers need to be thanked every now and then.

My WHOOP insight also expanded my thinking on *Gratitude*. During our coaching sessions in the past, I focused primarily on how a leader's demonstration of *Gratitude* unleashes their team members' unique potential and how it positively impacts team member energy renewal. However, I had lost sight of *Gratitude's* reciprocal, reinforcing nature. Expressions of *Gratitude* to both the giver and the receiver activate neurochemical releases of serotonin and dopamine. These help you decrease stress and regulate your emotions. Simple exchanges of *Gratitude* yield long-lasting, positive effects on neurological functioning.[12]

Robert Emmons, the world's foremost scientific expert on the subject, says *Gratitude* "magnifies positive emotions" by helping us focus on the present. When something is new—car, spouse, house—we initially feel excited, but that feeling wears off after a while. "But *Gratitude* makes us appreciate the value of something, and when we appreciate the value of something, we extract more benefits from it; we are less likely to take it for granted."[13] I often hear the phrase, "Have an attitude of *Gratitude*." However, a grateful attitude does not go far enough to evoke *Gratitude's* positive, neurological, and physiological effects. *Gratitude* is an action, not a mindset.

As leaders, you must be active participants in the work of *Gratitude*. In choosing to do so, you not only take another step toward building an enduring organization, but you also improve the health and *Resilience* of the employees under your care, not to mention your own.

TEAM THREE—THE BRAIN SCIENCE

The brain science of *Empathy, Inclusivity,* and *Gratitude,* taken collectively, shed light on their profound impact on social connections and personal growth. *Empathy* relies on a complex interplay of neural networks within the brain. Mirror neurons, found in regions like the insula and anterior cingulate cortex, fire when you perform an act of *Empathy* and witness someone else performing the same action, leading to an internal simulation of the observed experience.[14] The prefrontal cortex enables perspective-taking and Cognitive *Empathy.*

Neuroscientific research shows that *Inclusivity* activates the reward centers in the brain. When you demonstrate *Inclusivity,* the reward centers release neurotransmitters like dopamine, promoting a positive emotional response and reinforcing a sense of *Belonging.* Brain regions associated with social processing are activated during inclusive experiences, indicating the brain's inherent inclination towards social cohesion.[15]

Like *Inclusivity, Gratitude* also activates the brain's reward centers and releases feel-good neurotransmitters such as dopamine and serotonin. This enhances your mood, reduces stress, and improves overall mental health. The practice of *Gratitude* strengthens neural connections in the prefrontal cortex, facilitating emotion regulation and cognitive flexibility.[16] *Empathy, Inclusivity,* and *Gratitude* collectively nurture social cohesion and strengthen relationships. Understanding the brain science behind these Leader Touchstones illuminates the inherent capacity of the human brain for personal growth, compassion, and connection. You cultivate a safe environment that promotes *Resilience*, reducing divisiveness and creating a reciprocal cycle of positivity inside your organization.

~LEADER-FIRST SPOTLIGHT~

The brain science behind Leader Touchstones,
Empathy, Inclusivity, *and* Gratitude, *illuminate the inherent capacity of the human brain for compassion, connection, and personal growth.*

TOUCHSTONE TAI CHI—THE TEAM THREE

To grow as LF Leader who demonstrates *Empathy, Inclusivity,* and *Gratitude,* you must first examine your own beliefs, biases, and assumptions. Then think about how you contribute to and detract from the team's strength. By understanding your unique advantages, gaps, and potential blindspots, you can better navigate your biases and make conscious efforts to be more inclusive. LF Leaders recognize and appreciate the value of diversity in all its forms. Diversity goes beyond race, ethnicity, and gender. This requires you to explore and understand other types of diversity, such as age, socioeconomic background, sexual orientation, physical abilities, and religion.[6]

Seek out diverse perspectives and experiences when forming teams and making decisions. By embracing diversity, you can tap into the collective wisdom of difference. I will kick off Touchstone Tai Chi with a Leader Coaching Corner. Each time you engage with a team member, keep the Team Three touchstones in mind by asking yourself and answering these questions:

LEADER COACHING CORNER

✓ **Do I understand what's happening with this team member that might impact their success?** (*Empathy*)

✓ **What is this team member's perspective on this problem?** (*Empathy* and *Inclusivity*)

✓ **What does my team member need from me?** (*Empathy* and *Inclusivity*)

✓ **Do I truly understand this team member's talents, skills, interests, and unique advantages?** (*Inclusivity*)

✓ **Have I expressed *Gratitude* to this team member for their contribution throughout and after engagement?** (*Inclusivity* and *Gratitude*)

✓ **Do I understand how this team member wants to be thanked for their contribution?** (*Gratitude*)

In the following pages, you will find practical tactics to grow in the *Team Three* touchstones. You can use these with your team members to cultivate *Empathy*, *Inclusivity*, and *Gratitude* in them as well.

Cultivate the touchstones.

So much of what you need to lead with *Empathy*, *Inclusivity*, and *Gratitude* naturally develops as you cultivate the other Leader Touchstones. Stay curious about current diversity and inclusion trends, best practices, and research. Cultivate *EI*— self-awareness to open your mind to your biases and social awareness to grow as a tuned-in, empathetic leader. Push through discomfort to engage in courageous conversations about diversity, equity, and inclusion. Create safe spaces that encourage discussion of complex and challenging topics openly. Address sensitive issues such as bias, micro-aggressions, discrimination, and privilege to foster *Inclusivity* and provide opportunities to learn and to lead learning. Share yourself authentically, and grow your *Integrity*-baseline to inspire *Trust* and connection.

Practice perspective-taking.

Engage in perspective-taking by putting yourself in another person's shoes, and working to understand their experiences, beliefs, and values. Adopting different perspectives can broaden your understanding of how different team members perceive situations. This enables you to respond with greater sensitivity and compassion. Enhance perspective-taking by engaging in open-minded discussions, seeking diverse opinions, and encouraging feedback.

Improve transparent communication and active listening.

Active listening is a fundamental *Empathy* skill and extends to *EI* progressions of Social Awareness and Relationship Management. Be present when conversing with your team members by giving them your undivided attention, maintaining eye contact, and demonstrating genuine interest in their perspectives. By understanding and acknowledging your team members' perspectives, challenges, and accomplishments, you open up opportunities to provide meaningful *Gratitude* for their contributions.

~LEADER-FIRST SPOTLIGHT~

By understanding and acknowledging your team members' perspectives, challenges, and accomplishments, you open up opportunities to provide meaningful Gratitude *for their contributions.*

Promote transparent communication channels where all team members can express concerns and ideas. Actively listen to diverse viewpoints and encourage respectful dissent. Intuitively understand your personal communication style, and work to understand your team members' styles and preferences to promote equal participation and understanding. Table 12.1 includes several tactics you can use with your team members to enhance communication and listening.

ENHANCE COMMUNICATION AND LISTENING

REFLECTIVE LISTENING

One person speaks in pairs or small groups while the other listens attentively. After the speaker finishes, the listener repeats or paraphrases what they heard. This promotes focused listening and encourages the speaker to feel understood.

LISTENING TO AUDIO RECORDINGS OR PODCASTS

Select engaging audio recordings or podcasts and actively listen to them. Take notes on key points, summarize the content, and discuss it afterward. This exercise enhances concentration and comprehension skills.

GUIDED LISTENING EXERCISES

Find recorded guided listening exercises online or use a mindfulness app. These exercises often focus on specific sounds or sensations and help develop concentration and mindfulness, which are essential for active listening.

GROUP DISCUSSIONS

Facilitate and participate in group discussions where each team member takes turns speaking on a particular topic. Improve active listening by asking follow-up questions or requesting clarification. This activity enhances comprehension and encourages participants to pay close attention to others' viewpoints.

ACTIVE LISTENING GAMES

Play games that require active listening, such as "Whispers," where a message is whispered from person to person and compared to the original, or "20 Questions," where participants ask questions to determine a specific object or person. These games promote attentive listening and the ability to extract relevant information.

NONVERBAL COMMUNICATION EXERCISES

Practice noticing and interpreting nonverbal cues--facial expressions, body language, and tone of voice. Engage in role-playing activities where participants practice active listening by paying attention to these cues.

MINDFUL LISTENING WALK

Walk in a quiet, natural environment like a park or forest. Focus on the sounds you hear, whether birds chirping, leaves rustling, or water flowing. Concentrate on each sound individually, trying to identify as many as possible. This exercise enhances concentration and helps attune your ears to different sounds.

Table 12.1: Tactics to Enhance Communication and Listening

Understand bias. Challenge stereotypes.

Vigilantly identify and challenge your biases and stereotypes. Unconscious bias can influence decision-making and hinder *Inclusivity* and *Empathy*. Engage in self-reflection, education, and training to gain awareness of your biases and actively work to overcome them. Encourage open dialogue about bias by fostering an environment where team members feel safe to discuss and challenge stereotypes and prejudices. Table 12.2 provides some practices for understanding stereotypes and biases.

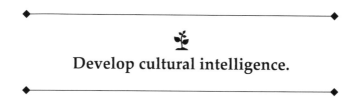

Develop cultural intelligence.

Cultivating *Empathy* and *Inclusivity* requires you to embrace and celebrate diversity in all its forms. By actively improving your cultural awareness and intelligence, you signal to your team that you celebrate diversity and care enough to understand who they are. *Cultural intelligence* is the ability to understand other cultures and to work effectively cross-culturally. You can enhance your cultural intelligence by seeking knowledge about various cultures, customs, and traditions. Organize cultural immersion experiences that expose you and

~KEY DEFINITION~
Cultural intelligence is the ability to understand other cultures and to work effectively cross-culturally.

UNDERSTANDING STEREOTYPES AND BIAS

START BY LEARNING ABOUT THE TYPES OF BIAS:

~KEY DEFINITIONS~

Unconscious bias (or implicit bias) operates outside your awareness. This type of bias is prejudice or unsupported judgments that occur with the brain automatically makes quick assumptions based on past experiences and pre-established constructs.[17]

Conscious bias (or explicit) is an extreme form of bias expressed through verbal and sometimes physical harassment and harm. You can also demonstrate conscious bias subtly but cognizantly through acts of exclusion.[18]

Confirmation bias is the tendency to favor information that aligns with your existing beliefs or attitudes.[19]

TAKE AN IMPLICIT ASSOCIATION TEST (IAT)

While the LF Leadership Touchstone Assessment generally measures *Inclusivity*, IATs help identify specific implicit biases outside your awareness. IATs can provide insights into biases related to various elements of diversity.

DO BIAS REFLECTION EXERCISES

Reflect on personal and professional experiences to identify where biases may have influenced your decisions or actions. Write down these instances and explore the underlying biases and their potential impact.

FACILITATE BIAS-BASED CASE STUDY GROUP DISCUSSIONS

Host case studies discussions or real-life scenarios that involve bias-related challenges. Openly explore the biases that might have influenced decision-making processes.

Table 12.2: Practices for Understanding Stereotypes and Bias

your team members to different cultures. Practice by adapting your leadership style to accommodate different cultural norms and values.

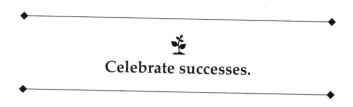

Celebrate successes.

Celebrate individual and collective successes. Don't reserve them for the big wins. Celebrate the small ones too. Celebrations can demonstrate your *Gratitude,* especially when they meaningfully exhibit your appreciation. Celebrations can be anything from public acknowledgments to team outings to personalized rewards and incentives.

Encourage peer-to-peer recognition.

While leaders should set the tone, *Gratitude* is not solely your responsibility or the sole responsibility of the leadership team. Boost peer-to-peer recognition by creating platforms or channels for team members to express appreciation for one another. Encourage team members to provide specific and timely recognition. When recognizing a peer, have your team members highlight the specific behaviors that made a positive impact. By creating an environment where appreciation and recognition become second nature, you deepen connections and strengthen relationships throughout the organization.

Collaborate and delegate.

Inclusive leaders understand the importance of collaboration and delegation. Actively involve team members in decision-making processes by seeking input, especially from those who bring unique perspectives. By giving team members ownership over projects and tasks, you empower them, grow their *Courage* and confidence, and reinforce the *Culture of Belonging*. To wrap up Chapter Twelve, take a look at this Leader-First Story contributed by Crescent Leadership Collaborator Diana del Monaco on inclusion and culture.

A LEADER-FIRST STORY
Red Rover—A Lesson Learned on
Disparity, Inclusion, and Culture
~Contributed by Diana del Monaco, PhD, MBA, MPH~
Acting Director, Trauma & Clinical Care Research Directorate
Defense Health Agency, 59th Medical Wing
Crescent Leadership Collaborator

It is time for parents to teach young people early on that in diversity, there is beauty and there is strength. ~ Maya Angelou

I can still hear the song playing over and over in my head. Red rover, red rover, let Kayla come over. Kayla and I were the last two 5-year-olds left on the west wing of the game. We felt left out and disheartened. It was a horrible feeling. Those feelings generated so many thoughts… so many questions at such a young age. Even in young children, fear and isolation can perpetuate self-doubt. The feelings transcend the playground. They move into the classroom and beyond. Self-doubt at that age meant not being good enough, and later on, it meant not having the confidence to share my voice and recognize my strengths.

Although the game is not as prevalent today in many child playgrounds, *are we still living and re-living Red Rover in the workplace?* It's a child's game that shouldn't mean anything, and yet today, we've learned to, consciously or unconsciously, include some people and exclude others. But why? Each person's life perspective has merit. Each person's knowledge has value. We decided to hire them. Yet we make assumptions about their interest, capacity, level of engagement, and fit. These assumptions limit their career trajectory and have a damaging effect on an organization's ability to innovate.

Some argue that people in leadership are tasked to assess who is the right fit for their organization. My challenge to leaders is to question whether the concept of "fit" is outdated. Consider how often we overlook history, knowledge, experience, and perspective from our more tenured team members. Conversely, how often do we discount ideas from the rookies because they need more experience to understand the problem? This only perpetuates a cycle of disparity and exclusion in the workplace. These actions can have a lasting impact on organizational culture that harvests fear of engagement and repression of voice.

The past few decades have brought some change. Traditional patriarchal leadership is shifting as more women ascend to the C-Suite. Women, by nature, exercise highly connected relationships through bonding. The level of connectedness varies based on a person's background, culture, education, self-awareness, and life experiences. While command-and-control management still happens, leadership styles have become more collaborative and relationship-based.

Awareness and understanding of diversity grow through self-exploration of biases and reading history that explores traditions and cultural influence. I frequently seek out past and present trailblazers who share my cultural and situational experiences to identify strengths and shortcomings that I might not instinctively consider in my journey. One of my favorites is Juana Bordas, a Latina community activist specializing in leadership development and diversity training. Her recent book, *The Power of Latino Leadership*, describes several actions a person must embrace to build a thriving organizational culture. For example, *personalismo*, or the "character of oneself," is a personal commitment to apply the belief that every person has inherent value and thus deserves respect.[20] For Latinos, *personalismo* is an inherent expectation in our culture and traditions. A person who embodies *personalismo* is seen as a leader and highly regarded.

As leaders, we must be cognizant of how actions could exclude the people we lead. Both inadvertent or overt acts break the bond of trust and have a long-term impact on the culture and success of the organization.

When leaders are faced with significant opportunities and challenges early in the life cycle of planning, they should seek the voices and the engagement of all members of their teams. These acts promote *Inclusion*, solidarity, respect, and value, reinforcing the organization's *Culture of Belonging*. Stakeholder buy-in and vision acceptance are the pillars of the change. It impacts their *Destino* or future paths. For the Latino, it solidifies fate and purpose. After all, one's *Destino* is but "a dance with the currents of life."

Having come from disparity, I watch for the people inside and outside my circle who need mentorship. Trailblazing is not meant to be a lonely path. It is an altruistic journey in which you constantly reach back and pull those behind you forward. That is the ultimate legacy you leave behind, and every person you meet has a part in creating that legacy.

CHAPTER THIRTEEN
Tap the Untapped Magic of Resilience

The best asset we have for making a contribution to the world is ourselves. If we underinvest in ourselves, and by that, I mean our minds, our bodies, and our spirits, we damage the very tool we need to make our highest contribution.
~ Greg McKeown

As a leader, I know the demands you face daily are incredible. In a fast-paced, ever-changing world, balance seems unattainable, even laughable. The pandemic made our lives even more challenging and tested our mettle. Sometimes, I find it difficult to identify what positive lessons we've learned over the past few years, but I have seen at least one constructive outcome of the pandemic. It has changed the landscape just enough, pushing many executives to the brink of personal health crises, that they are starting to understand the pricelessness of their well-being. Further, they see they can't pawn off wellness as a superficial, check-the-box initiative.

We are, and will forever be, stuck with 24 hours in a day. Trying to do more... and more... and more... with an unchanging space of time is the very definition of ignorance. The most common mistake made by Bottom-Line (BL) executives is this—working team members to the point of exhaustion *does not* increase productivity and high performance. Working late hours and long days, with no focused time to recuperate, not only catastrophically impairs performance but also endangers the health of their team members.

The integration of *Resilience* as a Leader Touchstone distinctly jumped out of the research. The last few years have shown that overcoming adversity is critical to leaders and team members. *The ability to overcome adversity* is the standard definition of *Resilience*. However, when developing the Leader-First (LF) Leadership model definition, I just couldn't get past the period at the end of the sentence. I kept remembering how many times I'd overcome adversity in my life and how utterly exhausted I felt by it all, simply because I'm the kind of person who can handle a great deal of stress. While overcoming adversity is necessary, it shouldn't come at the expense of your health and well-being or worse. So, I changed the question from:

"What are the characteristics of resilient people?"
to
"How do people build Resilience?"

Quickly, I started seeing the answer align with what I already knew about energy renewal. The dictionary definition of *Resilience* is a slippery slope. It leaves leaders open to overcoming adversity at work, no matter the personal cost. The

LF Leadership definition of *Resilience* gives specific guidance to leaders about how they should cultivate the *Resilience* touchstone. *Resilience* is your capacity to overcome adversity through the systematic renewal of the body's four energy wellsprings—physical, mental, emotional, and spiritual. This definition guides you in building an enduring organization while protecting you as a human being. Energy renewal is a prerequisite to preparing for adversity. Before I make you believe your energy renewal has the power to strengthen your *Resilience*, first, I need to show you the bottom-line impact for you and your organization if you don't.

A DEADLY REALITY—CULTURES OF FATIGUE

I often use discussion boards in my leadership classrooms to provoke deeper thought on surface-level topics. When my students respond, I'll add probing questions to challenge their thinking. Last year during a heated discussion, I posed these questions:

Why is building a foundation of psychological safety so important to building high-performing organizations? How are you doing it at your company?

One student responded with an unexpected perspective. He challenged the view that psychological safety builds high-performing organizations. He offered that while data demonstrates that psychological safety creates high-performing teams, he could not find data to support the notion that psychological safety creates high-performing organizations. He used the examples of Wal-Mart and Amazon, Fortune 500 and Global 500's #1 and #2 companies. Even though these are the top revenue-producing companies, both have become frequently mentioned demonstrations of low trust and psychologically unsafe environments. From these examples, my student deduced that while psychological safety improves team functionality and individual team member success, it minimally impacts high performance across large organizations.

I responded that if we're using the sole benchmark of total revenue to define "high-performing," I would agree. These two companies are the *highest-performing* corporations in the world. However, I would challenge the standard by which we define high-performing. Fear can drive performance but only to a certain point. You can scare your people into performing by threatening their jobs, working them to the point of exhaustion, limiting their growth opportunities, and making errors a death sentence instead of a chance to learn from the experience. But "the impact of fear on performance has diminishing returns."[1] At a certain point, the negative side of fear rears its ugly head. Fear reinforces *cultures of isolation, fatigue,* and *apathy* and can lead to avoidance, paralysis of action, or even aggression.

Karoshi 過労死, the word to describe Japanese work culture where working 70+ hours a week is considered honorable, means "death from overwork." The dangers of the Karoshi phenomenon have spread, afflicting nations worldwide. In 2021, the World Health Organization published the sobering results of a longitudinal study. Long working hours (55+ hours per week) caused 745,000 premature deaths and disabled 23 million additional people in 2016.[2] This number represents a 29% increase since 2000.

In 2018, Jeffrey Pfeffer of Stanford Graduate School of Business published a book with a harrowing title—*Dying for a Paycheck.*[3] If the title doesn't scare the book right off the bookshelf for you, his findings detailed in its pages, will. Toxic workplace conditions and job stress in the United States account for as many as 120,000 preventable deaths yearly, making it the fifth-highest cause of death. 8% of total healthcare spending, or $180 billion, covers additional healthcare costs caused by stress-related illness and disease. In China, an estimated 600,000 people die yearly due to overwork. That means more than 68 people drop dead in China every hour of every day simply from overtoiling their bodies. These numbers represent the tangible costs in human lives and actual dollars spent.

~BOTTOM-LINE EXECUTIVE BEHAVIOR~

Karoshi 過労死, *the word to describe Japanese work culture where working 70+ hours a week is considered honorable, means "death from overwork.*

Depression and anxiety cost the global economy approximately $1 trillion in lost productivity. An estimated 1 million workers are absent every day because of stress. Job stress annually costs the US economy more than $300 billion in losses due to absenteeism, diminished productivity, and accidents. "When fear becomes an entrenched marker of an organization's culture, it can have toxic effects over the long run. In addition to stifling creativity, it can inhibit collaboration and lead to burnout."[4]

The term "*burnout*" has been around since the 1970s but has been diluted over time, making the fear-mongering of BL executives easier to swallow. Productivity loss is significant and represents a high cost to organizations. Ultimately that cost doesn't get factored into total revenue. However, there is a far greater cost of fear and work-related stress—the cost of the health and sometimes the lives of actual breathing human beings. That cost is rarely acknowledged.

~BOTTOM-LINE EXECUTIVE BEHAVIOR~

*Job stress costs the US industry more than $300
billion in losses due to absenteeism, diminished
productivity, and accidents.*

RESILIENCE AND CULTURING

Your commitment to *Resilience* and energy renewal in all
four wellsprings directly and most significantly reinforces the
Culture of Vitality. But *Resilience* also reinforces the other three
culture dimensions. You create a *Culture of Trust* by designing
psychologically safe workplaces, eliminating fear-based tactics,
and reducing unhealthy forms of stress.

When you prioritize spiritual energy renewal for you
and your team members, you unlock their unique potential and
reinforce the *Culture of Belonging*. Freeing up your team
members to focus on the organization's purpose instead of
obscure metrics builds loyalty and endears them to the work.
The *Culture of Purpose* organically evolves as each team member
takes responsibility for achieving the organization's reason for
existence.

Playing the long game means defining high performance
differently. The organization's total performance (taking into
account both revenue *and* loss related to stress-related illness,
mortality, turnover, and lost productivity) would indeed be
even higher, more ethical and sustainable long-term, and at a
lower cost to your employees' lives—this means Amazon and
Wal-Mart too. Changing the conversation about high-
performance can only happen when you cultivate *Resilience* in
yourself and the entire organization.

TOUCHSTONE TAI CHI & THE SCIENCE—*RESILIENCE*

Most research about leadership focuses on the psychology. Not enough focus is given to the physiology of leadership. LF Leadership looks at both. While it is not a popular or pervasively studied concept, holistic wellness and energy renewal are inherently linked to how well people lead others. What's more, it *does* have a positive bottom-line impact. Schwartz and McCarthy showed us this in their ground-breaking study that found a positive correlation between energy renewal and work performance.[5] Before Wachovia merged, the company participated in an energy management pilot. The researchers measured their performance against a control group to determine how much energy renewal could positively impact bottom-line performance.

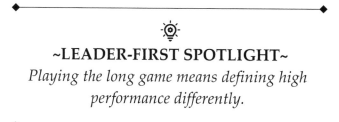

~LEADER-FIRST SPOTLIGHT~
Playing the long game means defining high performance differently.

The participants in the energy renewal program outperformed the control group on key financial metrics, such as the value of loans they generated. Specifically, test group participants produced 13% greater year-over-year revenues from loans than the control group and exceeded the control group's revenues from deposits by 20%. Further, they reported substantial improvements in customer relationships, work engagement, and personal satisfaction.

The concept of energy comes from the world of thermodynamics, so the definition of energy can get a bit

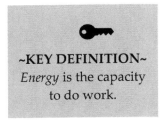

~KEY DEFINITION~
Energy is the capacity
to do work.

technical. But its fundamental meaning is the capacity to do work. Schwartz and McCarthy's research explored the four primary energy sources in humans—the body, mind, emotions, and spirit. They also looked at how each source of energy can be sustained and renewed. Shulbha Kothari took this research further in his 2017 article, Renew your Inner Energy through Human Internal Energy Sources. Kothari shared that as much as 80-85% of all disease and illness is caused by stress but could be prevented through sound energy management.[6] Through a remarkable symphony of biological mechanisms that sustain the health of the human body, energy is vital to functionality, influencing your daily life in countless ways.

~LEADER-FIRST SPOTLIGHT~

Through a remarkable symphony of biological mechanisms that sustain the health of the human body, energy is vital to functionality, influencing your daily life in countless ways.

From the moment you wake up and throughout the day, the human body can renew and replenish its energy levels. In the following sections, I've integrated brain and body science along with *Touchstone Tai Chi* for the four energy sources. Learning about the science also demonstrates how to renew each one. The human mind governs your thoughts, emotions, and behaviors. However, the mind is not an isolated system. The mind and body are intricately interconnected. Because of the symbiotic relationship between the body and mind, certain energy renewal habits boost multiple wellsprings, but in different ways. Therefore, I've broken these sections out by the cultivating action. In each, you'll find the specific body-mind mechanism that drives renewal in a particular wellspring.

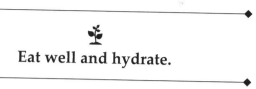

Eat well and hydrate.

Proper nutrition and hydration are fundamental to the body's physical, mental, and emotional energy renewal. A balanced diet provides essential macronutrients (proteins, carbohydrates, and fats) and micronutrients (vitamins and minerals) for energy production and cellular functioning. Cellular respiration is at the heart of the body's renewal of energy. The journey of cellular respiration begins when you ingest food. The body breaks down carbohydrates, fats, and proteins during digestion, releasing energy in the form of glucose.[7]

The body's preferred energy source is carbohydrates because they efficiently convert into glucose. Sources of complex carbohydrates that provide sustained energy include whole grains, fruits, vegetables, and legumes. Proteins, on the other hand, repair muscles and produce energy. Lean meats, fish, dairy products, and plant-based sources such as beans and tofu are rich in protein. Fats, although often demonized, when consumed in moderation, provide essential energy stores and insulation. Unsaturated fats in avocados, nuts, and olive oil renew energy while supporting cardiovascular health.

Optimal brain function requires a steady supply of nutrients. The Omega-3 fatty acids in walnuts, flaxseeds, and fatty fish such as salmon boost cognitive function and emotional regulation. Avoiding excessively processed foods, refined sugars, and heavy caffeine can help prevent mood fluctuations throughout your day. A nourishing diet supports mental energy renewal and contributes to overall physical well-being. Nutrients such as B vitamins and magnesium improve mood and emotional *Resilience*. An overall balanced diet stabilizes your blood sugar levels, averting energy crashes that negatively impact your ability to regulate emotions.

In addition to proper nutrition, hydration is paramount for energy renewal. Almost every bodily process involves water, including transporting nutrients and removing waste products. Dehydration can decrease energy levels, cause fatigue, and impair cognitive function. That's why water consumption spread throughout the day can maintain energy levels and drive energy renewal.

Sleep well and rest.

The first time I read the opening paragraph of Arianna Huffington's book, *Thrive*, I felt like she was writing directly to me.[8] At the time, I was raising my daughter, traveling all over the country for work, going through a divorce, and trying to maintain my sanity. Reading Arianna's words shook me. I think that's the intended response when you read, "I was lying on the floor in a pool of blood." Anytime I talk to leaders about energy renewal and sleep, I share the story from her book. I've never been a great sleeper, but I'm working on my sleep in the same way I trained for the

Houston Marathon—methodically and purposefully. Too much of your body's recovery relies on sleep. In addition to biochemical processes, all four wellsprings of energy renewal depend heavily on quality sleep and adequate rest. Sleep is a commanding energy renewal source.

~ LEADER-FIRST SPOTLIGHT~

Sleep is a commanding energy renewal source.

During sleep, the body undergoes vital restorative processes that replenish energy reserves and optimize physiological functions. Two stages of sleep—non-rapid eye movement (NREM) and rapid eye movement (REM)—promote different aspects of energy renewal. NREM sleep supports physical restoration and energy conservation, allowing the body to repair tissues, synthesize proteins, and release growth hormones. REM sleep, on the other hand, focuses on cognitive restoration and emotional processing. Both are essential for memory consolidation and emotional well-being. During REM sleep, the brain integrates emotional memories, facilitating emotional *Resilience* and energy renewal.

Restful periods interspersed throughout the day, such as breaks away from screens and other distractions, allow the body to recover from physical exertion and recharge energy levels. Engaging in activities that embody relaxation, such as meditation or deep breathing exercises, can also contribute to renewing physical and emotional energy. You also create a foundation for spiritual growth and renewal by prioritizing rest and self-care.

Chronic sleep deprivation impairs attention, memory, and decision-making abilities. Lack of sleep also increases susceptibility to stress and mental health disorders. Good sleep hygiene replenishes mental energy. This could include identifying a sleep accountability partner, instituting a regular sleep schedule, creating a sleep-friendly environment, and avoiding stimulants, such as technology, before bedtime.

Move more.

Unfortunately, I know I'm lying to myself when I say I'm too tired to work out or go for a run. Exercise and movement renew much more energy than it takes to engage in it. Physical activity supports energy renewal in all four wellsprings. When my husband, Brian, talks to his patients, he doesn't tell them to start some crazy, unrealistic exercise regimen. He says, "Just move more than you're currently moving." If you're sitting on the couch all day, start by taking a short walk around the block, but do that consistently to build a habit. If you're already walking, add some resistance movement with bands or weights. The key is small, incremental, and consistent changes.

Regular exercise improves cardiovascular function, enhances oxygen utilization, and increases the efficiency of energy production within the body. It also stimulates the release of endorphins—neurotransmitters that promote feelings of pleasure and reduce stress and anxiety. Exercise increases blood flow to the brain, delivering oxygen and nutrients that support optimal brain function, including emotional regulation. By incorporating exercise into your routine, you provide the body with an opportunity to renew emotional energy and promote overall emotional balance.

~ LEADER-FIRST SPOTLIGHT~
"Just move more than you're currently moving."
~Dr. Brian DeShields

I tell people I like to "lift heavy things." Lifting something heavy is one of the ways I relieve stress and clear my head.

Weightlifting properly has the reverse effect than you might expect, just like exercise in general. Resistance training strengthens more than just your muscles. It also fortifies your bones and connective tissues. Increased strength and stability help you ward off injuries and overcome injuries. Resistance training, especially later in life, helps eliminate the 3 to 8% of muscle mass and bone density loss you experience each decade, giving you more longevity for active energy renewal throughout your lifetime.

Aerobic exercises like running or swimming improve mental clarity and emotional regulation, reduce anxiety, and increase energy levels. Mind-body activities like yoga, tai chi, or dance connect you with your body, creating a sense of mindfulness in motion. The rhythmic movements and focus on breath during exercise can quiet your mind and form a harmonious union between the physical body and the spiritual experience.[9]

🌱

Reconnect with nature.

Richard Louv introduced nature-deficit disorder in his book, *Last Child in the Woods*. "Nature-deficit disorder describes the human costs of alienation from nature, among them: diminished use of the senses, attention difficulties, and higher rates of physical and emotional illnesses."[10] When you spend time outdoors, you unlock the transformative power of nature to renew your energy in all four wellsprings by giving you a break from a world dominated by technology and urbanization. "Reconnection to the natural world is fundamental to human health, well-being, spirit, and survival." Your physical energy gets a boost through the absorption of sunlight and the creation of Vitamin D. Vitamin D strengthens your immune system and supports the regulation of emotions. Natural environments, especially those abundant in lush vegetation, offer a greater supply of fresh air that enhances blood circulation, delivering oxygen to your cells and tissues.

The outdoors provides a sanctuary for your mental and emotional rejuvenation. Surrounded by peaceful landscapes, away from the noise and demands of modern life, your mind can escape the stressors that deplete your energy. Time spent in nature reduces cortisol levels—the hormone responsible for stress—leading to improved mental clarity and enhanced focus. Nature stimulates your senses, offering a respite from the constant influx of information and technological stimuli. This respite allows your brain to rest and recover, promoting cognitive restoration. When you allow your brain to relax, your ability to focus, problem-solve, and retain information improves, ultimately replenishing your mental energy.

~LEADER-FIRST SPOTLIGHT~

"Reconnection to the natural world is fundamental to human health, well-being, spirit, and survival." ~Richard Louv

Nature's beauty and tranquility have a profound impact on your emotional well-being. Experiencing awe-inspiring landscapes, hearing the soothing sounds of rustling leaves or flowing water, and observing the vibrant colors of flowers and wildlife rejuvenates your emotional energy. Fresh air elevates your mood and reduces negative emotions. Your spiritual energy gets a boost because nature offers a sense of connectedness and *Belonging* by reminding you of your place in the larger web of life. This connection promotes mindfulness, allowing you to be fully present in the moment and appreciate the beauty around you.

Stop multitasking. Create distraction-free spaces.

Contrary to decades of reinforcement that it is the only way to juggle the demands of a busy leader, multitasking is problematic. Studies show that multitasking kills your performance and damages your brain. Let me repeat--multitasking causes brain damage! Researchers at Stanford

University found that multitasking is less productive than doing a single thing at a time.[11] When you regularly get bombarded with several streams of information, it impedes your ability to pay attention, recall information, or switch from one job to another compared to someone who completes a single task at a time. Not only does multitasking abuse your mental energy, but it blocks energy renewal as well.

~BOTTOM-LINE EXECUTIVE BEHAVIOR~
Multitasking causes brain damage!

Creating distraction-free spaces preserves and renews mental and emotional energy. Unfocused workplaces riddled with distraction and micromanagement destroy productivity and performance, especially when work requires a high degree of cognitive processing. Distractions prevent you from fully engaging in a task, leading to fragmented attention and increased mental effort. This constant shifting of attention can quickly deplete your mental resources, causing exhaustion and reducing your ability to focus and concentrate effectively. As a result, you feel drained. Distractions increase your cognitive load by demanding constant attentional shifts and task-switching. This cognitive load taxes your mental resources and can lead to cognitive fatigue. Cognitive fatigue depletes your ability to think clearly, make good decisions, and solve problems efficiently.

In late 2020, during a session of virtual office hours, a student dropped in to ask me some questions about the syllabus. After I had answered her questions, she hesitated a bit and then asked if it was OK to stay on to talk about a challenge she was facing at work. When we were sure no one else would pop in, she let go of what felt like months of pent-up frustration and anxiety. She worked for a large company as a research scientist. The organization had moved to an entirely virtual environment earlier that year and started using productivity technologies like Microsoft Teams and Slack. Every time she would begin to get into deep work on her research... ping... ping... ping...

This high-performing team member expressed concerns to her supervisor and asked if she could turn these tools off for at least one-hour increments to focus on her research. He denied her request and said staying connected to team members was necessary since they were not physically sitting in an office. I have since reconnected with this student. She shared with me that she decided to leave when her work environment didn't change. The decisions of the BL executives in charge reinforced a *culture of fatigue*. They rigidly micromanaged time instead of prioritizing impact. She was unwilling to stay in an environment where those in charge did not understand or value the need for focus and rest.

Find flow.

Flow, a remarkable phenomenon first introduced by psychologist Mihaly Csikszentmihalyi, is the state of optimal human experience, where you fully immerse yourself in an activity.[12] During a state of flow, you experience a heightened sense of concentration, enjoyment, and effortless engagement. Time seems to dissolve, self-consciousness fades away, and you become completely absorbed in the present moment. Achieving flow requires a delicate balance between skill and challenge. Flow catalyzes energy renewal in the mental, emotional, and spiritual wellsprings.

Engaging in a task or activity you enjoy or find rewarding renews your spiritual energy. Flow offers you a respite from negative emotions, stress, and the daily grind, giving your mental and emotional resources time to recharge. It facilitates an effortless focus, where your attention diverts from external stressors and mental rumination and is entirely focused on the activity in front of you. Consequently, the mind revitalizes and rejuvenates, enhancing overall cognitive functioning, productivity, and energy renewal.

Annie Lamott said, "*No* is a complete sentence." I've found this tiny sentence to be one of the more difficult to say. However, once you've experienced a flow state, it equips you to more easily set boundaries, guardrail your time for activities and engagements that align with your interests, and renew your energy.

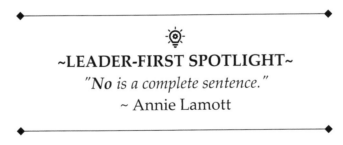

~LEADER-FIRST SPOTLIGHT~
"No is a complete sentence."
~ Annie Lamott

Flow experiences promote a sense of control and mastery over the activity and foster competence and self-efficacy, boosting your confidence and motivation. When you tap into your intrinsic motivation by engaging in activities that align with your natural advantages, core values, and interests, flow is a potent energy renewal source.

SHIFT THE PARADIGM—LIFE ACTUALIZATION

During The Industrial Revolution, *work was life*. Blue-collar workers would put in 12 to 16-hour days, six days a week, without any paid holidays or vacation. Even children worked punishing workdays until factories started banning children under the age of nine from working. Work was everything.[13] In 1926, Henry Ford, the founder of Ford Motor Company, adopted the five-day per week, 9-to-5 workday after discovering that productivity increased when his team members worked fewer hours.[14] Today, Ford gets blamed by frustrated workers locked into an archaic system of work that no longer matches the needs of society. But in the 1920s, Ford's move was revolutionary. Ford liked to disrupt the apple cart.

The phrase "work-life balance" didn't first appear until the 1980s in the UK as a part of the Women's Liberation Movement. But in the 1920s, Ford said, "It's high time to rid ourselves of the notion that leisure for workmen is either lost time or a class privilege." The 40-hour workweek was enshrined into US law in 1940 and adopted by companies worldwide.

Work is Life to Work-Life Balance

The concept of *work-life balance* picked up steam in the 1980s and 1990s as Gen Xers demanded a new relationship with work. They grew up watching their competitive, results-driven Baby Boomer parents give everything to the job. Baby Boomers' sense of identity is tied to work and career progression. This

yields some insight as to why they've held onto leadership positions longer than expected and struggle to develop the next layer of leadership.[15] The realization of true balance was and still is a myth. Balance conjures images of equal parts. That's unrealistic for a person juggling wide-ranging community, family, and leadership responsibilities.

Work-Life Balance to Work-Life Integration

With increased connectivity and the tech craze, we entered a new phase—*work-life integration*. The positive side of being able to work from anywhere means that working from

the office 100% of the time has become unnecessary. It allows us to challenge the 1920s outdated model and rethink the modern workday based on the needs of people right now. Technology provides team members with flexibility, only when executives can let go of control and use *Trust* to oversee the work of their team members. Regrettably, work-life integration has a dangerous side, too—always on, always accessible, with no meaningful time to unplug, recuperate, and focus on what matters.

Work-Life Integration to Life Actualization

What would happen if we summoned our inner-Henry Ford and shifted the work-life paradigm? Life is not about balance with work, and work is not life. Life is just life. Work is a cog in the wheel of life—a necessary means to achieve the essentials that give your life meaning.

~LEADER-FIRST SPOTLIGHT~

Life is not about balance with work, and work is not life. Life is just life. Work is a cog in the wheel of life—a necessary means to achieve the essentials that give your life meaning.

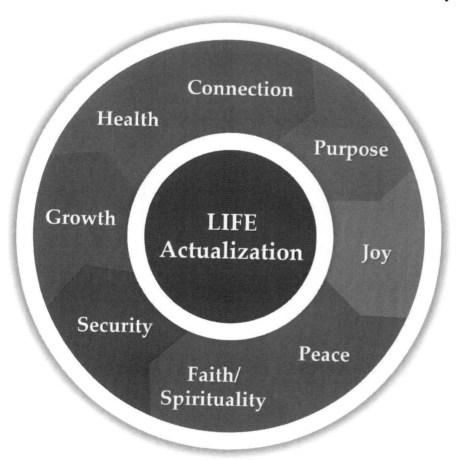

Figure 13.1: Life Actualization

As an LF Leader, I want to challenge you to think about work differently altogether. Prioritizing what matters most is called *Life Actualization*. When you actualize your life, sometimes you will work more and play less because doing so helps you move closer to your life's purpose. Sometimes you're going to focus on your personal growth. Sometimes connection and relationships will take priority. All are necessary for *Life Actualization*, but the ebb and flow happen based on realizing your fullest potential as a partner, a child, a parent, a sibling, a team member, and yes, as a leader of people. Work-life balance and work-life integration shackle you to the notion that work will always take significant priority, leaving no real space to work on you as a person. When you focus on life actualization instead of work-life balance or work-life integration, work can still be your priority when and how it needs to be.

> **~KEY DEFINITION~**
>
> *Life Actualization* is prioritizing what matters most at the right time so that you can realize your life's purpose and fullest potential as a partner, a child, a parent, a sibling, a team member, and a leader of people.

I have worked non-stop for the past few months to complete the final elements of this book. I'm doing that wholeheartedly supported by my family because this book fits into the bigger picture we have for our life. Whatever comes of it, *9 Leader Touchstones* is not just my accomplishment, it is *our* accomplishment. And when I'm done, I'm going to completely adjust my focus back to my family and community—getting ready for Emily's wedding in the fall, planning to celebrate my husband's 50th birthday in November, preparing Madi to start 5th grade and basketball, and working with my troop parents to get our Girl Scout Troop ready to begin the work on earning their Bronze Awards.

Shifting the paradigm of how work fits into the bigger picture of your life helps you reclaim the leverage work has over you so you can enjoy greater control over your decisions and actions. On that note, I want to end this chapter on *Resilience* and wrap up our journey through the nine Leader Touchstones with a poignant Leader-First Story about what is possible when you regain control of what's important, prioritize energy renewal, and reconnect with what matters most. This story is contributed by Crescent Leadership Client Jennifer Young, Partner, PhiloWilke Partnership.

·ı||·ıı·ı·

A LEADER-FIRST STORY
Leadership and Energy Renewal
~Contributed by Jennifer Young~
Partner, PhiloWilke Partnership
Crescent Leadership Client

Last year, several leaders from our organization went through the Leader-First Leadership program with Jes. We chose to make leadership development a focus so that as our organization grows, we have team members ready to step up to lead. Our primary goal was to prepare our team with skillsets not just to manage but to lead people well.

While each of us took away something personal from the engagement related to our leadership development, the most significant affirmation for me was how vital it is to prioritize my own health. Intuitively, we all know how important health is, but sometimes, we allow the busyness and chaos of life and work to de-prioritize our personal well-being. It is easy to overlook yourself to prioritize the good of your business, project work, team, and family.

The epiphany for me was understanding how my prioritization of health and wellness shapes my effectiveness as a leader in two ways. First, it directly influences how I show up for my team. When I'm low on energy or mental sharpness because I haven't prioritized my wellness, I can't fully connect with team members or bring my highest value to the workplace. Second, as a Partner in our company, my actions indirectly indicate my priorities to the team and the entire organization. Even if unwittingly, when I don't focus on my personal well-being, it signals to them that my health doesn't matter, so theirs doesn't really matter to me either.

Leader-First Leadership reminded me to stay true to my values and personal principles. That means focusing on my health, among other things. In our session, Jes coached us on creating three living value statements based on our core values. With my renewed epiphany for health, I developed one value that read:

"Honor your body without excuse!"

I vowed at that moment to honor my three living values and wrote them on my office whiteboard to keep as a constant reminder.

Over the past year, I have dug deep, making determinations of the root causes of health issues I'd been experiencing for years. With help, I have made small changes, strategically building each change upon the next and instilling consistent, healthy habits. Prioritizing a daily schedule of good sleep, healthy eating, and purposeful exercise are just a few of these building blocks that have positively impacted my life. Along with a renewed energy and clearer mind, I've decreased my cholesterol and blood pressure and now have lost almost 70 pounds! Although losing weight is a positive result of my process, it was not my intended focus. Being a better leader for my team, being more present in my life and work, and being healthier were the behaviors I wanted to prioritize.

During Leader-First Leadership, Jes said that when we focus on results instead of the actions to get us there, rarely are the results achieved. But when we focus on the right behaviors and implement them consistently, results flow naturally and are more sustainable over time. I cannot think of a more powerful message. It has really changed my life!"

CONCLUSION
Create a Ripple

*Everything we do, even the slightest thing we do, can
have a ripple effect and repercussions that emanate. If
you throw a pebble into the water on one side of the
ocean, it can create a tidal wave on the other side.*
~Victor Webster

At the start of this book, I asked you to take this
incredibly demanding yet rewarding journey with me. We've
made it to the final pages together, but our journey is just
beginning. There is still so much work to do if we are going to
restore the distinctive nature of leadership.

If you did get excited about the systems charts and
research, and enjoyed the systems diagrams from Chapter Two,
be sure to check out Appendices 14A, 14B, and 14C. 14A
includes a research chart for each Leader Touchstone showing
all the possible interconnections, reinforcements, and outflows
for each. 14B gives you an at-a-glance table of these details for
the entire system. Finally, 14C includes the final Dynamic,
Enduring Organization System diagram. This is the roadmap I
promised you in Chapter One. When you flood the system with
Leader Touchstones, you untangle unhealthy culture conditions
and tangle up the good ones. This diagram may overwhelm
some so I included it in the Appendices. But it gets me excited
to know what's possible when leaders intentionally build
organizational culture. Just think—when you tangle up healthy
culture, it creates an environment difficult to breach. Just as a
toxic organization is resistant to good change, a healthy

organization is resistant to harmful change and external destructive forces.

Throughout our journey, I've challenged you to look *first* to yourself by cultivating the Leader Touchstones so that you can create thriving organizational culture. I've asked you to rethink how you approach culturing, DEI, and wellness by tossing the typical platitudes aside and methodically cultivating them like the growth strategies they are. I've urged you to shift your sights away from the bottom line to the behaviors that drive growth. I've asked you to forego short-term outcomes for sustainable, long-term results. I've broken down organizational systems thinking in such a way that all leaders can move toward leading with a systems view. Truly, this is the only way to build dynamic, enduring organizations. Finally, my sincerest hope is that you walk ahead from this part of your journey equipped with the tools you need to lead people well and build more leaders. By reading this far, you've thrown the first stone into the water, and the ripple is already starting to move and expand.

When I started writing *9 Leader Touchstones*, I'd be lying if I told you I wasn't weary. This work feels so utterly personal and so big. To create the change that needs to happen in our workplaces and in greater society, like-minded people have to band together. But we can't do it in isolation from others who don't share our views. We have to meet people where they are on their journeys if we're going to truly change the state of work, fill the leadership gap, and ethically create value for all the organization's stakeholders.

As I progressed through my research, I was heartened to find that the greater ripple is swelling—maybe not as fast as I'd like, but movement is the first step to real change. In 2008, at the World Economic Forum, during his remarks, Bill Gates introduced the concept of creative capitalism—" an approach where governments, businesses, and nonprofits work together to stretch the reach of market forces so that more people can make a profit, or gain recognition, doing work that eases the world's inequities." Ideologically, creative capitalism aligns with Adam Smith's original definition.[1]

In 2010, John Mackey, co-founder of Whole Foods, joined with Raj Sisodia to found *Conscious Capitalism*. Their nonprofit organization spreads a socially responsible approach to capitalism. The philosophy represents a business's ethical pursuit of profits while serving all its stakeholders—yes, shareholders and management teams, but also employees, customers, suppliers, humanity, and the environment. The Credo of Conscious Capitalism states:

Conscious businesses are galvanized by higher purposes that serve, align, and integrate the interests of all their major stakeholders. Their higher state of consciousness makes visible to them the interdependencies that exist across all stakeholders, allowing them to discover and harvest synergies from situations that otherwise seem replete with trade-offs. They have conscious leaders who are driven by service to the company's purpose, all the people the business touches, and the planet we all share together. Conscious businesses have trusting, authentic, innovative, and caring cultures that make working there a source of both personal growth and professional fulfillment. They endeavor to create financial, intellectual, social, cultural, emotional, spiritual, physical, and ecological wealth for all their stakeholders.[2]

Conscious capitalism still embodies the fundamentals of capitalism—private ownership, competition, voluntary exchange, freedom of choice, profit motive, and minimal government intervention. But, according to Mackey, "It's capitalism, done in a more conscious way."[3]

~LEADER-FIRST SPOTLIGHT~

To create the change that needs to happen in our workplaces and in greater society, like-minded people have to band together. But we can't do it in isolation from others who don't share our views.

Over a 30-year history, BlackRock has grown to be the world's largest asset manager. Between 2008 and 2021, it grew from $1.31 trillion to $10.01 trillion in total assets under management. In 2012, founder and CEO Larry Fink released his first Letter to CEOs. Aside from 2013, Fink's letter has become an annual practice. Even as early as the first letter, he was already discussing "value-focused engagement," "long-term" approaches, and the company's approach to "social, ethical, and environmental issues." His first mention of environmental, social, and governance (ESG) issues came in his 2016 letter. Each year he writes a clearer message, and with an increasing sense of urgency. "In today's globally interconnected world, a company must create value for and be valued by its full range of stakeholders to deliver long-term value for its shareholders."[4]

Founded as an association in 1972, the Business Roundtable includes the CEOs of major companies in America. The organization focuses on serving as the voice of business in Washington to advance favorable economic policies. In 2019 at the Business Roundtable, nearly 200 CEOs of Fortune 500 companies deviated from decades-old corporate philosophy— that the corporation's sole purpose is to maximize profits at all costs. They issued a statement on the "purpose of a corporation" that shifts the focus away from advancing the interests of shareholders to all stakeholders.

"The Statement on the Purpose of a Corporation reflected the view of our members that to succeed and profit over the long term, they need to consider the interests of all their stakeholders—invest in their employees, keep the trust of their customers, partner with their suppliers, and be a good member of their communities, all to ensure that their enterprises flourish far into the future."[5]
~Joshua Bolton, President & CEO, Business Roundtable

Member corporations employ over 37 million people and generate as much as $10 trillion annually, accounting for 24% of the GDP. Their collective voices certainly give the debate some sway. Even though the group has been criticized for making this bold statement and not devising a plan of action, this is the most significant challenge to the status quo in fifty years. I say it's a great place to start.

Four years later, employees seek jobs that give them a sense of purpose, well-being and flexibility, personal growth and autonomy, fair compensation and benefits, recognition, good job design, and the tools to do their job well. The world is rich with insight and talent, but we just need to be bold enough to see it, take the time to understand and invest in it, grow from it, and unleash it. The plan gets activated when leaders look *first* to themselves, then roll up their sleeves, and start playing the long game.

There's no better time to start than now.

APPENDIX 6A
Leader Touchstones™ Assessment

STEP ONE: Visit our website and register for the Leader-First® Leadership Community:

https://crescent-leadership.com/lfl-community

STEP TWO: Follow the instructions to receive a link to take your complimentary assessment.

STEP THREE: Once you've completed the assessment, your baseline report will go to the email address you supplied when submitting your registration.

APPENDIX 6B
Touchstone Brain Science—Descriptions

BRAIN STRUCTURES

AMYGDALA
The amygdala, a critical limbic system component, regulates emotions, particularly fear and aggression. It evaluates the emotional significance of incoming stimuli, allowing for a rapid and automatic response to potential environmental threats or dangers. (Touchstones: *All*)

ANTERIOR CINGULATE CORTEX
The anterior cingulate cortex (ACC), located in the cerebral cortex, plays a role in attention, decision-making, error detection, conflict monitoring, and emotional regulation. The ACC helps evaluate potential rewards and risks, assess the value of different choices, and make adaptive decisions based on available information. It supports growth in self-awareness by monitoring self-actions, detecting errors or discrepancies between expected and actual outcomes, and making adjustments accordingly. This aids in learning from mistakes and adapting behavior. (Touchstones: *Curiosity, Emotional Intelligence, Integrity, Authenticity, Empathy, Resilience*)

ANTERIOR INSULA
The anterior insula regulates interoception, emotion, *Empathy*, self-awareness, and social cognition. It is a hub for integrating bodily sensations, emotional experiences, and cognitive functions. By making you aware of your bodily sensations, emotions, and internal states, you can monitor and regulate your behavior, decision-making, and social interactions. The insula is involved in processes such as *Empathy*, moral decision-making, and social emotions. (Touchstones: *Emotional Intelligence, Integrity, Authenticity, Empathy, Inclusivity, Gratitude, Resilience*)

BASAL GANGLIA
The basal ganglia, located deep within the brain, control and modulate voluntary movements, motor learning, cognitive and motivational processes, and emotional regulation. (Touchstones: *Curiosity, Emotional Intelligence, and Resilience*)

HIPPOCAMPUS

The hippocampus, located in the limbic system, forms, organizes, and retrieves memories. It also supports spatial navigation, and cognitive functions, making it a fundamental structure for navigating the world around you. (Touchstones: *All*)

LIMBIC SYSTEM

The limbic system consists of various interconnected structures that regulate emotions, motivation, learning, reward processing, and memory. (Touchstones: *All*)

MIRROR NEURONS

Mirror neurons are a class of specialized nerve cells found in the brains of humans and some other primates. These neurons are known for their unique property of "mirroring" the actions and intentions of others. Mirror neurons play a significant role in understanding the actions, intentions, and emotions of others. (Touchstones: *Curiosity, Emotional Intelligence, Courage, Empathy, Inclusivity,* and *Resilience*)

PREFRONTAL CORTEX

The prefrontal cortex, the executive center of the brain, is a highly evolved and complex area located just behind the forehead. It plays a vital role in higher-order cognitive abilities such as decision-making, abstract thinking, problem-solving, anticipation of consequences, planning, goal-setting, impulse control, attention, working memory, *Empathy,* and social behavior. (Touchstones: *All*)

REWARD CIRCUITRY

Reward circuitry is a network of brain regions that work together to detect and process rewarding stimuli, motivate behavior, and reinforce certain actions or experiences. Reward circuitry aids in the experience of pleasure, motivation, and the formation of habits. (Touchstones: *Curiosity, Gratitude,* and *Resilience*)

NEUROTRANSMITTERS

The interaction effects of neurotransmitters also provide insight into how the Touchstones influence each other. Dopamine and serotonin interact to regulate mood, motivation, and emotional well-being. Adrenaline can trigger the release of dopamine, enhancing arousal and attention. Oxytocin can modulate the effects of dopamine and serotonin, promoting social bonding and reducing stress. Cortisol can suppress the production and release of dopamine and serotonin, impacting mood and motivation.

ADRENALINE

The adrenal glands produce adrenaline in response to stress or danger. It triggers the body's "fight-or-flight" response, increasing heart rate, blood pressure, and energy levels. Adrenaline prepares the body for immediate action, enhancing focus, alertness, and physical performance. It plays a crucial role in survival instincts.

CORTISOL

Cortisol is a hormone released by the adrenal glands in response to stress. It helps the body manage and adapt to stressors, regulates metabolism, and influences the immune system. Cortisol increases blood sugar levels, suppresses the immune response, and aids in metabolizing proteins, carbohydrates, and fats. In appropriate amounts, cortisol is essential for survival. However, chronic high levels of cortisol due to long-term stress can negatively affect physical and mental health.

DOPAMINE

Dopamine is a neurotransmitter associated with pleasure, motivation, and reward. Dopamine also affects movement, memory, attention, and learning.

OXYTOCIN

Oxytocin is often called the "love hormone" or "bonding hormone." It promotes feelings of trust, *Empathy*, and connection and is involved in various social functions.

SEROTONIN

Serotonin regulates mood, sleep, appetite, and social behavior. It is often referred to as the "feel-good" neurotransmitter, as it contributes to feelings of well-being and happiness. Serotonin also helps regulate anxiety, depression, and aggression.

CURIOSITY

Original Hypothesis: Curiosity→ Culture of Purpose→
Commitment and Motivation

FINDINGS

CULTURE DIMENSIONS

Curiosity primarily reinforces a *Culture of Purpose*

Curiosity secondarily reinforces a *Culture of Trust*

Curiosity secondarily reinforces a *Culture of Belonging*

Curiosity secondarily reinforces a *Culture of Vitality*

OTHER LEADER TOUCHSTONES

Curiosity creates a reinforcing feedback loop with *EI*

Curiosity creates a reinforcing feedback loop with *Courage*

Curiosity creates a reinforcing feedback loop with *Resilience*

Curiosity creates a reinforcing feedback loop with *Integrity*

Curiosity creates a reinforcing feedback loop with *Empathy*

Curiosity reinforces *Authenticity*

Curiosity reinforces *Inclusivity*

Curiosity reinforces *Gratitude*

RESULTS (OUTFLOWS)

Curiosity creates conditions for *performance and innovation* through a *Culture of Trust*

Curiosity creates conditions for *commitment and motivation* through a *Culture of Purpose*

Curiosity creates conditions for *collaboration* through a *Culture of Belonging*

Curiosity creates conditions for *productivity and engagement* through a *Culture of Vitality*

EMOTIONAL INTELLIGENCE (EI)

Original Hypothesis: EI→ Culture of Belonging→ Collaboration and Connection

FINDINGS

CULTURE DIMENSIONS

EI primarily reinforces a *Culture of Belonging*

EI primarily reinforces a *Culture of Trust*

EI secondarily reinforces a *Culture of Belonging*

EI secondarily reinforces a *Culture of Vitality*

OTHER LEADER TOUCHSTONES

EI creates a reinforcing feedback loop with *Curiosity*

EI creates a reinforcing feedback loop with *Courage*

EI creates a reinforcing feedback loop with *Resilience*

EI creates a reinforcing feedback loop with *Authenticity*

EI creates a reinforcing feedback loop with *Empathy*

EI creates a reinforcing feedback loop with *Inclusivity*

EI creates a reinforcing feedback loop with *Gratitude*

EI creates a reinforcing feedback loop with *Integrity*

RESULTS (OUTFLOWS)

EI creates conditions for *performance, innovation, and collaboration* through a *Culture of Trust*

EI creates conditions for *commitment, motivation, innovation, and engagement* through a *Culture of Purpose*

EI creates conditions for *connection, innovation, motivation, and collaboration* through a *Culture of Belonging*

EI creates conditions for *productivity* through a *Culture of Vitality*

COURAGE

Original Hypothesis: Courage→ Culture of Trust→ Innovation and Performance

FINDINGS

CULTURE DIMENSIONS

Courage primarily reinforces a *Culture of Trust*

Courage secondarily reinforces a *Culture of Belonging*

Courage secondarily reinforces a *Culture of Purpose*

Courage secondarily reinforces a *Culture of Vitality*

OTHER LEADER TOUCHSTONES

Courage creates a reinforcing feedback loop with *Curiosity*

Courage creates a reinforcing feedback loop with *EI*

Courage creates a reinforcing feedback loop with *Resilience*

Courage creates a reinforcing feedback loop with *Integrity*

Courage creates a reinforcing feedback loop with *Authenticity*

Courage creates a reinforcing feedback loop with *Empathy*

Courage creates a reinforcing feedback loop with *Inclusivity*

Courage creates a reinforcing feedback loop with *Gratitude*

RESULTS (OUTFLOWS)

Courage creates conditions for *performance, innovation, and collaboration* through a *Culture of Trust*

Courage creates conditions for *innovation, commitment, and motivation* through a *Culture of Purpose*

Courage creates conditions for *collaboration* through a *Culture of Belonging*

Courage creates conditions for *productivity, engagement, and motivation* through a *Culture of Vitality*

INTEGRITY

Original Hypothesis: Integrity→ Culture of Purpose→ Commitment and Motivation

FINDINGS

CULTURE DIMENSIONS

Integrity primarily reinforces a *Culture of Trust*

Integrity primarily reinforces a *Culture of Purpose*

Integrity secondarily reinforces a *Culture of Vitality*

Integrity tertiarily reinforces a *Culture of Belonging*

OTHER LEADER TOUCHSTONES

Integrity creates a reinforcing feedback loop with *Authenticity*

Integrity creates a reinforcing feedback loop with *Resilience*

Integrity creates a reinforcing feedback loop with *Curiosity*

Integrity creates a reinforcing feedback loop with *Courage*

Integrity reinforces *EI*

Integrity reinforces *Empathy*

Integrity reinforces *Inclusivity*

Integrity reinforces *Gratitude*

RESULTS (OUTFLOWS)

Integrity creates conditions for *performance, innovation, and collaboration* through a *Culture of Trust*

Integrity creates conditions for *engagement, innovation, connection, and motivation* through a *Culture of Purpose*

Integrity creates conditions for *collaboration* and *innovation* through a *Culture of Belonging*

Integrity creates conditions for *productivity and motivation* through a *Culture of Vitality*

AUTHENTICITY

Original Hypothesis: Authenticity → Culture of Belonging → Collaboration and Connection

FINDINGS

CULTURE DIMENSIONS

Authenticity primarily reinforces a *Culture of Belonging*

Authenticity primarily reinforces a *Culture of Trust*

Authenticity secondarily reinforces a *Culture of Vitality*

Authenticity secondarily reinforces a *Culture of Purpose*

OTHER LEADER TOUCHSTONES

Authenticity creates a reinforcing feedback loop with *Curiosity*

Authenticity creates a reinforcing feedback loop with *Courage*

Authenticity creates a reinforcing feedback loop with *Resilience*

Authenticity creates a reinforcing feedback loop with *EI*

Authenticity creates a reinforcing feedback loop with *Empathy*

Authenticity creates a reinforcing feedback loop with *Inclusivity*

Authenticity creates a reinforcing feedback loop with *Gratitude*

Authenticity creates a reinforcing feedback loop with *Integrity*

RESULTS (OUTFLOWS)

Authenticity creates conditions for *engagement, commitment, and productivity* through a *Culture of Trust*

Authenticity creates conditions for *commitment, motivation, and performance* through a *Culture of Purpose*

Authenticity creates conditions for *innovation, connection, and collaboration* through a *Culture of Belonging*

Authenticity creates conditions for *productivity* and *innovation* through a *Culture of Vitality*

EMPATHY

Original Hypothesis: Empathy→ Culture of Trust→ Innovation and Performance

FINDINGS

CULTURE DIMENSIONS

Empathy primarily reinforces a *Culture of Belonging*

Empathy primarily reinforces a *Culture of Trust*

Empathy secondarily reinforces a *Culture of Vitality*

Empathy tertiarily reinforces a *Culture of Purpose*

OTHER LEADER TOUCHSTONES

Empathy creates a reinforcing feedback loop with *EI*

Empathy creates a reinforcing feedback loop with *Inclusivity*

Empathy creates a reinforcing feedback loop with *Gratitude*

Empathy creates a reinforcing feedback loop with *Courage*

Empathy creates a reinforcing feedback loop with *Resilience*

Empathy creates a reinforcing feedback loop with *Curiosity*

Empathy reinforces *Integrity*

Empathy reinforces *Authenticity*

RESULTS (OUTFLOWS)

Empathy creates conditions for *performance, commitment, innovation, and productivity* through a *Culture of Trust*

Empathy creates conditions for *engagement and productivity* through a *Culture of Purpose*

Empathy creates conditions for *innovation, connection, and engagement* through a *Culture of Belonging*

Empathy creates conditions for *productivity, collaboration, and motivation* through a *Culture of Vitality*

INCLUSIVITY

Original Hypothesis: Inclusivity→ Culture of Belonging→ Collaboration and Connection

FINDINGS

CULTURE DIMENSIONS

Inclusivity primarily reinforces a *Culture of Belonging*

Inclusivity secondarily reinforces a *Culture of Trust*

Inclusivity secondarily reinforces a *Culture of Vitality*

Inclusivity tertiarily reinforces a *Culture of Purpose*

OTHER LEADER TOUCHSTONES

Inclusivity creates a reinforcing feedback loop with *Authenticity*

Inclusivity creates a reinforcing feedback loop with *Resilience*

Inclusivity creates a reinforcing feedback loop with *Gratitude*

Inclusivity creates a reinforcing feedback loop with *Courage*

Inclusivity creates a reinforcing feedback loop with *EI*

Inclusivity creates a reinforcing feedback loop with *Empathy*

Inclusivity reinforces *Integrity*

Inclusivity reinforces *Curiosity*

RESULTS (OUTFLOWS)

Inclusivity creates conditions for *performance, innovation, productivity, and collaboration* through a *Culture of Trust*

Inclusivity creates conditions for *commitment, performance, and motivation* through a *Culture of Purpose*

Inclusivity creates conditions for *motivation, engagement, collaboration, connection, and commitment* through a *Culture of Belonging*

Inclusivity creates conditions for *innovation and engagement* through a *Culture of Vitality*

GRATITUDE
Original Hypothesis: Gratitude → Culture of Vitality→ Productivity and Engagement

FINDINGS

CULTURE DIMENSIONS

Gratitude primarily reinforces a *Culture of Vitality*

Gratitude secondarily reinforces a *Culture of Purpose*

Gratitude secondarily reinforces a *Culture of Trust*

Gratitude secondarily reinforces a *Culture of Belonging*

OTHER LEADER TOUCHSTONES

Gratitude creates a reinforcing feedback loop with *Resilience*

Gratitude creates a reinforcing feedback loop with *Empathy*

Gratitude creates a reinforcing feedback loop with *Inclusivity*

Gratitude creates a reinforcing feedback loop with *EI*

Gratitude creates a reinforcing feedback loop with *Courage*

Gratitude reinforces *Integrity*

Gratitude reinforces *Authenticity*

Gratitude reinforces *Curiosity*

RESULTS (OUTFLOWS)

Gratitude creates conditions for *collaboration, motivation, and performance* through a *Culture of Trust*

Gratitude creates conditions for *commitment and performance* through a *Culture of Purpose*

Gratitude creates conditions for *connection and collaboration* through a *Culture of Belonging*

Gratitude creates conditions for *productivity, commitment, engagement,* and *innovation* through a *Culture of Vitality*

RESILIENCE

Original Hypothesis: Resilience→ Culture of Vitality→ Productivity and Engagement

FINDINGS

CULTURE DIMENSIONS

Resilience primarily reinforces a *Culture of Vitality*

Resilience secondarily reinforces a *Culture of Purpose*

Resilience secondarily reinforces a *Culture of Trust*

Resilience tertiarily reinforces a *Culture of Belonging*

OTHER LEADER TOUCHSTONES

Resilience creates a reinforcing feedback loop with *Curiosity*

Resilience creates a reinforcing feedback loop with *EI*

Resilience creates a reinforcing feedback loop with *Gratitude*

Resilience creates a reinforcing feedback loop with *Integrity*

Resilience creates a reinforcing feedback loop with *Authenticity*

Resilience creates a reinforcing feedback loop with *Courage*

Resilience creates a reinforcing feedback loop with *Empathy*

Resilience creates a reinforcing feedback loop with *Inclusivity*

RESULTS (OUTFLOWS)

Resilience creates conditions for *performance* and *innovation* through a *Culture of Trust*

Resilience creates conditions for *motivation and performance* through a *Culture of Purpose*

Resilience creates conditions for *connection* through a *Culture of Belonging*

Resilience creates conditions for *productivity, innovation, and performance* through a *Culture of Vitality*

How the Leader Touchstones fuel the Enduring Organization System

System Elements	Curiosity	Emotional Intelligence	Courage	Integrity	Authenticity	Empathy	Inclusivity	Gratitude	Resilience
Culture Dimensions (Stocks) Reinforced 1-PRIMARY 2-Secondary 3-Tertiary	PURPOSE Trust Belonging Vitality	BELONGING Purpose Vitality	TRUST Belonging Purpose Vitality	TRUST PURPOSE Vitality Belonging	BELONGING TRUST Purpose Vitality	BELONGING TRUST Vitality Purpose	BELONGING Vitality Trust Purpose	VITALITY Purpose Trust Belonging	VITALITY Purpose Trust Belonging
Other Touchstones (Inflows) Reinforced (Reinforcing Feedback Loops)	EI Courage Resilience Integrity Empathy Authenticity Inclusivity Gratitude	Curiosity Courage Authenticity Empathy Inclusivity Gratitude Resilience Integrity	Curiosity EI Resilience Integrity Authenticity Empathy Inclusivity Gratitude	Authenticity Resilience Curiosity Courage EI Empathy Inclusivity Gratitude	Integrity Resilience Curiosity EI Courage Empathy Inclusivity Gratitude	Inclusivity Gratitude EI Courage Resilience Curiosity Integrity Authenticity	Authenticity Empathy Gratitude Resilience EI Courage Integrity Curiosity	Resilience Empathy Inclusivity EI Courage Integrity Authenticity Curiosity	Curiosity EI Integrity Gratitude Authenticity Courage Empathy Inclusivity
Bottom-Line Impact: Results (Outflows)	**Increases:** Performance Innovation Engagement Collaboration Motivation Productivity Commitment	**Increases:** Performance Innovation Engagement Collaboration Motivation Productivity Commitment Connection	**Increases:** Performance Innovation Engagement Collaboration Motivation Productivity Commitment Connection	**Increases:** Performance Innovation Engagement Collaboration Motivation Productivity Commitment Connection	**Increases:** Performance Innovation Engagement Collaboration Motivation Productivity Commitment Connection	**Increases:** Performance Innovation Engagement Collaboration Motivation Productivity Commitment Connection	**Increases:** Performance Innovation Engagement Collaboration Motivation Productivity Commitment Connection	**Increases:** Performance Innovation Engagement Collaboration Motivation Productivity Commitment Connection	**Increases:** Performance Innovation Engagement Collaboration Motivation Productivity Commitment Connection

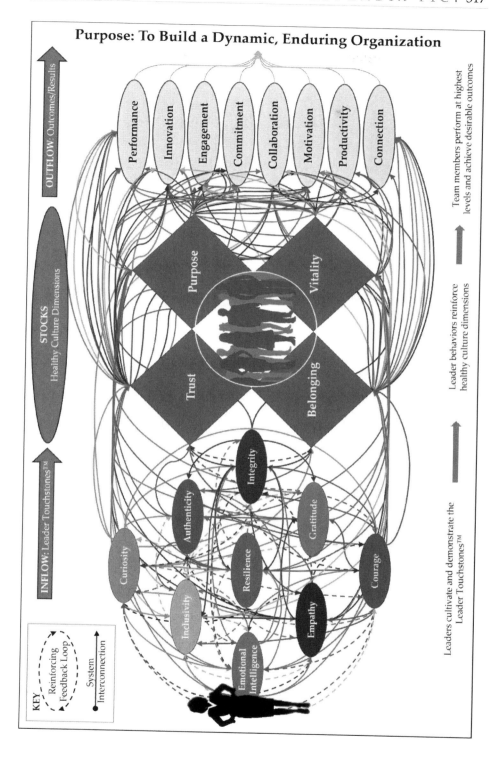

Purpose: To Build a Dynamic, Enduring Organization

KEY DEFINITIONS

AMYGDALA
The *amygdala*, a key component of the limbic system, regulates emotions, particularly fear and aggression. It evaluates the emotional significance of incoming stimuli allowing for a rapid and automatic response to potential threats or dangers in the environment. The amygdala plays a role in the function and development of every Leader Touchstone.

AUTHENTICITY TOUCHSTONE
Authenticity is the daily practice of letting go of who you think you're supposed to be and embracing who you are through the interpretation and ownership of your life experiences. (Part of the definition adopted from Brené Brown)

BEHAVIORAL LEADERSHIP
Behavioral Leadership is leader success based on a set of learned behaviors.

BOTTOM-LINE (BL) EXECUTIVE
A *bottom-line (BL) executive* is a person who has been given the power to supervise others but is doing it poorly because other BL executives are misguiding them, they have not received the proper training to teach them how to lead people well, or they are engaging in unethical or illegal activity. BL executives focus on bottom-line results at the expense of everything else and fail to define the behaviors necessary to achieve the desired results.

BOTTOM-LINE MENTALITY
Bottom-line mentality is one-dimensional thinking that revolves around securing bottom-line outcomes while neglecting all other competing priorities and failing to define the behaviors that achieve desired bottom-line outcomes.

CAMOUFLAGE SOLUTIONS
Camouflage solutions are quick, easily-controllable fixes to organizational problems that typically have nothing to do with the actual problem.

CHALLENGE STRESS

Challenge stress is a unique form of stress that has positive effects on cognitive, emotional, and physical well-being. When a person perceives demanding situations as opportunities for growth and achievement, it enhances their performance.

COGNITIVE EMPATHY

Cognitive Empathy is also known as perspective-taking *Empathy* or "thinking" *Empathy*. It means to understand another person's emotions and point of view.

COLLABORATION

Collaboration refers to team members working harmoniously towards shared goals by leveraging diverse skills, knowledge, and perspectives.

COMMITMENT

Commitment reflects team members' dedication and loyalty toward their work to go the extra mile, take ownership, and stay focused on realizing the organization's purpose.

COMPASSIONATE EMPATHY

Compassionate Empathy means to understand another's perspective and share their emotions, motivating you to take action and provide support.

CONFIRMATION BIAS

Confirmation bias is the tendency to favor information that aligns with your existing beliefs or attitudes.[19]

CONNECTION

Connection is a team member's ability to foster trust-based, internal relationships through respect and effective, transparent communication.

CONSCIOUS OR EXPLICIT BIAS

Conscious bias (or explicit) is an extreme form of bias expressed through verbal and sometimes physical harassment and harm. You can also demonstrate conscious bias subtly but cognizantly through acts of exclusion.

COURAGE TOUCHSTONE

Courage is acting on what is right, despite being afraid or uncomfortable, when facing situations involving pain, risk, opportunity, uncertainty, or intimidation. (Definition adopted from Bill Treasurer)

CRESCENDO

A Crescendo is a transformational life experience that happens as a result of pressure building in intensity when you repeatedly face expectations that fall outside of your values or purpose. Your internal compass screams that something is wrong and you need to reorient. When the intensity becomes so significant, a moment arrives when you must make a shift, despite the circumstances or potential outcomes.

CULTURAL INTELLIGENCE

Cultural intelligence is the ability to understand other cultures and to work effectively cross-culturally.

CULTURE DIMENSION

A *culture dimension* is a measurable continuum that describes the properties and characteristics of an organizational system stock.

CULTURE OF APATHY

A *culture of apathy* is a disconnected environment where mediocrity and avoidance rules and team members are detached and reclusive.

CULTURE OF BELONGING

A *Culture of Belonging* is an environment where human connection thrives, diversity is valued, and team members are encouraged to lean into their *Authenticity* by showcasing their unique advantages.

CULTURE OF FATIGUE

A *culture of fatigue* is an environment where exhaustion is worn as a badge of honor, team members are disengaged, and executives micromanage time through rigid and inflexible expectations that reward effort over impact.

CULTURE OF FEAR

A *culture of fear* is a low transparency, psychologically-unsafe environment where micromanagement, compulsion, silos, and politics prevent the organization from making forward progress.

CULTURE OF ISOLATION

A *culture of isolation* is a disconnected, self-focused environment of information hoarding, favoritism, ego, and suppression of individuality.

CULTURE OF PURPOSE

A *Culture of Purpose* is an environment where team members feel that they make meaningful contributions, and each takes ownership of helping the organization realize its reason for existence.

CULTURE OF TRUST

A *Culture of Trust* is an environment where multi-directional feedback flourishes, risk-taking and safe-fail zones encourage learning, and team members feel empowered to express ideas and concerns.

CULTURE OF VITALITY

A *Culture of Vitality* is an environment of *Resilience* where physical, mental, emotional, and spiritual energy renewal is prioritized above "time" and exhaustion. Team members feel appreciated for their efforts, and *Gratitude* is openly expressed and received.

CULTURE SIGNAL

A *culture signal* is an intentional or subconscious behavior—channeled through communication, actions, or decisions—by a top-level executive that signals to team members how they should act and what they should prioritize.

CULTURING

Culturing creates and maintains conditions suitable for growth through methodical and intentional planning, execution, cultivation, and measurement.

CURIOSITY TOUCHSTONE
Curiosity is the insatiable desire to know and understand unfamiliar things and then to put wonder into action.

EMOTIONAL COURAGE
Emotional Courage is embracing emotions, even uncomfortable ones.

EMOTIONAL (AFFECTIVE) EMPATHY
Emotional or Affective Empathy means to experience and share the emotional experiences of others.

EMOTIONAL INTELLIGENCE (EI) TOUCHSTONE
Emotional Intelligence (EI) is the motivation to understand and the ability to apply emotional knowledge in a way that brings about positive outcomes for yourself and others.

EMPATHY TOUCHSTONE
Rooted in sincere care for others' well-being, *Empathy* is the ability to understand and share someone else's emotions and perspectives.

ENDURING ORGANIZATION
An *enduring organization* is a dynamic system that learns, evolves, innovates, and optimizes, fueled by the behavior of people through carefully and ethically cultivated relationships. It stands the test of time by sustainably growing over its lifespan and transcending destructive external interferences.

ENERGY
Energy is the capacity to do work.

ENGAGEMENT
Engagement describes team members' emotional and intellectual investment in delivering high-quality work and achieving the organization's goals.

ETHICAL CREVICE
An *ethical crevice* is the gap between a minimum standard of behavior defined by an established law and the highest standard of ethical behavior.

ETHICAL FADING
Ethical fading is a cognitive phenomenon in which people fail to recognize or consider all the ethical ramifications of their decisions. They become so focused on other aspects, such as financial gains, personal interests, or behavioral pressures, that they unintentionally overlook or downplay the moral implications of their actions.

FEEDBACK LOOPS
Feedback loops are pathways where information feeds back to influence future inflows, processes, or decisions.

GRATITUDE TOUCHSTONE
Gratitude is reflecting an appreciation for what brings meaning to your life and recognizing and expressing that the source of value falls outside of yourself. (Part of the definition adopted from Robert Emmons)

HEALTHY IDEOLOGICAL CONFLICT
Healthy ideological conflict is constructive and respectful exchanges of divergent ideas, beliefs, values, or perspectives on a team.

INCLUSIVITY TOUCHSTONE
Inclusivity is fostering an environment that values authentic contributions and empowers the full participation and acceptance of all people.

INFLOWS
Inflows (or inputs) come into the system through various sources and initiate and sustain the system-shaping process.

INNOVATION
Innovation is a team member's identification and implementation of fresh ideas, processes, products, or services that identify cost savings or create a competitive advantage for the organization.

INTEGRITY TOUCHSTONE

Integrity is adhering consistently to morals, ethical principles, and values to do what is right, not expedient.

INTELLECTUAL COURAGE

Intellectual Courage is challenging ideas, questioning your thinking, risk-taking, and making mistakes for the sake of growth.

INTERCONNECTIONS

Interconnections represent the dependent, influential relationships between inflows, stocks, and outflows.

LEADER-FIRST LEADERSHIP

See *Leader-First® Leadership Manifesto* in Chapter One.

LEADER TOUCHSTONES

Leader Touchstones are healthy or constructive leader behaviors that fuel the dynamic, enduring organizational system.

LIFE ACTUALIZATION

Life Actualization is prioritizing what matters most at the right time so that you can realize your life's purpose and fullest potential as a partner, a child, a parent, a sibling, a team member, and a leader of people.

LIVING VALUE STATEMENTS

Living Value Statements are meaningful, action-oriented core values. These tangible tools are a crucial part of the Integrity baseline and provide a clear guide for behavior.

THE LONG GAME

Playing the *long game* means building dynamic organizations that not only endure but sustainably thrive by ethically creating value for all of the organizations' stakeholders. You acknowledge that consideration for the human element will maximize results to the highest degree possible over time.

MORAL COURAGE

Moral Courage is doing the right thing even when difficult, unpopular, or uncomfortable.

MOTIVATION

Motivation is a team members' internal drive and desire to excel at their job.

MULTI-DIRECTIONAL ACCOUNTABILITY

Multi-directional accountability is the practice of holding leaders, colleagues, and yourself responsible for actions, behaviors, performance, and adherence to shared goals and values.

NEUROPLASTICITY

Neuroplasticity modifies the brain's structure and function in response to experiences, learning, and environmental changes by triggering changes in neural pathways, forming new connections, and strengthening existing ones.

NORTH STARS

The North Stars are an organization's, team's, or individual's purpose, vision, mission, and values used to positively guide action and decision-making.

ORGANIZATIONAL MISSION

Organizational Mission is *what* you do each day. It represents the current state.

ORGANIZATIONAL PURPOSE

Organizational Purpose is *why* you exist.

ORGANIZATIONAL VALUES

Organizational Values are the filters for *how* you do your work.

ORGANIZATIONAL VISION

Organizational Vision is *where* you ultimately want to go. It represents a future state.

OUTCOME
Outcomes are desirable and measurable results.

OUTFLOWS
Outflows (or outputs) are released from the system's stocks and represent the output generated by system processes.

OUTPUT
Outputs are the behaviors that produce outcomes—desirable and measurable results.

PAC-MAN® ANOMALY
The *Pac-man® Anomaly* occurs when independent yet correlated metrics should have the same behavior—to increase or decrease—but one increases while the other decreases. This should signal an underlying problem with delivery, service, or measurement.

PERFORMANCE
Performance is a team member's ability to consistently deliver exceptional quality, timely, and relevant work products.

PERFORMANCE MYOPIA
Performance myopia is a type of cognitive bias that occurs when team members excessively focus on short-term performance metrics or goals, often at the expense of long-term sustainability and overall success.

PHYSICAL COURAGE
Physical Courage is developing your strength, Resilience, and awareness.

PRODUCTIVITY
Productivity refers to team members' astute prioritization and effective energy management to maximize high-quality work output.

PSYCHOLOGICAL SAFETY
Psychological safety is the belief that the work environment is safe for interpersonal risk-taking, where you can speak up with relevant ideas, questions, or concerns. (Definition adopted from Amy Edmondson).

REFRAMING

Reframing is reconceptualizing a problem to see it from a different perspective.

REGULATION OF EMOTIONS

Regulation of emotions is emotional self-management by separating emotion from logic, choosing how to respond to emotions, and thinking before acting.

RELATIONSHIP MANAGEMENT

Relationship management is the fourth progression of emotional intelligence, where you use what you know about emotions to facilitate a positive outcome for yourself and others.

RESILIENCE TOUCHSTONE

Resilience is your capacity to overcome adversity by systematically renewing the four energy wellsprings—physical, emotional, mental, and spiritual.

RESTORATIVE SOLUTIONS

Restorative solutions heal the organization by addressing the core problem and simultaneously addressing the interconnected system problems.

RIPPLE EFFECT

A *ripple effect* creates a chain reaction, starting with a single action. It flows outward and expands incrementally. The effect organically grows unless something interrupts it.

SELF-AWARENESS

Self-Awareness is understanding your emotions as they happen and expressing them naturally, and understanding how your emotions affect other people.

SHARED LEADERSHIP

In a *Shared Leadership* model, a single point of ultimate accountability still exists, however, the top-level leader collaboratively shares responsibility and accountability throughout the leadership structure in an organization.

SMART FAILURE

Smart failure is a constructive, strategic approach of intentionally pursuing ideas or endeavors that carry a risk of failure but to gain valuable insights, learning, and improving future outcomes.

SOCIAL-AWARENESS

Social-Awareness is sensing and understanding other people's emotions and needs.

SOCIAL COURAGE

Social Courage is acting at the risk of social embarrassment or exclusion, rejection, or unpopularity.

STOCK

A system *stock* is a reservoir that stores information like memories of historical events and experiences.

SUNK COST FALLACY

The *sunk cost fallacy* refers to a cognitive bias where individuals, teams, or organizations continue to invest in a project or decision even when it is no longer rational because they have already invested significant resources, such as time, money, or effort, into it.

SYSTEM

A system is an interconnected set of elements coherently organized in a way that achieves something. (Definition adopted from Dana Meadows)

SYSTEM'S PURPOSE

The *system's purpose* represents the reason why the system exists and provides a sense of direction or intentionality.

SYSTEMS LEADERSHIP

A *Systems Leader* sees the whole, not just the parts of the organization. They understand that their behavior fuels how the organizational system gets shaped and, ultimately, how it behaves. They constantly seek to interpret the dynamic environmental context in which their organizations operate and catalyze shared leadership to identify relevant systematic transformations that solve the most complex organizational problems. They adapt approaches using evolving internal and external information to inform real-time decisions.

TOUCHSTONE TAI CHI

Touchstone Tai Chi is the disciplined practice of activating Leader-First Leadership by cultivating the Leader Touchstones.

UNCONSCIOUS BIAS

Unconscious bias (or implicit bias) operates outside your awareness. This type of bias is prejudice or unsupported judgments that occur with the brain automatically makes quick assumptions based on past experiences and pre-established constructs.

LIST OF FIGURES AND TABLES

NOTES AND REFERENCES

Introduction: Restore the Distinctive Nature of Leadership

1. Gittleman, M. (2022, July). *The "Great Resignation" in perspective, Monthly Labor Review*. U.S. Bureau of Labor Statistics.
2. McLean & Company. (2022). *2022 HR Trends Report*.
3. World Economic Forum. (2015). *Outlook on the global agenda 2015*.
4. Weisman, R. (2021, November 29). *At the top, a generational shakeup unfolds as boomers begin to step aside*. BostonGlobe.com.
5. Fry, R. (2021, May 28). *Millennials overtake baby boomers as America's largest generation*. Pew Research Center.
6. Deloitte. (2014, January). *Big demands and high expectations. The Deloitte Millennial Survey*.
7. Garelli, S. (2022, September 9). *Why you will probably live longer than most big companies*. Imd.org.
8. Statista. (2021, August 27). *Average company lifespan 2020*. Statista.
9. Greenbaum, R. L., Mawritz, M. B., & Eissa, G. (2012). Bottom-line mentality as an antecedent of social undermining and the moderating roles of core self-evaluations and conscientiousness. Journal of Applied Psychology, 97(2), 343–359.
10. Wan, W., Liu, L., Long, J., Fan, Q., & Wu, Y. J. (2021, June 7). *The bottom-line mentality of leaders in education and training institutions: Where to go for innovation?* Frontiers.
11. Meadows, D. H., & Wright, D. (2015). *Thinking in systems: A Primer*. Chelsea Green Publishing.
12. Smith, A. (1776). *An inquiry into the nature and causes of the wealth of nations*. W. Strahan and T. Cadell. London.
13. Friedman, M. (1970, September 13). *The Friedman Doctrine—The social responsibility of business is to increase its profits*.

Chapter One: Look to the Past Through a New Lens

1. DeShields, J. (2021). *The Crescent Leadership Manifesto*. Crescent Leadership. https://crescent-leadership.com/what-we-believe.
2. Watson, J. B. (1970). *Behaviorism*. Norton.

Chapter Two: The Stubborn Brilliant System

1. Meadows, D. H., & Wright, D. (2015). *Thinking in systems: A Primer*. Chelsea Green Publishing.

2. Dizikes, P. (2020, February 11). *When the Butterfly Effect took flight.* MIT Technology Review.

3. Williams, J. A. (2014). *A Qualitative Case Study Analyzing How a Community Eliminated the Racial Achievement Gap* (dissertation). ProQuest, Ann Arbor, MI.

4. Lesnick, J., Goerge, R., & Smithgall, C. (2010). *Third Grade Reading Level Predictive of Later Life Outcomes.* Chapin Hall.

5. Zak, P. (2021, August 31). *The Neuroscience of Trust.* Harvard Business Review.

6. Feintzeig, R. (2014, October 31). *Flexibility at work: Worth skipping a raise?* The Wall Street Journal.

7. Mcleod, S. (2023, March 21). *Maslow's hierarchy of needs theory.* Simply Psychology.

8. BetterUp. (2019). *Betterup's new, industry-leading research shows companies that fail at belonging lose tens of millions in revenue:* betterup.com.

9. DeWall, C. N., Baumeister, R., & Vohs, K. (2008). *Satiated with belongingness? effects of acceptance, rejection, and task framing on self-regulatory performance.* Journal of personality and social psychology.

10. Brown, B. (2019). *Braving the Wilderness: The Quest for true belonging and the Courage to stand alone.* Random House.

11. Hagerty, B., Lynch-Sauer, J., Patusky, K., & Bouwsema, M. (1993). *An Emerging Theory of Human Relatedness.* Sigma Theta Tau International Honor Society of Nursing.

12. Patagonia. (2023). Patagonia Outdoor Clothing & Gear. https://www.patagonia.com/

13. Coyle, D. (2019). *The Culture Code.* Random House UK.

Chapter Three: Culture is a Verb

1. Benioff, M. (2020). *Trailblazer: The power of business as the greatest platform for Change.* Simon & Schuster LTD.

2. Jaques, E. (1957). *The changing culture of a factory.* Tavistock Publications.

3. Kotter, J., & Heskett, J. (1992). *Corporate culture and performance.* New York: Free Press.

4. Rajgopal, S. (2019, January 2). *Why corporate culture is hard.* Ideas & Insights. Columbia University.

5. Oxford Dictionary. (2023). *Word meanings—Culturing.* Oxford English Dictionary.

Chapter Four: The System Fuel—Leader Behaviors

1. Watson, J. B. (1970). *Behaviorism.* Norton.

2. Milgram, S. (1963). Behavioral study of obedience. *The Journal of Abnormal and Social Psychology, 67*(4), 371–378.

3. Tenbrunsel, A. E., & Messick, D. M. (2004). Ethical fading: The role of self-deception in unethical behavior. *Social Justice Research, 17*(2), 223–236.

4. US Department of Justice. (2020, February 21). *Wells Fargo agrees to pay $3 billion to resolve criminal and civil investigations into sales practices involving the opening of millions of accounts without customer authorization.*

5. Wells Fargo. (2022). *History of Wells Fargo*. History of Wells Fargo – Wells Fargo.

6. Ordóñez, L. D., Schweitzer, M. E., Galinsky, A. D., & Bazerman, M. H. (2009). *Goals gone wild: The systematic side effects of over-prescribing goal* ... https://www.hbs.edu/.

7. Netflix. (2020). The Wagon Wheel. *Dirty Money*.

8. Reckard, S. (2013, December 21). *Wells Fargo's pressure-cooker sales culture comes at a cost*. Los Angeles Times.

9. Society for HR Management. (2022, April 26). *How-to guides: How to Develop and Implement a New Company Policy*. SHRM.

Additional Resources on Bereavement Policies

- Mallick, M. (2020). It's Time to Rethink Corporate Bereavement Policies. Harvard Business Review.
- Maitlis, S. and Petriglieri, G. (2019). When a Colleague is Grieving; How to Provide the Right Kind of Support. Harvard Business Review.
- Rabasca Roepe, L. (2017) How to Support Employees Through Grief and Loss. SHRM.
- Schumway, E. (2021) Why It May Be Time for a More Compassionate Bereavement Policy. HR Dive.
- Ward, M. (2020) American jobs aren't allowing a grieving nation the time needed to mourn the deaths of loved ones. Business Insider.

Chapter Five: Shared Leadership—Lend Your Superpowers

1. Davies, D. (2022, June 1). Short-term profits and long-term consequences - did Jack Welch break capitalism?

2. Gelles, D. (2022). *The Man Who Broke Capitalism: How Jack Welch Gutted the Heartland and Crushed the Soul of Corporate America and How to undo his legacy.* Simon & Schuster.

3. Securities and Exchange Commission. (2009, August 4). *SEC charges General Electric with accounting fraud. GE Agrees to Pay $50 Million to Settle SEC's Charges; 2009-178; Aug. 4, 2009.*

4. Tong, S. (2016, June 14). *How shareholders jumped to first in line for profits.* Marketplace.

5. Frail, P. (2002, January 17). *GE reports record fourth quarter and full-year results; 2001 earnings grow 11% to $14.1 billion; cash from operating activities grows 12% to $17.2 billion.* GE News.

6. Follett, M. P. (1954). *The illusion of final authority; authority must be functional and functional authority carries with it functional responsibility.* U.S. Bureau of Public Assistance.

7. Crutchfield, L. R., & Grant, H. M. (2012). *Forces for good the six practices of high-impact nonprofits.* Jossey-Bass.

8. UnidosUS. (2022, November 18). *Latino civil rights and advocacy.* UnidosUS.

9. Monsen, K. A., & De Blok, J. (2013). Buurtzorg: Nurse-led community care. Creative Nursing, 19(3), 122–127.

10. Stoll, J. (2020, May 15). *Corporate America's most underrated innovation strategy: 3M's 15% rule.* The Wall Street Journal.

11. Kruse, K. (2016, August 29). The Big Company that has no rules. Forbes.

12. Snavely, B. (2016, July 21). *Google, 3D printing keeps Ford's ex-CEO Alan Mulally on the forefront.* Detroit Free Press.

13. Klayman, B. (2014, May 1). *Mulally to hand over Ford CEO job earlier than expected.* Reuters.

Chapter Six: The Leader-First® Leadership Journey

1. Caldicott, S. M. (2014, June 25). *Why Ford's Alan Mulally is an innovation CEO for the record books.* Forbes.

2. Vakil, T. (2021, July 9). *Organizational culture change example - Alan Mulally Ford turnaround story.* New Age Leadership.

3. Guzzetta, M. (2017). *The four keys to one of the biggest turnarounds in business history - inc.com.* Inc.com.

4. Hoffman, B. G. (2013). *American icon: Alan Mulally and the fight to save Ford Motor Company.* Crown.

Chapter Seven: Be Annoyingly Curious

1. Scholz, J., & Klein, M. C. (2019). The plastic brain: from synaptic to structural plasticity. Cell and Tissue Research, 377(1), 3-14.

2. Andreatta, B. (2019). *Wired to Grow: Harness the power of brain science to master any Skill.* 7th Mind Publishing.

3. McLean, B., & Elkind, P. (2013). *The smartest guys in the room: The amazing rise and scandalous fall of Enron.* Portfolio.

4. McLean, B. (2021, April 24). *Is Enron overpriced? (Fortune, 2001).* Fortune.

5. Goodwyn, W. (2006, April 25). *Former Enron chairman blames others for collapse.* NPR. https://www.npr.org/2006/04/25/5361073/former-enron-chairman-blames-others-for-collapse

6. Dizikes, P. (2002, February 26). *Enron Showdown: Skilling Fires Away in Congress.* ABC News.

7. Hampton, L. (2021, June 3). *Ex-Enron CEO Taps McKinsey Colleagues for Energy Investment Venture-Sources.* Reuters.

8. Oppel, R. (2001, November 22). Employees' retirement plan is a victim as Enron tumbles. The New York Times.

9. Schein, E. H. (2013). Humble Inquiry: The Gentle Art of Asking Instead of Telling. Berrett-Koehler Publishers.

10. Kenney, C. (2010). Transforming Health Care: Virginia Mason Medical Center's Pursuit of the Perfect Patient Experience. CRC Press.

11. Bungay Stanier, M. (2016). *The Coaching Habit.* Box of Crayons Press.

12. Kahneman, D. (2011). *Thinking fast and slow.* Penguin Books.

13. Lauren, Keating, et al. "Good Leaders Are Good Learners." *Harvard Business Review*, 23 Jan. 2018.

14. Perrin, A. (2015). *Slightly fewer Americans are reading print books, new survey finds.* Pew Research Center.

15. Elkins, K. (2015). *A self-made millionaire who studied 1,200 wealthy people found they all have one free pastime in common.* Business Insider.

16. Kingsley, J. (2017, April 30). *4 reasons good leaders are readers.* Jeremy Kingsley | Leadership Expert, Inspirational Speaker and Best-Selling Author.

Chapter Eight: Shape the Game—Emotional Intelligence

1. Cherry, K. (2019, August 21). *How the Fight or Flight Response Works.* The American Institute of Stress.

2. Rowden, A. (2021). *Amygdala hijack: Symptoms, causes, and prevention.* Medical News Today.

3. Goleman, D. (1996). *Emotional intelligence: Why it can matter more than IQ.* Bloomsbury.

4. Bradberry, T., & Greaves, J. (2009). *Emotional intelligence 2.0.* TalentSmart.

5. Eurich, T. (2023, April 6). *What self-awareness really is (and how to cultivate it).* Harvard Business Review.

6. Bradberry, T. (2020). *The massive benefits of Boosting Your Emotional Intelligence.* World Economic Forum.

7. Lee, H. J. (2017). How emotional intelligence relates to job satisfaction and burnout in public service jobs. *International Review of Administrative Sciences, 84*(4), 729–745.

8. Nink, M., & Robison, J. (2023, March 28). *The damage inflicted by poor managers*. Gallup.com.

9. Jung, Y. H., Shin, N. Y., Jang, J. H., Lee, W. J., Lee, D., Choi, Y., Choi, S. H., & Kang, D. H. (2019, May). *Relationships among stress, emotional intelligence, cognitive intelligence, and cytokines*. Medicine.

10. Pert, C. B., Ruff, M. R., Weber, R. J., & Herkenham, M. (1985). *Neuropeptides and their receptors: A psychosomatic network*. Journal of Immunology (Baltimore, Md.: 1950).

11. Goleman, D. (2012). *Emotional intelligence, social intelligence, and ecological intelligence*. Daniel Goleman: Q & A. Retrieved from http://www.danielgoleman.info/eq-in-the-workplace/.

12. Espy, L. (2023, April 8). *5 Ways Emotional Intelligence Builds Trust through Communication*. PMWorld 360 Magazine.

13. Andreatta, B. (2018). *Wired to connect: The brain science of teams and a new model for creating collaboration and inclusion*. 7th Mind Publishing.

14. Jung, Y. H., Shin, N. Y., Jang, J. H., Lee, W. J., Lee, D., Choi, Y., Choi, S. H., & Kang, D. H. (2019, May). *Relationships among stress, emotional intelligence, cognitive intelligence, and cytokines*. Medicine.

15. Pert, C. B., Ruff, M. R., Weber, R. J., & Herkenham, M. (1985). *Neuropeptides and their receptors: A psychosomatic network*. Journal of Immunology (Baltimore, Md.: 1950).

16. Hogshead, S. (2014). *How the World Sees You*. HarperCollins.

17. Cuddy, A. (2018). *Presence: Bringing your boldest self to your biggest challenges*. Back Bay Books, Little, Brown, and Company.

18. Brown, B. (2020). *The gifts of imperfection*. Random House.

19. Harvard Business Review Press. (2019). *Self-awareness (HBR Emotional Intelligence series)*.

20. Guy-Evans, O. (2023, February 9). *Pareto principle (the 80-20 rule)*. Simply Psychology.

21. Collins, B. (2022, October 12). *The Pomodoro Technique explained*. Forbes.

22. Kouzes, J. M., & Posner, B. Z. (2011). *Credibility: How leaders gain and lose it, why people demand it*. Jossey-Bass.

23. Newport, C. (2021). *Deep work: Rules for focused success in a distracted world new*. Manjul Publishing House.

24. McKeown, G. (2014). *Essentialism*. Virgin Books.

25. Huffington, A. S. (2015). *Thrive*. WH Allen.

26. Brown, B. (2022). *Atlas of the heart: Mapping meaningful connection and the language of human experience*. Random House Large Print.

27. Gladwell, M. (2021). *Talking to Strangers. What we should know about the people we don't know*. Back Bay Books.

28. Patterson, K., Grenny, J., Maxfield, D. G., McMillan, R., & Switzler, A. (2018). *Crucial Accountability: Tools for resolving violated expectations, broken commitments, and bad behavior, Second edition.* McGraw-Hill.

29. Patterson, K. (2005). *Crucial confrontations: Tools for resolving broken promises, violated expectations, and bad behavior.* McGraw-Hill.

30. Patterson, K., Grenny, J., McMillan, R., Switzler, A., & Maxfield, D. G. (2012). *Crucial conversations: Tools for talking when stakes are high.* McGraw-Hill.

31. Brown, J. (2022). *How to be an inclusive leader: Your role in creating cultures of belonging where everyone can thrive.* Berrett-Koehler Publishers.

32. Chapman, G. D., & White, P. E. (2019). *The five languages of appreciation in the workplace: Empowering organizations by encouraging people.* Northfield Publishing.

33. Edmondson, A. C. (2019). *The Fearless Organization: Creating Psychological Safety in the Workplace for Learning, Innovation, and Growth.* John Wiley & Sons, Inc.

Chapter Nine: Take the Risk — Everyday Courage

1. Rate, C. R., Clarke, J. A., Lindsay, D. R., & Sternberg, R. J. (2007). Implicit theories of courage. *The Journal of Positive Psychology, 2*(2), 80–98.

2. Treasurer, B. (2008). *Courage goes to work: How to build backbones, boost performance, and get results.* Berrett-Koehler.

3. Detert, J. (2018, November 6). *Cultivating Everyday Courage. The right way to speak truth to power.* Harvard Business Review.

4. Hayes, E., & Dill, S. (2018). *Free Solo* [Film]. United States; National Geographic Partners.

5. AbuHasan, Q., Reddy, V., & Siddiqui, W. (2022, July 19). *Neuroanatomy, Amygdala.* National Library of Medicine.

6. Brown, B. (2015). *Daring greatly: How the courage to be vulnerable transforms the way we live, Love, parent, and lead.* Penguin Life.

7. White, A. (2008). *From Comfort Zone to Performance Management.* Research Gate.

8. Schneiderman, N., Ironson, G., & Siegel, S. D. (2005). Stress and health: Psychological, behavioral, and biological determinants. *Annual Review of Clinical Psychology, 1*(1), 607–628.

9. Keller, A., Litzelman, K., Wisk, L. E., Maddox, T., Cheng, E. R., Creswell, P. D., & Witt, W. P. (2012*). Does the perception that stress affects health matter? The association with health and mortality.* Health Psychology, 31(5), 677–684.

10. Zak, P. (2017). *Trust factor: The science of creating high-performance companies*. Amacon.

11. Apter, M. J. (1992). *The dangerous edge: The psychology of excitement*. Free Press.

12. Edmondson, A. C. (2019). *The Fearless Organization: Creating Psychological Safety in the Workplace for Learning, Innovation, and Growth*. John Wiley & Sons, Inc.

13. Woodard, C. R., & Pury, C. L. (2007). The construct of Courage: Categorization and measurement. *Consulting Psychology Journal: Practice and Research, 59*(2), 135–147.

14. Schwartz, T., & McCarthy, C. (2023, February 8). *Manage your energy, not your time*. Harvard Business Review.

Chapter Ten: Establish Your Moral Center—Integrity

1. Hakim, D., Kessler, A. M., & Ewing, J. (2015, September 26). *As Volkswagen pushed to be no. 1, ambitions fueled a scandal*. The New York Times.

2. Environmental Protection Agency. (2022). Basic Information about the Emission Standards Reference Guide for On-road and Nonroad Vehicles and Engines. EPA.

3. Clean Carbon Energy. (2022). NOx emissions – formation, reduction, and abatement. NOx emissions from diesel engines.

4. Singh, P. (2018). Volkswagen emissions scandal - A case study report. International Journal of Human Resource Management and Research, 8(5), 11–18.

5. Ewing, J. (2017a). *Faster, higher, farther: The Volkswagen scandal*. Bantam Press.

6. US Department of Justice. (2017, January 11). Volkswagen AG agrees to plead guilty and pay $4.3 billion in criminal and civil penalties; six Volkswagen executives and employees are indicted in connection with conspiracy to cheat U.S. emissions tests.

7. Barrett, S. R., Speth, R. L., Eastham, S. D., Dedoussi, I. C., Ashok, A., Malina, R., & Keith, D. W. (2015). Impact of the Volkswagen Emissions Control defeat device on US Public Health. Environmental Research Letters, 10(11), 114005.

8. Simons, T., McLean Parks, J., & Tomlinson, E. C. (2017). The benefits of walking your talk: Aggregate effects of behavioral integrity on guest satisfaction, turnover, and hotel profitability. *Cornell Hospitality Quarterly, 59*(3), 257–274.

9. Kouzes, J. M., & Posner, B. Z. (2011). *Credibility: How leaders gain and lose it, why people demand it.* Jossey-Bass.
10. Decker, B. (2008). *You've got to be believed to be heard.* ST. Martin's Press.

Chapter Eleven: Harness the Unicorn—Authenticity

1. Brown, B. (2020). *The gifts of imperfection.* Random House.
2. George, B., & Sims, P. (2007). *True North: Discover your authentic leadership.* Jossey-Bass/John Wiley & Sons.
3. Hogshead, S. (2014). *How the World Sees You.* HarperCollins.
4. Creswell, J. D., Welch, W. T., Taylor, S. E., Sherman, D. K., Gruenewald, T. L., & Mann, T. (2005). Affirmation of personal values buffers neuroendocrine and psychological stress responses. *Psychological Science, 16*(11), 846–851.
5. Cuddy, A. (2018). *Presence: Bringing your boldest self to your biggest challenges.* Back Bay Books, Little, Brown, and Company.
6. Cable, D. M., Gino, F., & Staats, B. R. (2013). Breaking them in or eliciting their best? reframing socialization around newcomers' authentic self-expression. *Administrative Science Quarterly, 58*(1), 1–36.

Chapter Twelve: Love Your Team—Empathy, Inclusivity, Gratitude

1. Goleman, D., Hallowell, E., & Daniel Goleman, R. E. B. (2018, December 20). *The focused leader.* Harvard Business Review.
2. Bariso, J. (2018, September 19). *There are actually 3 types of empathy. here's how they differ.* Inc.com.
3. Emmons, R. A. (2007). Thanks! How the new science of gratitude can make you happier. Houghton Mifflin Co.
4. Han, S., & Noland, M. (2020, August 27). *Companies with women in leadership positions are more profitable than those without.* PIIE.
5. Baeza, C. (2022, March 9). *Half of the candidates for management posts at BBVA Are Women.* NEWS BBVA.
6. Anoshiravani, A., & Drake, E. (2016, March 14). *Grads of Life Brandvoice: 4 reasons why diversity will boost your company's performance.* Forbes.
7. Badal, S. B. (2023, July 27). The business benefits of gender diversity. Gallup.com.
8. WHOOP. (2023, July 17). Your Personal Digital Fitness and health coach. WHOOP. https://www.whoop.com/
9. Chowdhury, M. R. (2022, August 2). The neuroscience of gratitude and its effects on the brain. PositivePsychology.com.
10. Riordan, C. M. (2014, August 7). Foster a culture of gratitude. Harvard Business Review

11. Grant, A. M., & Gino, F. (2010). A little thanks goes a long way: Explaining why gratitude expressions motivate prosocial behavior. American Psychological Association.

12. Zahn, M. R., Krueger, F., Huey, E. D., Garrido, G., & Grafman, J. (2007). Social concepts are represented in the superior anterior. The Proceedings of the National Academy of Sciences (PNAS).

13. Emmons, R. (2010). Why gratitude is good. Greater Good.

14. Armstrong, K. (2017, December 29). "I feel your pain": The Neuroscience of Empathy. Association for Psychological Science (APS).

15. Erfesoglou, L. (2023, February 14). The neuroscience of inclusion. How science can help businesses thrive. Cultural Awareness International.

16. Zahn, R., Moll, J., Paiva, M., Garrido, G., Krueger, F., Huey, E. D., & Grafman, J. (2009, February). The neural basis of human social values: Evidence from functional MRI. Cerebral cortex (New York, N.Y.: 1991).

17. Fox, B. (1970, December 19). Unconscious bias. Vanderbilt University.

18. Papillon, K. (2023). Two types of Bias. NCCC.

19. Healy, P. (2016, August 18). Confirmation bias: How it affects your organization: HBS Online. Business Insights Blog.

20. Bordas J. (2013). The Power of Latino Leadership: Culture, Inclusion, and Contribution. Berrett Koehler Publishers.

Chapter Thirteen: Tap the Untapped Magic of Resilience

1. Treasurer, B. (2019). Courage goes to work: How to build backbones, boost performance and get results. Berrett-Koehler Publishers, Inc.

2. Johnson, C. (2021, May 17). Long working hours increasing deaths from heart disease and stroke: Who. World Health Organization.

3. Pfeffer, J. (2018). Dying for a paycheck: How modern management harms employee health and company performance—and what we can do about it. HarperBusiness, an imprint of HarperCollins Publishers.

4. Carton, A., Barsade, S., & Creary, S. (2018). Does fear motivate workers—or make things worse? Knowledge at Wharton.

5. Schwartz, T., & McCarthy, C. (2023, February 8). *Manage your energy, not your time*. Harvard Business Review.

6. Kothari, S., & Lal, S. (2017). Renew your inner energy through human internal energy sources. Research Gate.

7. Dunn, J., & Grider, M. (2023, February 13). Physiology, adenosine triphosphate - statpearls - NCBI bookshelf. National Library of Medicine.

8. Huffington, A. S. (2015). *Thrive*. WH Allen.

9. Hawley, L., Padesky, C., Hollon, S., Mancuso, E., Laposa, J., Brozina, K., & Segal, Z. (2017). Cognitive-behavioral therapy for depression using

Mind over Mood: CBT skill use and differential symptom alleviation. Behavior therapy.

10. Louv, R. (2006). Last Child in the Woods. Algonquin Books. Chapel Hill.

11. Bates, S. (2018, October 25). Heavy multitaskers have reduced memory. Stanford News.

12. Csikszentmihalyi, M. (2009). Flow: The psychology of optimal experience. Harper and Row.

13. History on the Net. (2023, June 16). Industrial Revolution working conditions: What were they like? History on the Net.

14. Reiderer, R. (2022, November 15). Did you know? A brief history of the 5-day workweek. Morning Brew.

15. Leibow, C. (2014, December 16). Work/life balance for the generations. HuffPost.

Conclusion: Create a Ripple

1. Gates, B. (2008, January 24). *Bill Gates - 2008 World Economic Forum*. Bill and Melinda Gates Foundation.

2. Conscious capitalism. (2023). Conscious capitalism. Lead with Love.

3. Moore, M. (2020, October 6). *Whole Foods CEO on how business can be better than just "a bunch of selfish, greedy bastards."* Fortune.

4. Fink, L. (2012-2023). *Larry Fink's letters to CEOS*. BlackRock.

5. Business Roundtable. (2023, February 15). *Our commitment. Business Roundtable - Opportunity Agenda.*

Index

GRATITUDE

I could fill a book with words of appreciation for those who have supported me throughout the writing of *9 Leader Touchstones*. My deepest, heartfelt *Gratitude* goes to the following people for their invaluable support and contributions.

First and foremost, thank you to Brian, Madi, and Emily for putting up with me the last few years during the research and writing of this book. Your unwavering belief in me, constant encouragement, and love kept me motivated even when the writing process wore me down.

I also want to thank my amazing team of Crescent Leadership Collaborators—Alison Wilcox (my writing buddy), Diana Cardenas del Monaco, Jada Tullos Anderson, James Lovaas, Jenn Osman, Kerry Connolly, Lisa Austin, Maryann Dwyer, Michelle Taylor, Savannah Ray, and Shefali Chudgar. You never hesitate to give me tough feedback, and you never hold back on the love. Ours is the kind of team euphoria so few teams ever find. I'm so honored to journey with you on our quest to restore the distinctive nature of leadership.

I am indebted my team of beta readers—Abraham Thomas, Anne Manner-McLarty, Brian DeShields, Carolyn Moyers, Caitríona Taylor, Diana Cardenas del Monaco, Gerardo Berthin, Jada Tullos Anderson, James Lovaas, Jenn Osman, Kady Griffin, Kerry Connolly, Maryann Dwyer, Nichelle Howe, Paula Bookidis, Russel Statham, Saumil Chudgar, Savannah Ray, Shefali Chudgar, and Thea Dirton—whose guidance and expertise have invaluably shaped this book. Your profound insights, questions, constructive feedback, and continued support have elevated the quality of my research, writing, and subsequently, our work with leaders and teams.

I would like to extend my *Gratitude* to my leaders, teachers, and team members who have shaped me across a lifetime. There are too many to list here, but your guidance led me to where I am today. I also want to thank the leaders who generously shared their expertise and stories—Alison Wilcox, Brian DeShields, Diana Cardenas del Monaco, Elizabeth Gilbert, Jada Tullos Anderson, James Lovaas, Jennifer Young, Jenn Osman, Kady Griffin, Madelyn Ridgeway, Maryann Dwyer, Paula Bookidis, and Shefali Chudgar. Your insights and perspectives have greatly enriched me, our work, and the content of *9 Leader Touchstones*. I am truly fortunate to have had the opportunity to learn from you.

I want to thank the members of the book launch team. I can't list you all here because we're still gearing up to bring *9 Leader Touchstones* to the world. Just know you have my heartfelt love.

Lastly, I want to express my appreciation to all future readers and supporters of this book. Your interest in joining me on this journey and your enthusiasm for leadership have been a constant source of inspiration to me.

Although I have attempted to mention everyone who has contributed to this book, I understand that there may be individuals inadvertently left out. Please accept my sincere apologies if that is the case. Your contributions are no less appreciated. Thank you *all* for your unwavering support, patience, and belief in me. *9 Leader Touchstones* would not have been possible without each and every one of you.

ABOUT JES DESHIELDS

For the past 25 years, Dr. Jes DeShields has studied, evaluated, and applied models of leadership, organizational behavior, and systems change across multiple sectors. From Fortune 250 and privately-owned companies to national nonprofits to entire communities, Jes's work ranges from preparing leaders to successfully run their organizations to improving the trajectory of organizations in crisis and those poised for growth. Jes founded Crescent Leadership, a business consulting and leader coaching firm based on Leader-First® strategies, her distinct methodology for organizational change. Leader-First® strategies challenge leaders and teams of leaders first to examine how their behavior reinforces conditions for enduring growth and vitality or stagnation and decline.

Known as a passionate and engaging storyteller, Jes cultivates relationships of transparency, trust, and authentic connection. Her consulting approach focuses on the long game, applying the appropriate infusion of innovation with endurance-based strategies and conscientious culturing.

Jes earned her Ph.D. in Management-Leadership and Organizational Change in 2014. She teaches as a guest lecturer for Cornell University at the Brooks School of Public Policy and as an instructor in eCornell's Executive Leadership, Women's Leadership, Change Leadership, and Nonprofit Management Certificate programs. Jes regularly speaks and writes on leadership, team dynamics, and organizational change.

While Jes is zealous about leadership, equity, and causes related to self-sustainability and women, her first love is family. Jes and her husband, Dr. Brian DeShields, reside in Greenville, SC with their daughters, Madeleine and Emily, and their furry companions, Amos, Atlas, and Archer, where they regularly fulfill their curiosity and passion for adventure and nature.

ABOUT CRESCENT LEADERSHIP

Located in Greenville, South Carolina, Crescent Leadership is a consulting and executive coaching firm founded on the principles of its distinct approach—Leader-First® Leadership. Leader-First® strategies challenge leaders first to examine how their behaviors reinforce conditions for enduring growth and vitality or stagnation and decline. While Crescent Leadership works with organizations of all types and sizes, our more than 200 years of collective experience gives us a particular lean to Professional Service, Manufacturing, Nonprofit, Government, Military, and Healthcare Sectors.

Our Mission

Using Leader-First® strategies, we transform the systems that inhibit organizations from learning, evolving, innovating, optimizing, and enduring.

Our Vision

To restore the distinctive nature of leadership.

Our Purpose

To develop leaders who embrace the Leader Touchstones so that they build enduring organizations committed to improving the human experience.

Our Living Values

Be annoyingly curious. Own our nerd.
Protect health like our life depends on it.
Laugh-cry more.
Live just beyond our comfort zones.
Love first… period.

Leaders *first* look to themselves.

Made in the USA
Columbia, SC
15 April 2024

34217034R00204